DATE NIGHT COOKBOOK FOR COUPLES

TASTY HOMEMADE ROMANTIC RECIPES

JANE F GARRAWAY

THE DATE NIGHT COOKBOOK FOR COUPLES

By

JANE F. GARRAWAY

Copyright © 2024

Copyright © 2024 by Jane F. Garraway

All rights reserved. No part of this publication may be reproduced, distributed, or transmitted in any form or by any means, including photocopying, recording, or other electronic or mechanical methods, without the prior written permission of the publisher, except in the case of brief quotations embodied in critical reviews and certain other noncommercial uses permitted by copyright law.

CONTENT

THE DATE NIGHT COOKBOOK FOR COUPLES 1
   Copyright © 2024 3
AUTHOR'S NOTE 9
INTRODUCTION 10
MEAT DISHES 13
   Parmesan Pork Medallions 14
   Cast Iron Skillet Steak 16
   Air Fryer Garlic Butter Steak 17
   Cranberry Short Ribs 18
   Pork Tenderloin with Herb Sauce 20
   Slow-Cooked Beef Tips 21
   Merlot Filet Mignon 22
   Steak Strips with Dumplings 24
   Beef Fillet with Portobello Sauce 25
   Beef Steak with Blue Cheese 26
   Sirloin Strips over Rice 28
   Grilled Five Spice Flank Steak 29
   Slow-Cooked Pork Ribs 30
   Beef Wellington with Madeira Sauce 32
   Pressure-Cooked Mushroom Pork Ragout 34
   Air Fryer Smoked Pork Chops 35
   Bacon-Wrapped Filet with Scotch Mushrooms 37
POULTRY DISHES 38
   Cheesy Chicken Parmigiana 39
   Slow-Cooked Italian Chicken 41
   Turkey Cutlets with Pan Gravy 42
   Chicken Reuben Roll-Ups 43
   Goat Cheese and Spinach Stuffed Chicken 45
   Corsican Chicken 46
   Spinach and Feta Stuffed Chicken 47

- Italian Chicken Skillet 49
- Chicken Parmesan 50
- Asparagus-Stuffed Air Fryer Chicken Rolls 51
- Herb-Stuffed Cornish Hen 53
- Chicken Scampi 54
- Pressure Cooked Chicken Paprika 55
- Air Fryer Almond Chicken 57

SEAFOOD DISHES 58
- Walnut and Oat-Crusted Salmon 59
- Air Fryer Scallops 61
- Flavorful Salmon Fillets 62
- Seared Scallops with Citrus Herbed Sauce 63
- Garlic Lemon Shrimp 65
- Lobster Mac 'n' Cheese 66
- Pan-Seared Salmon with Lemon Garlic Butter Sauce 67
- Asparagus and Shrimp with Angel Hair 69
- Salmon with Spinach Sauce 70
- Air Fryer Tilapia 71
- Balsamic Salmon and Spinach Salad 73
- Sun-Dried Tomatoes Seafood Linguine 74
- Shrimp in Garlic Wine Sauce 75
- Pan-Seared Scallops with Bacon Cream Sauce 77
- Butter-Poached Lobster 78

VEGAN/VEGETARIAN DISHES 79
- Spinach Lasagna Roll-Ups 80
- Mushroom and Cabbage Dumplings 82
- Vegan Broccoli Pesto Pasta with Whipped Tofu Ricotta 84
- Vegan BLT Pizza 85
- Creamy Vegan Rigatoni with Roasted Cauliflower 87
- Vegan Teriyaki Oyster Mushrooms 88
- Vegan Lasagna Stuffed Portobello Mushrooms 89
- Oyster Mushroom and Jackfruit Vegan Pot Roast 91
- BBQ Vegan Lentil Meatballs 92
- Lemon Millet Rice with Asparagus 93

- Vegan Sri Lankan Curry 95
- Spaghetti Squash Burrito Bowls 96
- Vegetarian Sausage Sheet Pan Dinner 97
- Toaster Oven-Baked Potatoes 99
- Asparagus Couscous Bowls 100
- Vegetable Calzones 101
- Vegetable Pot Pie 103

PASTA DISHES 104
- Fettuccine Alfredo 105
- Quick One-Pan Carbonara 107
- Sweet Potato Tortellini with Hazelnut Sauce 108
- Four Cheese Stuffed Shells 109
- Ricotta Gnocchi with Spinach & Gorgonzola 111
- Garlic Salmon Linguine 112
- Shrimp Scampi 113
- Crab-Stuffed Manicotti 115
- Creamy Roasted Garlic and Beets Pasta 116
- Roasted Red Pepper Fettuccine with Creamy Feta Sauce 117
- Mozzarella Penne Rosa with Sun-Dried Tomatoes 119
- Thai Red Curry Vegetable Soup 120
- Creamy Tuscan Chicken Pasta 121

APPETIZERS 123
- Caprese Phyllo Cups 124
- Pizza Roses 126
- Baked Brie in Puff Pastry 127
- Cheese Fondue 128
- Roasted Potato Hearts 130
- Candied Bacon Roses 131
- Mini Bacon Ranch Cheese Balls 132
- Avocado Cucumber Shrimp Salad 134
- Monte Cristo Sliders 135
- Pink Moscato Strawberries 136
- Colored Deviled Eggs 138
- Mini Deep Dish Pizzas 139

Air Fryer Mozzarella Sticks ... 140
Chicken Fritters ... 142
Hot Mini Italian Sliders ... 143
Crab Cakes ... 144

DRINKS ... 146
Chocolate Truffle Martini ... 147
Chocolate Covered Strawberry Shooters ... 149
Valentine Cupid's Float ... 150
Strawberries and Champagne Margarita ... 151
Strawberry Grapefruit Mimosa ... 153
Raspberry Rose Bellinis ... 154
Cotton Candy Champagne ... 155
Love Potion Cocktail ... 157
Love Bug Cocktail ... 158
Raspberry Kiss Cocktail ... 159
Valentine Moscow Mule Cocktail ... 161
Pink Squirrel ... 162
Love Martini ... 163

DESSERTS ... 165
Chocolate Strawberries ... 166
Shortbread Heart-Shaped Cookies ... 168
Chocolate-Covered Strawberry Brownies ... 170
Red Velvet Cheesecake Bites ... 172
Sparkle Heart Cookies ... 175
Double Chocolate Mascarpone Raspberry Pie ... 177
French Silk Pie ... 179
Nutella Cheesecakes ... 182
Red Velvet Cake Mix Bars ... 184
Dark Chocolate Cherry Brownies ... 186
Frosted Sugar Cookie Bars ... 189
Chocolate Pillows ... 191
Mini Red Velvet Donuts ... 193

KITCHEN CONVERSION CHART ... 196
CONCLUSION ... 199

BONUS - SPECIAL PLAYLIST

Here's a playlist of popular romantic songs perfect for setting the mood on date nights:

1. "Perfect" - Ed Sheeran
2. "All of Me" - John Legend
3. "Amazed" - Lonestar
4. "At Last" - Etta James
5. "I Will Always Love You" - Whitney Houston
6. "Thinking Out Loud" - Ed Sheeran
7. "Unchained Melody" - The Righteous Brothers
8. "Can't Help Falling in Love" - Elvis Presley
9. "Your Song" - Elton John
10. "Un-break My Heart" - Toni Braxton
11. "Fly Me To The Moon" - Frank Sinatra
12. "Bleeding Love" - Leona Lewis
13. "Something" - The Beatles
14. "How Deep Is Your Love" - Bee Gees
15. "Just the Way You Are" - Bruno Mars
16. "I Don't Want to Miss a Thing" - Aerosmith
17. "Truly Madly Deeply" - Savage Garden
18. "Endless Love" - Lionel Richie & Diana Ross
19. "Eternal Flame" - The Bangles
20. "Unconditionally" - Katy Perry
21. "Have I Told You Lately" - Rod Stewart
22. "Everything" - Michael Bublé
23. "When a Man Loves a Woman" - Percy Sledge
24. "Crazy for You" - Madonna
25. "I Just Called to Say I Love You" - Stevie Wonder
26. "Make You Feel My Love" - Adele
27. "Kiss Me" - Sixpence None The Richer
28. "The Way You Look Tonight" - Tony Bennett
29. "Crazy Little Thing Called Love" - Queen
30. "Can't Take My Eyes Off You" - Frankie Valli

This playlist should provide a diverse mix of romantic tunes for a memorable date night. Enjoy!

consensus among experts and celebrities is that cooking together can be a powerful and enjoyable way to strengthen the emotional connection in a relationship.

HOW TO MAKE COOKING TOGETHER SPECIAL

1. **Choose a Theme or Cuisine:**
   - Select a theme or type of cuisine that resonates with both you and your partner. It could be a shared favorite or something new you both want to explore together.

2. **Plan Together:**
   - Collaborate on the planning process. Discuss the menu, choose recipes, and make a shopping list as a team. This involvement enhances the experience and makes it a joint effort.

3. **Create a Romantic Atmosphere:**
   - Set the mood with elements like soft lighting, candles, or background music. Creating a romantic ambiance transforms the cooking process into a special and intimate occasion.

4. **Personalized Touch:**
   - Add a personal element to the meal, whether it's incorporating a favorite ingredient, preparing a dish with sentimental value, or creating a handwritten menu. This touch makes the experience uniquely yours.

5. **Share Responsibilities:**
   - Divide tasks in the kitchen so that both partners actively contribute. This not only streamlines the cooking process but also reinforces teamwork, communication, and cooperation.

6. **Experiment and Be Playful:**
   - Embrace creativity and experimentation in the kitchen. Try new recipes, put your unique spin on familiar dishes, and have fun with the process. Cooking together is an opportunity to playfully explore culinary adventures.

7. **Savor the Moment:**
   - Once the meal is ready, take the time to sit down together without distractions. Enjoy the food, engage in meaningful conversation, and savor the shared experience. It's about more than just the end result; it's about the journey together.

8. **Celebrate Achievements:**
   - Acknowledge and celebrate the effort put into the meal. Whether it's successfully executing a recipe or sharing a light-hearted moment while cooking, recognizing these achievements enhances the overall experience and strengthens the connection.

In summary, making cooking together special involves thoughtful planning, collaboration, personalization, and a focus on creating a delightful, shared experience.

INTRODUCTION

Imagine preparing a candlelit dinner together for a romantic Valentine's Day. From choosing ingredients to preparing the meal side by side, the shared effort becomes a cherished memory. Alternatively, surprise your partner with a thoughtfully prepared dinner after a long day, showing appreciation and care. Cooking together can also be a playful activity—think of making heart-shaped cookies or a themed dinner for a fun and lighthearted experience. These scenarios create special moments and strengthen the bond between partners.

Cooking for or with your partner on special occasions like date nights and Valentine's Day can create a memorable and intimate experience. It allows you to share a meaningful activity, fostering connection and creating lasting memories together.

Cooking together adds an element of teamwork, communication, and shared creativity. It can be a fun way to bond, discover new recipes, and appreciate each other's culinary skills. The act of preparing a meal for your partner demonstrates thoughtfulness and care, making the occasion more personal and special. It's not just about the food; it's about the shared experience and the effort put into creating something together.

Furthermore, it often involves cooperation and coordination, enhancing your ability to work as a team. It can be a relaxed and enjoyable way to spend quality time, providing a break from routine and allowing you to focus on each other. The shared effort and the pleasure of savoring a meal you've both created can deepen the emotional connection and create a sense of closeness. It's a unique way to express love and create a lasting connection through the shared joy of a homemade meal.

Consider a cozy weekend brunch where you both contribute to making pancakes, omelets, or any favorite breakfast dishes. It's an informal and delightful way to start the day, fostering a sense of togetherness. Another choice is recreating a favorite restaurant dish at home; this not only showcases your culinary skills but also adds a personalized touch to a shared meal. Whether it's a casual weeknight or a special celebration, cooking together brings joy and intimacy to various occasions in your relationship.

Notable figures like Jamie Oliver and relationship experts like Dr. John Gottman often speak about the positive impact of cooking together on connection and communication in a relationship. It's always interesting to explore their insights for inspiration on creating meaningful moments with your partner.

Celebrity chefs like Gordon Ramsay and Nigella Lawson have also praised the idea of couples cooking together. They often highlight how the collaborative nature of the kitchen fosters teamwork and enhances the overall relationship. Relationship experts like Esther Perel emphasize the sensual and intimate aspects of cooking together, turning the process into a shared adventure that transcends the practical act of preparing a meal. Overall, the

AUTHOR'S NOTE

Hello and welcome to "The Date Night Cookbook for Couples!" I am thrilled to share this flavorful recipes with you, offering guidance to those exploring tasty homemade dishes for you and your partner.

This cookbook is thoughtfully tailored for beginners, providing straightforward instructions, useful tips, and a diverse array of recipes spanning from savory meat dishes to mouthwatering pasta dishes and refreshing drinks.

Each recipe in this compilation presents you with the opportunity to whip up luscious appetizing dishes with your partner in the comfort of your kitchen. Preparing romantic dishes is about relishing the tastes of wholesome ingredients, cruelty-free alternatives, and the sheer delight of indulging in companionship and quality time together.

Whether you're a novice or an experienced cook, I invite you to explore through the world of various homemade romantic dishes. Together, let's unlock the magic of cruelty-free indulgence and infuse your home with the joy of lovely dishes.

Enjoy,

Jane Garraway

MEAT DISHES

Parmesan Pork Medallions

Servings: 2 | **Prep Time:** 15 minutes | **Total Time:** 25 minutes

INGREDIENTS:
- 2 pork tenderloin medallions (about 6-8 ounces each)
- 1/2 cup grated Parmesan cheese
- 1/4 cup breadcrumbs
- 2 tablespoons olive oil
- 1 teaspoon dried oregano
- Salt and black pepper, to taste
- 2 tablespoons Dijon mustard
- 2 tablespoons unsalted butter

INSTRUCTIONS:
1. *Preheat the Oven:*
   - Preheat your oven to 375°F (190°C).
2. *Prepare the Pork Medallions:*
   - Pat the pork medallions dry with paper towels.
   - Season with salt and black pepper.
3. *Coat with Parmesan Mixture:*
   - In a bowl, mix grated Parmesan, breadcrumbs, dried oregano, and a pinch of black pepper.
   - Brush each pork medallion with Dijon mustard, then coat them in the Parmesan mixture, pressing it onto the surface.
4. *Sear in a Skillet:*
   - Heat olive oil in an oven-safe skillet over medium-high heat.
   - Sear the pork medallions for 2-3 minutes on each side until golden brown.
5. *Finish in the Oven:*
   - Transfer the skillet to the preheated oven and bake for 12-15 minutes or until the internal temperature reaches 145°F (63°C).
6. *Create a Pan Sauce:*
   - In the same skillet, add butter and melt over medium heat.
   - Spoon the melted butter over the pork medallions, coating them in the rich flavor.
7. *Garnish and Serve:*
   - Sprinkle fresh parsley over the pork for a burst of color and freshness.
   - Serve the Parmesan pork medallions with your favorite sides.

EXPERT TIPS & VARIATIONS:
- For a gluten-free version, use almond flour instead of breadcrumbs.
- Customize the seasoning by adding garlic powder or smoked paprika to the Parmesan mixture.

PAIRING SUGGESTIONS:
- Lemon herb roasted potatoes
- Steamed green beans or a crisp arugula salad

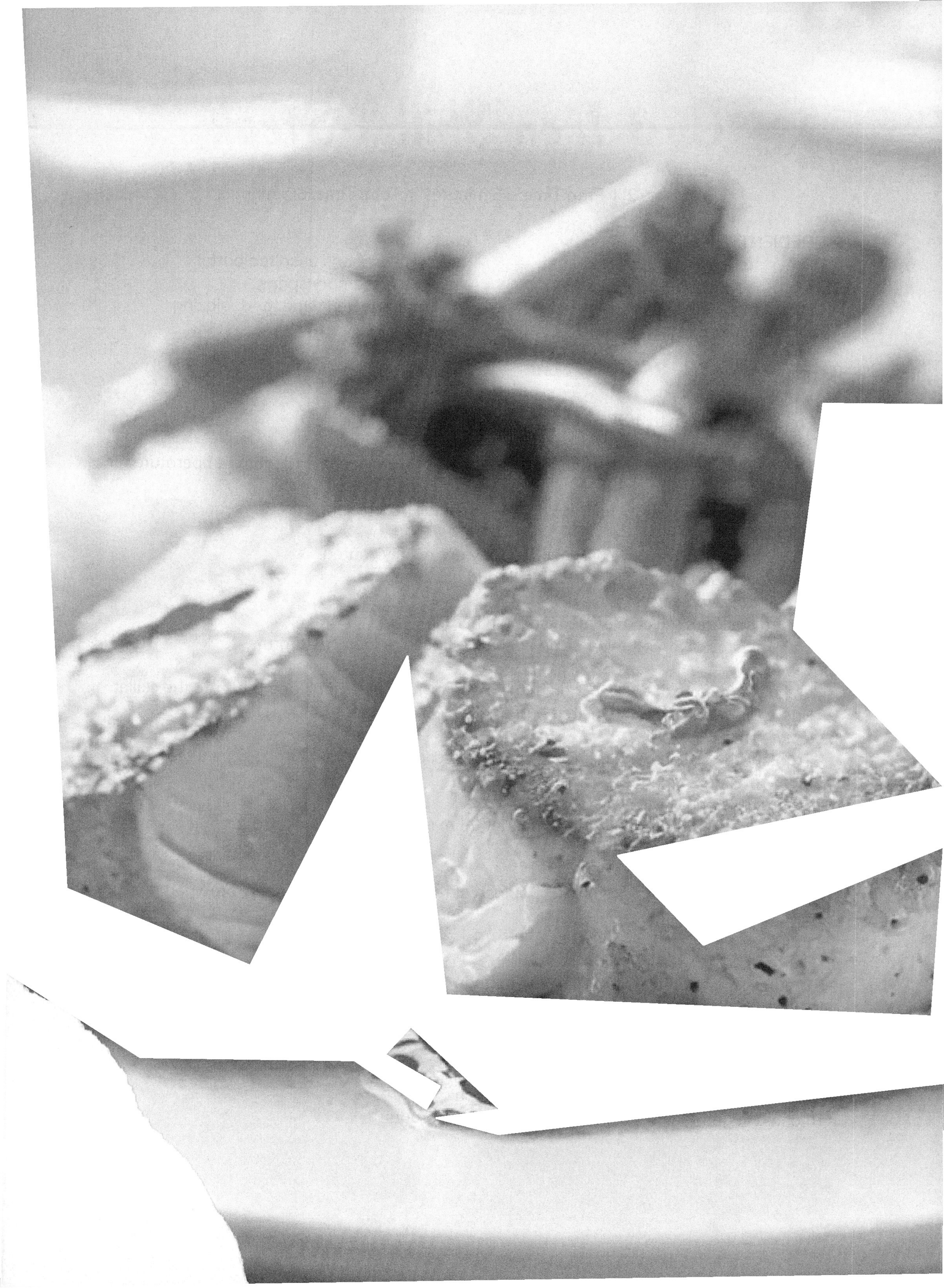

Cast Iron Skillet Steak

Servings: 2 | **Prep Time:** 15 minutes | **Total Time:** 30 minutes

INGREDIENTS:
- 2 ribeye steaks (8-10 ounces each)
- 2 tablespoons olive oil
- Salt and black pepper, to taste
- 2 cloves garlic, minced
- 2 tablespoons unsalted butter
- Fresh rosemary sprigs
- Optional: Red wine for deglazing

INSTRUCTIONS:
1. *Preheat the Oven:*
   - Preheat your oven to 400°F (200°C).
2. *Prepare the Steaks:*
   - Take the ribeye steaks out of the refrigerator and let them come to room temperature for about 30 minutes.
   - Pat the steaks dry with paper towels, which helps in achieving a better sear.
3. *Season the Steaks:*
   - Rub each steak with olive oil, ensuring they are evenly coated.
   - Generously season both sides with salt and black pepper.
4. *Sear in Cast Iron Skillet:*
   - Heat a cast iron skillet over medium-high heat.
   - Sear the steaks for 3-4 minutes on each side until a golden crust forms.
5. *Add Flavor:*
   - In the last minute of cooking, add minced garlic, fresh rosemary, and butter to the skillet.
   - Baste the steaks with the melted butter, garlic, and rosemary.
6. *Finish in the Oven:*
   - Transfer the skillet to the preheated oven and cook for an additional 5-8 minutes for medium-rare, depending on thickness.
7. *Rest the Steaks:*
   - Remove the steaks from the oven and let them rest on a cutting board for at least 5 minutes.
8. *Optional Red Wine Deglaze:*
   - If desired, deglaze the skillet with a splash of red wine, scraping up any browned bits for a flavorful sauce.

EXPERT TIPS & VARIATIONS:
- Experiment with different cuts like filet mignon for a leaner option.
- Infuse additional flavors by adding a pinch of smoked paprika or dried herbs to the seasoning.

PAIRING SUGGESTIONS:
- Creamy mashed potatoes or cauliflower mash
- Roasted vegetables like asparagus or Brussels sprouts

Air Fryer Garlic Butter Steak

Servings: 2 | **Prep Time:** 10 minutes | **Total Time:** 20 minutes

INGREDIENTS:
- 2 sirloin or ribeye steaks (6-8 ounces each)
- 3 tablespoons unsalted butter, melted
- 4 cloves garlic, minced
- 1 teaspoon dried thyme
- Salt and black pepper, to taste
- Olive oil spray for the air fryer basket

INSTRUCTIONS:
1. *Preheat the Air Fryer:*
   - Preheat your air fryer to 400°F (200°C) for about 5 minutes.
2. *Prepare the Steaks:*
   - Pat the steaks dry with paper towels.
   - Season both sides with salt and black pepper.
3. *Garlic Butter Mixture:*
   - In a small bowl, mix melted butter, minced garlic, and dried thyme.
4. *Coat the Steaks:*
   - Brush the steaks with the garlic butter mixture, ensuring an even coating on both sides.
5. *Prep the Air Fryer Basket:*
   - Lightly spray the air fryer basket with olive oil to prevent sticking.
6. *Air Fry the Steaks:*
   - Place the steaks in the air fryer basket in a single layer, ensuring they're not crowded.
   - Cook for 8-10 minutes, flipping halfway for medium-rare. Adjust the time for desired doneness.
7. *Rest and Serve:*
   - Remove the steaks from the air fryer and let them rest for a few minutes.
8. *Drizzle with Remaining Garlic Butter:*
   - Drizzle the remaining garlic butter mixture over the steaks before serving.

EXPERT TIPS & VARIATIONS:
- Add a dash of smoked paprika to the garlic butter for a hint of smokiness.
- For a spicy kick, include a pinch of red pepper flakes in the garlic butter mixture.

PAIRING SUGGESTIONS:
- Cauliflower mash or creamy polenta
- Grilled asparagus or a simple mixed greens salad

Cranberry Short Ribs

Servings: 2 | Prep Time: 20 minutes | Total Time: 4 hours (including cooking time)

INGREDIENTS:
- 2 lbs beef short ribs
- Salt and black pepper, to taste
- 2 tablespoons olive oil
- 1 large onion, diced
- 2 carrots, peeled and sliced
- 3 cloves garlic, minced
- 1 cup cranberry juice
- 1/2 cup red wine
- 1 cup beef broth
- 1/4 cup soy sauce
- 2 tablespoons balsamic vinegar
- 2 sprigs fresh rosemary
- 1 cup fresh or frozen cranberries

INSTRUCTIONS:
1. *Preheat the Oven:*
   - Preheat your oven to 325°F (163°C).
2. *Season and Sear the Short Ribs:*
   - Season short ribs with salt and black pepper.
   - Heat olive oil in an oven-safe pot over medium-high heat.
   - Sear short ribs until browned on all sides. Remove from pot and set aside.
3. *Sauté Aromatics:*
   - In the same pot, sauté diced onion, sliced carrots, and minced garlic until softened.
4. *Deglaze the Pot:*
   - Pour in cranberry juice, red wine, beef broth, soy sauce, and balsamic vinegar.
   - Scrape up any browned bits from the bottom of the pot for added flavor.
5. *Combine and Add Short Ribs:*
   - Return the seared short ribs to the pot.
   - Add fresh rosemary sprigs and cranberries.
6. *Braise in the Oven:*
   - Cover the pot and transfer it to the preheated oven.
   - Braise for 3-3.5 hours or until the short ribs are tender and falling off the bone.
7. *Serve:*
   - Carefully remove the pot from the oven.
   - Discard rosemary sprigs and skim off any excess fat from the surface and serve.

EXPERT TIPS & VARIATIONS:
- For a richer sauce, reduce it on the stovetop after braising.
- Add a touch of honey or maple syrup for sweetness if desired.

PAIRING SUGGESTIONS:
- Creamy polenta or mashed sweet potatoes
- Sautéed green beans or roasted Brussels sprouts

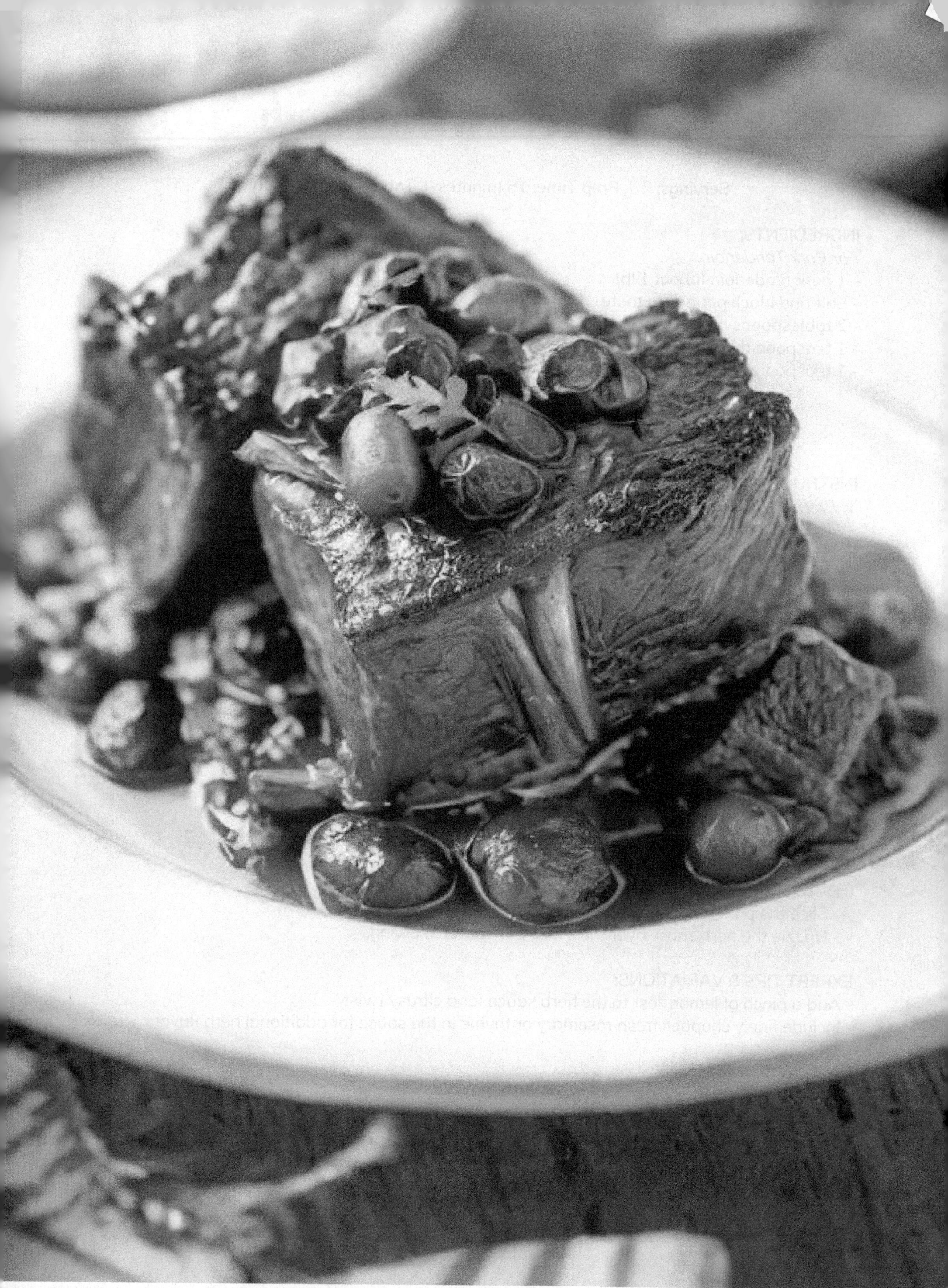

Pork Tenderloin with Herb Sauce

Servings: 2 | Prep Time: 15 minutes | Total Time: 30 minutes

INGREDIENTS:

For Pork Tenderloin:
- 1 pork tenderloin (about 1 lb)
- Salt and black pepper, to taste
- 2 tablespoons olive oil
- 1 teaspoon dried thyme
- 1 teaspoon smoked paprika

For Herb Sauce:
- 1/2 cup fresh parsley, chopped
- 2 tablespoons fresh chives, chopped
- 1 clove garlic, minced
- 2 tablespoons Dijon mustard
- 3 tablespoons red wine vinegar
- 1/4 cup extra virgin olive oil
- Salt and black pepper, to taste

INSTRUCTIONS:

1. *Preheat the Oven:*
   - Preheat your oven to 400°F (200°C).
2. *Prepare the Pork Tenderloin:*
   - Pat the pork tenderloin dry with paper towels.
   - Season with salt, black pepper, dried thyme, and smoked paprika.
3. *Sear and Roast:*
   - In an oven-safe skillet, heat olive oil over medium-high heat.
   - Sear the pork tenderloin on all sides until golden brown.
   - Transfer the skillet to the preheated oven and roast for about 20 minutes or until the internal temperature reaches 145°F (63°C).
4. *Rest the Pork:*
   - Remove the pork from the oven and let it rest for 5 minutes before slicing.
5. *Prepare Herb Sauce:*
   - In a bowl, combine chopped parsley, chives, minced garlic, Dijon mustard, and red wine vinegar.
   - Slowly whisk in extra virgin olive oil until the sauce is well combined.
   - Season with salt and black pepper to taste.
6. *Slice and Serve:*
   - Slice the pork tenderloin into medallions.
   - Drizzle the herb sauce over the sliced pork before serving.

EXPERT TIPS & VARIATIONS:
- Add a pinch of lemon zest to the herb sauce for a citrusy twist.
- Include finely chopped fresh rosemary or thyme in the sauce for additional herb flavors.

PAIRING SUGGESTIONS:
- Garlic mashed potatoes or wild rice
- Roasted vegetables like carrots and Brussels sprouts

Slow-Cooked Beef Tips

Servings: 2 | **Prep Time:** 15 minutes | **Total Time:** 6-8 hours (Slow Cooker time)

INGREDIENTS:
- 1 lb beef sirloin tips, cubed
- Salt and black pepper, to taste
- 2 tablespoons olive oil
- 1 onion, diced
- 2 carrots, peeled and sliced
- 2 cloves garlic, minced
- 1 cup beef broth
- 1/2 cup red wine
- 2 tablespoons tomato paste
- 1 teaspoon dried thyme
- 1 teaspoon dried rosemary
- 1 bay leaf
- 2 tablespoons all-purpose flour (optional, for thickening)
- Chopped fresh parsley, for garnish

INSTRUCTIONS:
1. *Season and Sear the Beef Tips:*
   - Season the beef tips with salt and black pepper.
   - In a skillet, heat olive oil over medium-high heat.
   - Sear the beef tips until browned on all sides. Transfer to the slow cooker.
2. *Sauté Vegetables:*
   - In the same skillet, sauté diced onion, sliced carrots, and minced garlic until softened.
3. *Combine Ingredients in Slow Cooker:*
   - Place the sautéed vegetables in the slow cooker with the seared beef tips.
   - Add beef broth, red wine, tomato paste, dried thyme, dried rosemary, and the bay leaf.
4. *Slow Cook:*
   - Set the slow cooker on low and cook for 6-8 hours or until the beef is tender.
5. *Optional Thickening:*
   - If desired, mix flour with a little water to create a slurry.
   - Stir the slurry into the slow cooker during the last 30 minutes for a thicker sauce.
6. *Serve:*
   - Discard the bay leaf before serving.
   - Garnish with chopped fresh parsley.

EXPERT TIPS & VARIATIONS:
- Add mushrooms during the last hour of cooking for extra flavor.
- For a richer sauce, add a splash of balsamic vinegar or Worcestershire sauce.

PAIRING SUGGESTIONS:
- Creamy mashed potatoes or buttered egg noodles
- Steamed green beans or a side salad

Merlot Filet Mignon

Servings: 2 | Prep Time: 15 minutes | Total Time: 30 minutes

INGREDIENTS:
- 2 filet mignon steaks (6-8 ounces each)
- Salt and black pepper, to taste
- 2 tablespoons olive oil
- 2 cloves garlic, minced
- 1/2 cup Merlot red wine
- 2 tablespoons unsalted butter
- 1 teaspoon Dijon mustard
- Fresh thyme sprigs for garnish (optional)

INSTRUCTIONS:
1. *Preheat the Oven:*
   - Preheat your oven to 400°F (200°C).
2. *Season and Sear the Filet Mignon:*
   - Pat the filet mignon steaks dry with paper towels.
   - Season with salt and black pepper.
   - In an oven-safe skillet, heat olive oil over medium-high heat.
   - Sear the steaks for 2-3 minutes on each side until a golden crust forms.
3. *Roast in the Oven:*
   - Transfer the skillet to the preheated oven and roast for 8-10 minutes for medium-rare, or adjust for preferred doneness.
4. *Create Merlot Sauce:*
   - In the same skillet, remove the steaks and set them aside.
   - Add minced garlic to the skillet and sauté for a minute.
   - Pour in Merlot red wine, scraping up any browned bits.
   - Stir in unsalted butter and Dijon mustard, creating a rich Merlot sauce.
5. *Finish and Garnish:*
   - Return the filet mignon to the skillet, coating them in the Merlot sauce.
   - Spoon the sauce over the steaks and garnish with fresh thyme sprigs.

EXPERT TIPS & VARIATIONS:
- For a bolder flavor, marinate the filet mignon in Merlot for 1-2 hours before cooking.
- Add a touch of honey or maple syrup to the sauce for a hint of sweetness.

PAIRING SUGGESTIONS:
- Creamy mashed potatoes or cauliflower mash
- Roasted Brussels sprouts or a side of sautéed mushrooms

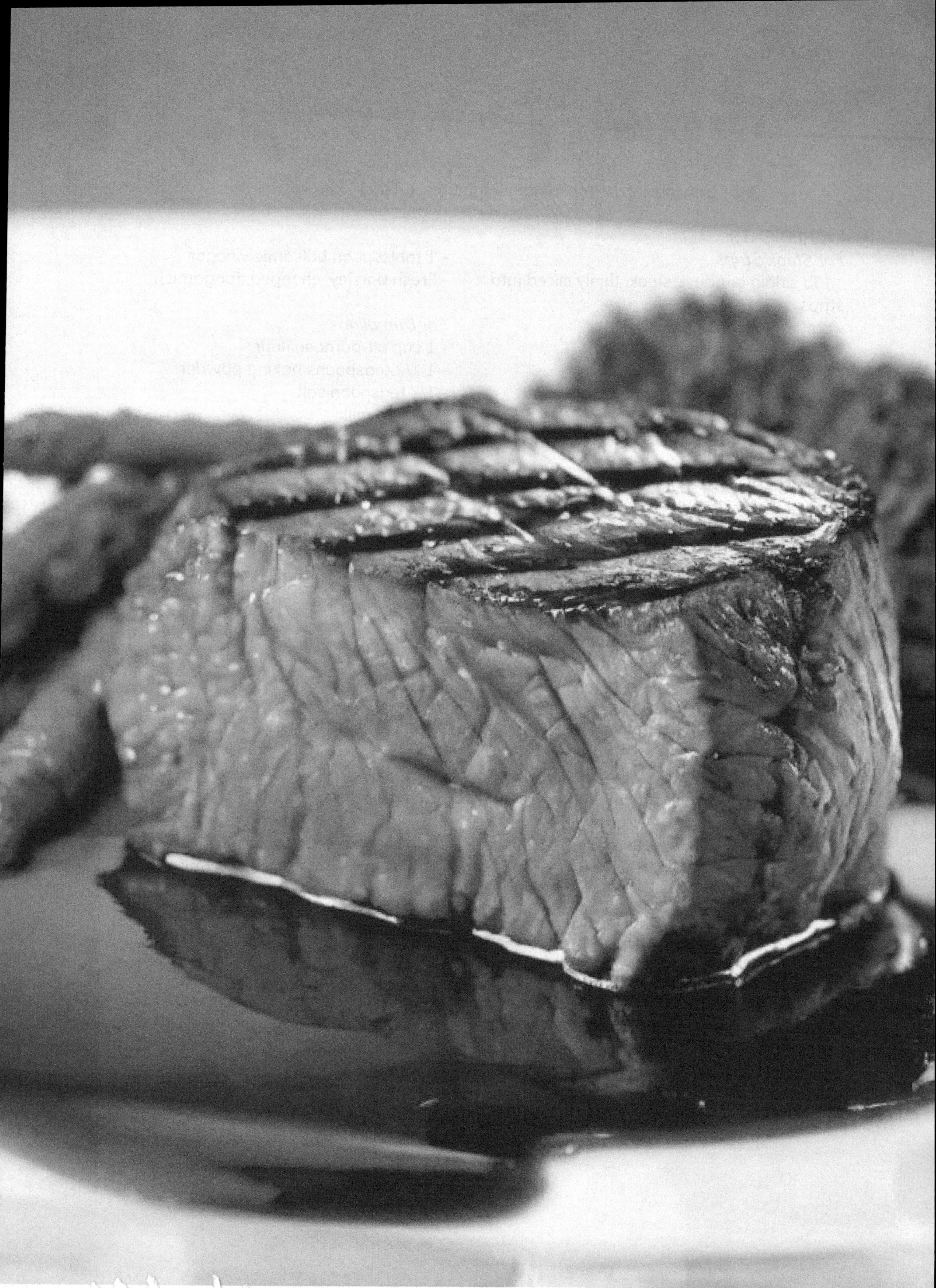

Steak Strips with Dumplings

Servings: 2 | Prep Time: 20 minutes | Total Time: 40 minutes

INGREDIENTS:

For Steak Strips:
- 1 lb sirloin or ribeye steak, thinly sliced into strips
- Salt and black pepper, to taste
- 2 tablespoons olive oil
- 1 onion, thinly sliced
- 2 cloves garlic, minced
- 1 tablespoon soy sauce
- 1 tablespoon Worcestershire sauce
- 1 tablespoon balsamic vinegar
- Fresh parsley, chopped, for garnish

For Dumplings:
- 1 cup all-purpose flour
- 1 1/2 teaspoons baking powder
- 1/2 teaspoon salt
- 1/2 cup milk
- 2 tablespoons unsalted butter, melted

INSTRUCTIONS:

1. *Sear Steak Strips:*
   - Season steak strips with salt and black pepper.
   - In a skillet, heat olive oil over medium-high heat.
   - Sear the steak strips until browned on all sides. Remove from the skillet and set aside.
2. *Sauté Onion and Garlic:*
   - In the same skillet, add sliced onion and minced garlic.
   - Sauté until softened and golden.
3. *Combine Steak Strips and Sauces:*
   - Return the seared steak strips to the skillet with sautéed onion and garlic.
   - Add soy sauce, Worcestershire sauce, and balsamic vinegar.
   - Cook for an additional 3-4 minutes until the steak is cooked to your liking.
4. *Prepare Dumplings:*
   - In a mixing bowl, combine flour, baking powder, and salt.
   - Gradually add milk and melted butter, stirring until a soft dough forms.
5. *Drop Dumplings:*
   - Drop spoonfuls of the dumpling dough onto the simmering steak mixture.
   - Cover and cook for 15-20 minutes until dumplings are cooked through and puffed up.
6. *Serve:*
   - Spoon steak strips and dumplings onto plates.
   - Garnish with fresh chopped parsley.

EXPERT TIPS & VARIATIONS:
- Add a touch of cream to the steak mixture for a creamier sauce.
- Incorporate fresh herbs like thyme or rosemary into the dumpling dough for added flavor.

PAIRING SUGGESTIONS:
- Mashed potatoes or buttered noodles
- Steamed broccoli or a side salad

Beef Fillet with Portobello Sauce

Servings: 2 | Prep Time: 15 minutes | Total Time: 25 minutes

INGREDIENTS:
For Beef Fillet:
- 2 beef fillet steaks (6-8 ounces each)
- Salt and black pepper, to taste
- 2 tablespoons olive oil
- 2 cloves garlic, minced
- 1 teaspoon dried thyme

For Portobello Sauce:

- 2 tablespoons unsalted butter
- 1 cup Portobello mushrooms, sliced
- 1/2 cup beef broth
- 1/4 cup heavy cream
- 2 tablespoons red wine (optional)
- Salt and black pepper, to taste
- Fresh parsley, chopped, for garnish

INSTRUCTIONS:
1. *Preheat the Oven:*
   - Preheat your oven to 400°F (200°C).
2. *Season and Sear the Beef Fillet:*
   - Pat the beef fillet steaks dry with paper towels.
   - Season with salt, black pepper, and dried thyme.
   - In an oven-safe skillet, heat olive oil over medium-high heat.
   - Sear the fillet steaks for 2-3 minutes on each side until a golden crust forms.
3. *Finish in the Oven:*
   - Transfer the skillet to the preheated oven and roast for 10-12 minutes for medium-rare, or adjust for preferred doneness.
4. *Prepare Portobello Sauce:*
   - In a separate skillet, melt unsalted butter over medium heat.
   - Add sliced Portobello mushrooms and sauté until they release their moisture.
5. *Create Sauce:*
   - Pour in beef broth, heavy cream, and red wine (if using).
   - Simmer for 5-7 minutes until the sauce thickens.
   - Season with salt and black pepper to taste.
6. *Serve:*
   - Place the beef fillet steaks on plates.
   - Spoon the Portobello sauce over the steaks.
   - Garnish with fresh chopped parsley.

EXPERT TIPS & VARIATIONS:
- Add a splash of balsamic vinegar to the Portobello sauce for depth of flavor.
- Incorporate a touch of Dijon mustard into the sauce for a subtle tang.

PAIRING SUGGESTIONS:
- Garlic mashed potatoes or roasted sweet potatoes
- Steamed green beans or sautéed spinach

Beef Steak with Blue Cheese

Servings: 2 | Prep Time: 15 minutes | Total Time: 25 minutes

INGREDIENTS:
For Beef Steak:
- 2 beef steaks (ribeye or sirloin, 8-10 ounces each)
- Salt and black pepper, to taste
- 2 tablespoons olive oil
- 2 cloves garlic, minced
- 1 teaspoon dried rosemary

For Blue Cheese Sauce:
- 1/2 cup crumbled blue cheese
- 1/2 cup heavy cream
- 2 tablespoons unsalted butter
- Salt and black pepper, to taste

INSTRUCTIONS:
1. *Preheat the Oven:*
   - Preheat your oven to 400°F (200°C).
2. *Season and Sear the Beef Steak:*
   - Pat the beef steaks dry with paper towels.
   - Season with salt, black pepper, and dried rosemary.
   - In an oven-safe skillet, heat olive oil over medium-high heat.
   - Sear the steaks for 2-3 minutes on each side until a golden crust forms.
3. *Finish in the Oven:*
   - Transfer the skillet to the preheated oven and roast for 10-12 minutes for medium-rare, or adjust for preferred doneness.
4. *Prepare Blue Cheese Sauce:*
   - In a saucepan, melt unsalted butter over medium heat.
   - Add heavy cream and crumbled blue cheese, stirring until the cheese is melted and the sauce is smooth.
   - Season with salt and black pepper to taste.
5. *Serve:*
   - Place the beef steaks on plates.
   - Spoon the rich blue cheese sauce over the steaks.

EXPERT TIPS & VARIATIONS:
- Add a splash of Worcestershire sauce to the blue cheese sauce for an extra layer of umami.
- Incorporate finely chopped chives into the sauce for a fresh herbaceous flavor.

PAIRING SUGGESTIONS:
- Loaded baked potatoes or creamy mashed cauliflower
- Sautéed spinach or a side of roasted Brussels sprouts

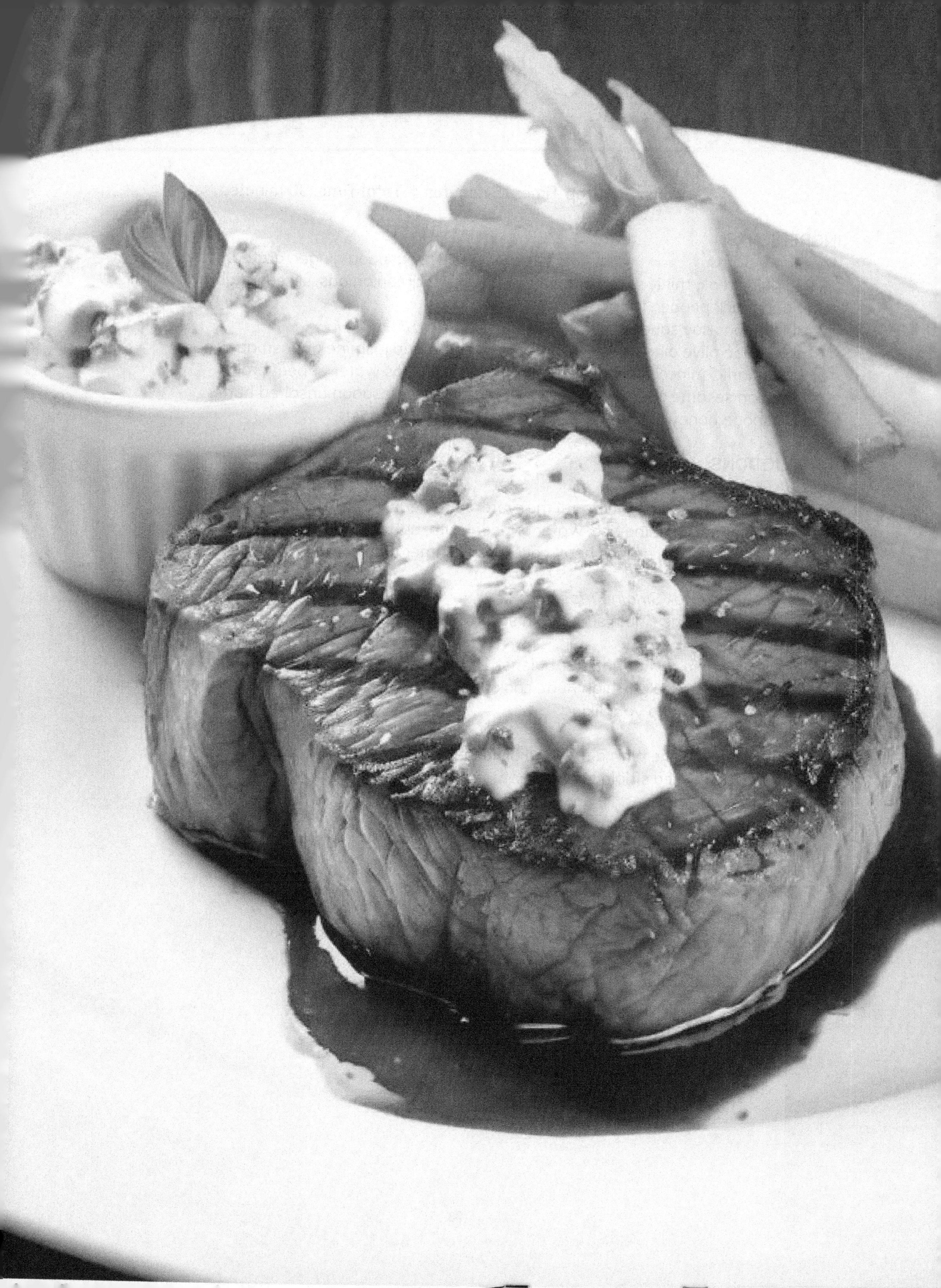

Sirloin Strips over Rice

Servings: 2 | Prep Time: 15 minutes | Total Time: 30 minutes

INGREDIENTS:

For Sirloin Strips:
- 1 lb sirloin steak, thinly sliced into strips
- Salt and black pepper, to taste
- 2 tablespoons soy sauce
- 1 tablespoon olive oil
- 2 cloves garlic, minced
- 1 teaspoon sesame oil
- 1 tablespoon honey
- 1 teaspoon ginger, grated
- 2 green onions, sliced for garnish

For Rice:
- 1 cup jasmine or basmati rice
- 2 cups water or beef broth
- 1 tablespoon unsalted butter
- Salt, to taste

INSTRUCTIONS:

1. *Cook Rice:*
   - Rinse rice under cold water until the water runs clear.
   - In a saucepan, combine rice, water or beef broth, butter, and a pinch of salt.
   - Bring to a boil, then reduce heat, cover, and simmer until rice is tender and liquid is absorbed.
2. *Marinate and Cook Sirloin Strips:*
   - In a bowl, combine sirloin strips with soy sauce, olive oil, minced garlic, sesame oil, honey, and grated ginger.
   - Allow the sirloin to marinate for at least 10 minutes.
   - In a skillet over medium-high heat, cook the sirloin strips for 2-3 minutes on each side until browned and cooked to your liking.
3. *Serve Over Rice:*
   - Fluff the cooked rice with a fork and divide it between two plates.
   - Arrange the cooked sirloin strips over the rice.
4. *Garnish and Enjoy:*
   - Garnish with sliced green onions.
   - Drizzle any remaining marinade over the sirloin strips for extra flavor.

EXPERT TIPS & VARIATIONS:
- Add a splash of lime juice to the sirloin marinade for a citrusy kick.
- Include colorful bell peppers or snap peas for added texture and flavor.

PAIRING SUGGESTIONS:
- Steamed broccoli or sautéed bok choy
- A side of sweet chili sauce or teriyaki sauce for dipping

Grilled Five Spice Flank Steak

Servings: 2 | **Prep Time:** 15 minutes | **Marinating Time:** 1-4 hours | **Grilling Time:** 10-12 minutes

INGREDIENTS:
For Five Spice Marinade:
- 1 lb flank steak
- 2 tablespoons soy sauce
- 1 tablespoon hoisin sauce
- 1 tablespoon sesame oil
- 1 tablespoon honey
- 1 teaspoon Chinese five-spice powder
- 2 cloves garlic, minced
- 1 teaspoon ginger, grated
- 2 green onions, finely chopped (reserve some for garnish)

INSTRUCTIONS:
1. *Prepare the Marinade:*
   - In a bowl, whisk together soy sauce, hoisin sauce, sesame oil, honey, Chinese five-spice powder, minced garlic, grated ginger, and chopped green onions.
2. *Marinate the Flank Steak:*
   - Place the flank steak in a shallow dish or a resealable plastic bag.
   - Pour the marinade over the steak, ensuring it's well-coated.
   - Marinate in the refrigerator for at least 1-4 hours, allowing the flavors to infuse.
3. *Preheat the Grill:*
   - Preheat your grill to medium-high heat.
4. *Grill the Flank Steak:*
   - Remove the flank steak from the marinade, letting excess drip off.
   - Grill the steak for 5-6 minutes per side for medium-rare, adjusting the time for desired doneness.
5. *Rest and Slice:*
   - Allow the grilled flank steak to rest for 5 minutes before slicing it against the grain into thin strips.
6. *Serve and Garnish:*
   - Arrange the sliced steak on a serving platter.
   - Garnish with reserved chopped green onions.

EXPERT TIPS & VARIATIONS:
- Add a dash of rice vinegar or lime juice to the marinade for a tangy twist.
- For extra heat, incorporate a pinch of red pepper flakes or a drizzle of Sriracha.

PAIRING SUGGESTIONS:
- Fragrant jasmine rice or Asian-style noodles
- Grilled vegetables or a side of Asian slaw

Slow-Cooked Pork Ribs

Servings: 2 | **Prep Time:** 15 minutes | **Slow Cooking Time:** 6-8 hours

INGREDIENTS:
- 1 rack of pork ribs (about 2 lbs)
- Salt and black pepper, to taste
- 1 tablespoon smoked paprika
- 1 tablespoon brown sugar
- 1 teaspoon garlic powder
- 1 teaspoon onion powder
- 1/2 teaspoon cayenne pepper (adjust to taste)
- 1 cup barbecue sauce
- 1/4 cup apple cider vinegar
- 1/4 cup honey
- 2 tablespoons Dijon mustard

INSTRUCTIONS:
1. *Prep the Pork Ribs:*
   - Remove the membrane from the back of the ribs.
   - Season both sides with salt and black pepper.
2. *Create Dry Rub:*
   - In a bowl, mix smoked paprika, brown sugar, garlic powder, onion powder, and cayenne pepper.
   - Rub the dry mixture onto both sides of the ribs.
3. *Slow Cook the Ribs:*
   - Place the seasoned ribs in the slow cooker.
   - In a separate bowl, combine barbecue sauce, apple cider vinegar, honey, and Dijon mustard.
   - Pour the sauce over the ribs, ensuring they are well-coated.
   - Cook on low for 6-8 hours until the meat is tender and easily pulls away from the bones.
4. *Finish Under Broiler (Optional):*
   - Preheat your broiler.
   - Transfer the cooked ribs to a baking sheet and brush with additional barbecue sauce.
   - Broil for 5-7 minutes for a caramelized finish.
5. *Serve:*
   - Slice the ribs between the bones and serve with extra sauce on the side.

EXPERT TIPS & VARIATIONS:
- Adjust the cayenne pepper to control the level of spiciness.
- For a smokier flavor, add a teaspoon of liquid smoke to the barbecue sauce.

PAIRING SUGGESTIONS:
- Creamy coleslaw or macaroni and cheese
- Cornbread or baked sweet potatoes

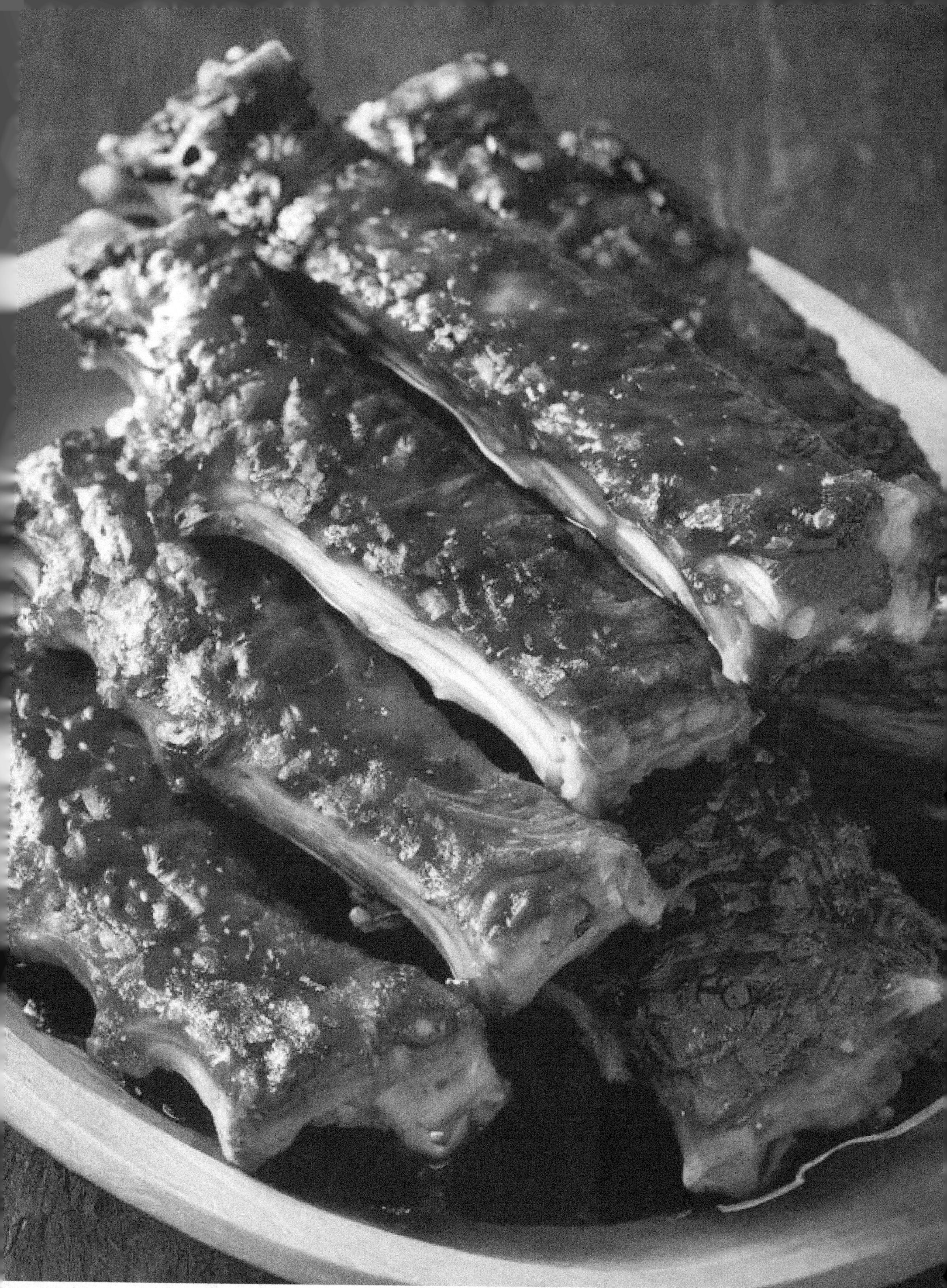

Beef Wellington with Madeira Sauce

Servings: 2 | Prep Time: 30 minutes | Cooking Time: 40 minutes

INGREDIENTS:

For Beef Wellington:
- 2 beef fillet steaks (6-8 ounces each)
- Salt and black pepper, to taste
- 1 tablespoon olive oil
- 1 tablespoon Dijon mustard
- 4 slices prosciutto
- 1 sheet puff pastry, thawed
- 1 egg, beaten (for egg wash)

For Madeira Sauce:
- 1 cup Madeira wine
- 1 cup beef broth
- 1 tablespoon unsalted butter
- 1 tablespoon all-purpose flour
- Salt and black pepper, to taste

INSTRUCTIONS:

1. *Prepare the Beef Fillet:*
   - Pat the beef fillet steaks dry with paper towels.
   - Season with salt and black pepper.
   - Heat olive oil in a skillet over high heat and sear the fillet steaks for 1-2 minutes on each side until browned.
   - Remove from heat and let them cool. Brush with Dijon mustard.
2. *Wrap in Prosciutto and Puff Pastry:*
   - Lay out the prosciutto slices on plastic wrap.
   - Place each fillet steak on the prosciutto and roll them tightly.
   - Roll out the puff pastry and wrap each fillet with the pastry, sealing the edges. Brush with egg wash.
3. *Chill and Preheat Oven:*
   - Chill the wrapped fillets in the refrigerator for 15 minutes.
   - Preheat your oven to 400°F (200°C).
4. *Bake Beef Wellington:*
   - Place the chilled Wellingtons on a baking sheet and bake for 20-25 minutes or until the pastry is golden brown.
5. *Prepare Madeira Sauce:*
   - In a saucepan, melt butter over medium heat. Add flour and cook for 1-2 minutes to create a roux.
   - Pour in Madeira wine and beef broth, stirring continuously until the sauce thickens.
   - Season with salt and black pepper to taste.
6. *Serve:*
   - Slice the Beef Wellington and serve with the Madeira sauce drizzled over the top.

EXPERT TIPS & VARIATIONS:
- Add sautéed mushrooms in Dijon mustard for an extra layer of flavor inside the Wellington.

- Garnish with fresh herbs like thyme or rosemary for a fragrant touch.

PAIRING SUGGESTIONS:
- Mashed potatoes or truffle mashed cauliflower
- Roasted vegetables or a side of asparagus

Pressure-Cooked Mushroom Pork Ragout

Servings: 2 | **Prep Time:** 15 minutes | **Pressure Cooking Time:** 35 minutes

INGREDIENTS:
- 1 lb pork shoulder, cut into cubes
- Salt and black pepper, to taste
- 2 tablespoons olive oil
- 1 onion, finely chopped
- 2 cloves garlic, minced
- 1 cup cremini mushrooms, sliced
- 1/2 cup red wine
- 1 can (14 oz) crushed tomatoes
- 1 teaspoon dried thyme
- 1 teaspoon dried rosemary
- 1 bay leaf
- 1/2 cup beef or vegetable broth
- Fresh parsley, chopped, for garnish

INSTRUCTIONS:
1. *Season and Sear Pork:*
   - Season pork cubes with salt and black pepper.
   - In the pressure cooker, heat olive oil and sear the pork until browned on all sides. Remove and set aside.
2. *Sauté Onion, Garlic, and Mushrooms:*
   - In the same pressure cooker, sauté chopped onion until softened.
   - Add minced garlic and sliced mushrooms, cooking until mushrooms release their moisture.
3. *Deglaze and Add Ingredients:*
   - Pour in red wine to deglaze the pot, scraping up any browned bits.
   - Return the seared pork to the pot.
   - Add crushed tomatoes, dried thyme, dried rosemary, bay leaf, and beef or vegetable broth.
4. *Pressure Cook:*
   - Close the pressure cooker lid and cook on high pressure for 25 minutes.
5. *Release Pressure and Serve:*
   - Allow natural pressure release for 10 minutes, then quick release any remaining pressure.
   - Open the lid and stir the ragout.
   - Discard the bay leaf and adjust seasoning if necessary.
6. *Garnish and Enjoy:*
   - Serve the mushroom pork ragout over pasta, rice, or mashed potatoes.

EXPERT TIPS & VARIATIONS:
- Add a splash of balsamic vinegar for a touch of acidity.
- Include a handful of baby spinach or kale for added freshness.

PAIRING SUGGESTIONS:
- Creamy polenta or mashed cauliflower
- Steamed green beans or a side of roasted Brussels sprouts

Air Fryer Smoked Pork Chops

Servings: 2 | **Prep Time:** 15 minutes | **Cooking Time:** 15 minutes

INGREDIENTS:
- 2 bone-in pork chops (about 1 inch thick)
- Salt and black pepper, to taste
- 1 tablespoon smoked paprika
- 1 teaspoon garlic powder
- 1 teaspoon onion powder
- 1/2 teaspoon dried thyme
- Olive oil spray

INSTRUCTIONS:
1. *Preheat the Air Fryer:*
   - Preheat your air fryer to 400°F (200°C) for about 5 minutes.
2. *Season the Pork Chops:*
   - Pat the pork chops dry with paper towels.
   - Season both sides with salt, black pepper, smoked paprika, garlic powder, onion powder, and dried thyme.
3. *Spray with Olive Oil:*
   - Lightly spray the seasoned pork chops with olive oil to help achieve a crispy exterior.
4. *Air Fry the Pork Chops:*
   - Place the pork chops in the air fryer basket in a single layer, ensuring they are not crowded.
   - Cook for 12-15 minutes, flipping halfway through, until the internal temperature reaches 145°F (63°C) for medium doneness.
5. *Rest and Serve:*
   - Allow the pork chops to rest for a few minutes before serving.

EXPERT TIPS & VARIATIONS:
- For an extra smoky flavor, add a pinch of smoked sea salt.
- Customize the seasoning with your favorite herbs and spices.

PAIRING SUGGESTIONS:
- Loaded baked sweet potatoes or mashed cauliflower
- Grilled vegetables or a side salad

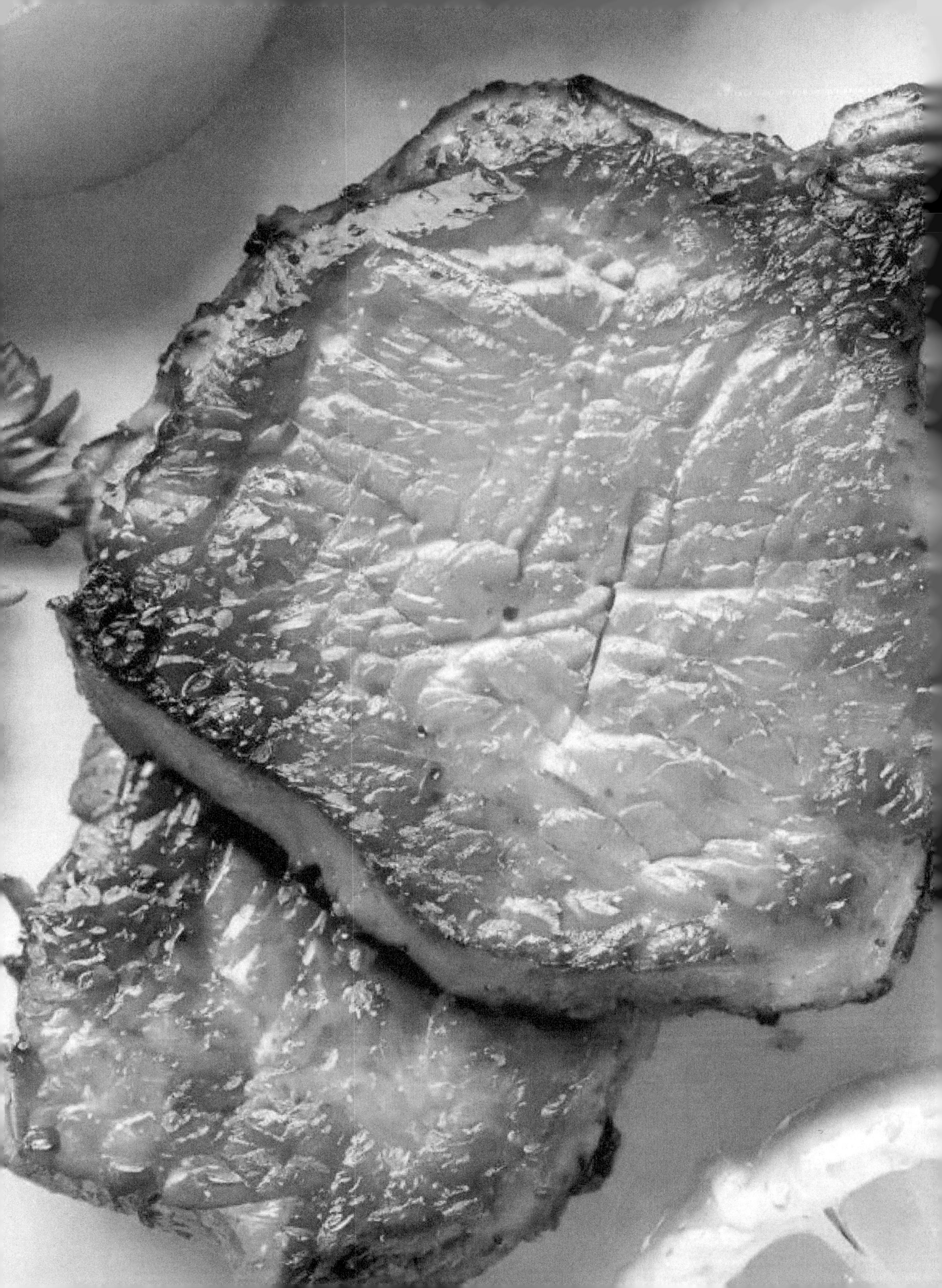

Bacon-Wrapped Filet with Scotch Mushrooms

Servings: 2 | Prep Time: 20 minutes | Cooking Time: 20 minutes

INGREDIENTS:

For Bacon-Wrapped Filet:
- 2 beef filet mignon steaks (6-8 ounces each)
- Salt and black pepper, to taste
- 4 slices bacon
- 2 tablespoons olive oil
- 2 cloves garlic, minced
- Fresh thyme sprigs for garnish

For Scotch Mushrooms:
- 2 cups cremini or button mushrooms, quartered
- 2 tablespoons unsalted butter
- 1/4 cup Scotch whisky
- Salt and black pepper, to taste
- Fresh parsley, chopped, for garnish

INSTRUCTIONS:

1. *Preheat the Oven:*
   - Preheat your oven to 400°F (200°C).
2. *Season and Wrap Filet:*
   - Pat the filet mignon steaks dry with paper towels. Season with salt and black pepper.
   - Wrap each steak with 2 slices of bacon, securing with toothpicks.
3. *Sear Bacon-Wrapped Filets:*
   - In an oven-safe skillet, heat olive oil over medium-high heat.
   - Sear the bacon-wrapped filets for 2-3 minutes on each side until bacon is partially cooked.
4. *Roast in the Oven:*
   - Transfer the skillet to the preheated oven and roast for 12-15 minutes for medium-rare, or adjust for preferred doneness.
5. *Prepare Scotch Mushrooms:*
   - In a separate skillet, melt unsalted butter over medium heat.
   - Add quartered mushrooms and sauté until browned.
   - Pour in Scotch whisky and let it simmer until the alcohol evaporates.
   - Season with salt and black pepper to taste.
6. *Serve and Garnish:*
   - Plate the bacon-wrapped filets and spoon Scotch mushrooms over the top.
   - Garnish with chopped fresh parsley and thyme sprigs.

EXPERT TIPS & VARIATIONS:
- Add a touch of Dijon mustard to the bacon-wrapped filets before roasting.
- Include a splash of heavy cream to the Scotch mushrooms for a creamy sauce.

PAIRING SUGGESTIONS:
- Truffle mashed potatoes or roasted sweet potatoes
- Sautéed spinach or a side of grilled asparagus

POULTRY DISHES

Cheesy Chicken Parmigiana

Servings: 2 | Prep Time: 20 minutes | Baking Time: 25 minutes

INGREDIENTS:

For Chicken Parmigiana:
- 2 boneless, skinless chicken breasts
- Salt and black pepper, to taste
- 1 cup all-purpose flour
- 2 large eggs, beaten
- 1 cup breadcrumbs
- 1 cup marinara sauce
- 1 cup shredded mozzarella cheese
- 1/2 cup grated Parmesan cheese
- Fresh basil leaves, for garnish

For Marinara Sauce:
- 1 can (14 oz) crushed tomatoes
- 2 cloves garlic, minced
- 1 teaspoon dried oregano
- 1 teaspoon dried basil
- Salt and black pepper, to taste
- 1 tablespoon olive oil

INSTRUCTIONS:

1. *Preheat the Oven:*
   - Preheat your oven to 400°F (200°C).
2. *Prepare Marinara Sauce:*
   - In a saucepan, heat olive oil over medium heat.
   - Add minced garlic and sauté until fragrant.
   - Pour in crushed tomatoes, dried oregano, dried basil, salt, and black pepper.
   - Simmer for 10-15 minutes, stirring occasionally.
3. *Prep Chicken Breasts:*
   - Season chicken breasts with salt and black pepper.
   - Dredge each chicken breast in flour, dip into beaten eggs, and coat with breadcrumbs.
4. *Cook Chicken:*
   - In an oven-safe skillet, heat olive oil over medium-high heat.
   - Sear the chicken breasts for 2-3 minutes on each side until golden brown.
5. *Layer and Bake:*
   - Spoon marinara sauce over each chicken breast.
   - Sprinkle shredded mozzarella and grated Parmesan over the top.
   - Transfer the skillet to the preheated oven and bake for 20-25 minutes until the cheese is melted and bubbly.
6. *Serve and Garnish:*
   - Garnish with fresh basil leaves before serving.

EXPERT TIPS & VARIATIONS:
- Add a layer of thinly sliced prosciutto between the chicken and cheese for extra flavor.
- Mix chopped fresh basil into the breadcrumbs for a herb-infused crust.

PAIRING SUGGESTIONS:
- Spaghetti or zucchini noodles
- Roasted vegetables or a side salad

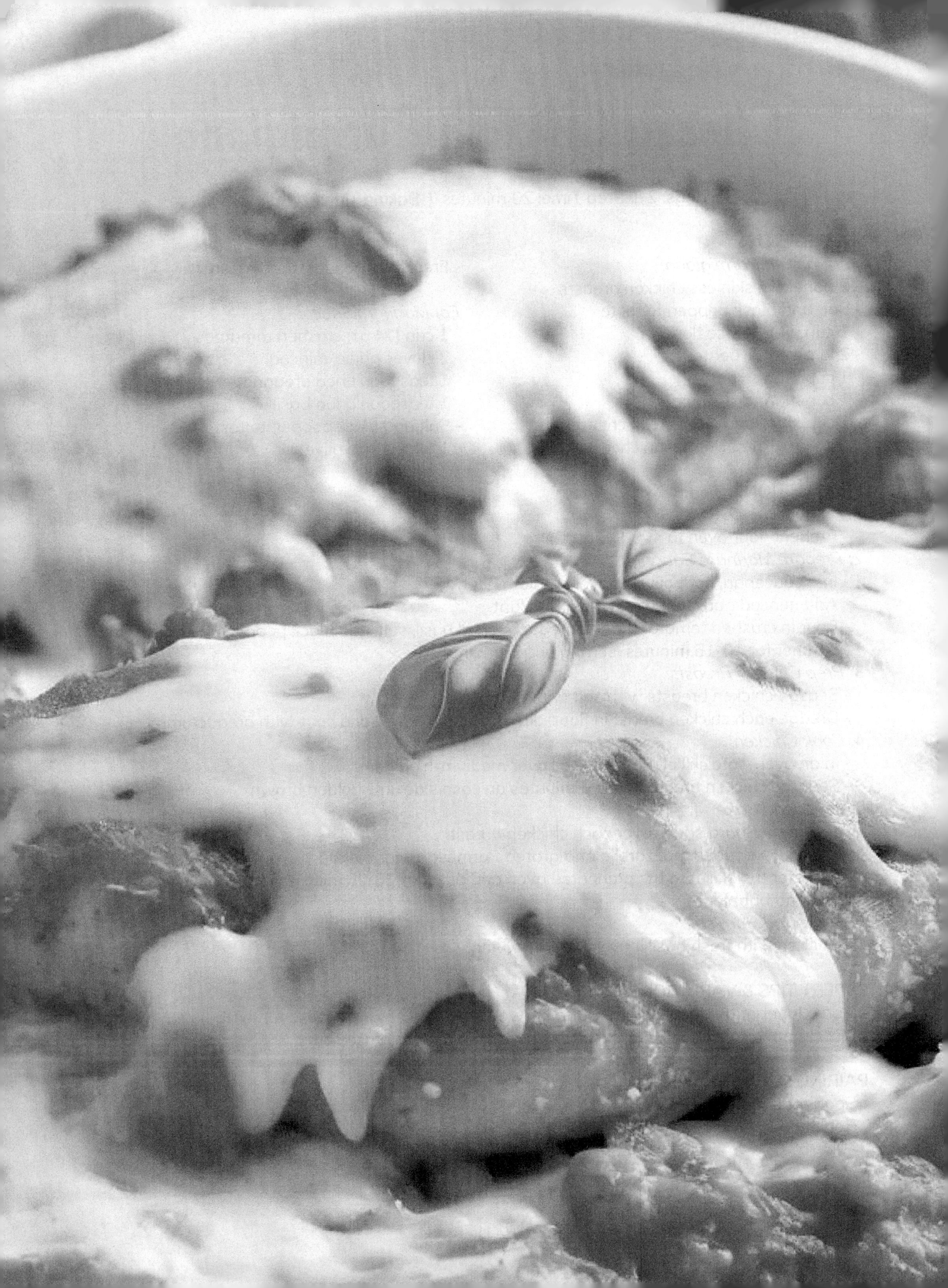

Slow-Cooked Italian Chicken

Servings: 2 | Prep Time: 15 minutes | Slow Cooking Time: 4-6 hours

INGREDIENTS:
- 2 boneless, skinless chicken breasts
- Salt and black pepper, to taste
- 1 tablespoon olive oil
- 1 onion, finely chopped
- 2 cloves garlic, minced
- 1 can (14 oz) diced tomatoes
- 1/2 cup chicken broth
- 1 teaspoon dried oregano
- 1 teaspoon dried basil
- 1/2 teaspoon dried thyme
- 1/4 teaspoon red pepper flakes (optional)
- 1/2 cup black olives, sliced
- 1/4 cup capers, drained
- Fresh parsley, chopped, for garnish
- Grated Parmesan cheese, for serving

INSTRUCTIONS:
1. *Season and Sear Chicken:*
   - Season chicken breasts with salt and black pepper.
   - In a skillet, heat olive oil over medium-high heat.
   - Sear the chicken breasts for 2-3 minutes on each side until browned.
2. *Sauté Onion and Garlic:*
   - In the same skillet, sauté chopped onion and minced garlic until softened.
3. *Combine Ingredients in Slow Cooker:*
   - Transfer the seared chicken, sautéed onion, and garlic to the slow cooker.
   - Add diced tomatoes, chicken broth, dried oregano, dried basil, dried thyme, and red pepper flakes (if using).
4. *Slow Cook:*
   - Cover and cook on low for 4-6 hours until the chicken is tender and cooked through.
5. *Add Olives and Capers:*
   - Stir in sliced black olives and drained capers during the last 30 minutes of cooking.
6. *Serve and Garnish:*
   - Serve the slow-cooked Italian chicken over pasta or rice.
   - Garnish with chopped fresh parsley and grated Parmesan cheese.

EXPERT TIPS & VARIATIONS:
- For a richer flavor, add a splash of white wine to the slow cooker.
- Include sun-dried tomatoes for an extra burst of sweetness.

PAIRING SUGGESTIONS:
- Garlic bread or crusty Italian bread
- Steamed broccoli or a side of sautéed spinach

Turkey Cutlets with Pan Gravy

Servings: 2 | Prep Time: 15 minutes | Cooking Time: 20 minutes

INGREDIENTS:

For Turkey Cutlets:
- 2 turkey cutlets
- Salt and black pepper, to taste
- 2 tablespoons olive oil
- 1 teaspoon dried thyme
- 1 teaspoon garlic powder
- 1/2 cup all-purpose flour (for dredging)

For Pan Gravy:
- 2 tablespoons unsalted butter
- 2 tablespoons all-purpose flour
- 1 1/2 cups chicken broth
- 1/4 cup dry white wine (optional)
- Salt and black pepper, to taste
- Fresh parsley, chopped, for garnish

INSTRUCTIONS:

1. *Season and Dredge Turkey Cutlets:*
   - Season turkey cutlets with salt, black pepper, dried thyme, and garlic powder.
   - Dredge each cutlet in flour, shaking off excess.
2. *Sear Turkey Cutlets:*
   - In a skillet, heat olive oil over medium-high heat.
   - Sear turkey cutlets for 3-4 minutes on each side until golden brown and cooked through.
3. *Make Pan Gravy:*
   - In the same skillet, melt unsalted butter over medium heat.
   - Sprinkle in flour and whisk continuously to create a roux.
   - Slowly pour in chicken broth and white wine (if using), whisking to avoid lumps.
   - Simmer until the gravy thickens. Season with salt and black pepper.
4. *Serve:*
   - Plate the turkey cutlets and spoon pan gravy over the top.
   - Garnish with chopped fresh parsley.

EXPERT TIPS & VARIATIONS:
- Add a splash of heavy cream to the pan gravy for richness.
- Include finely chopped shallots or onions for extra flavor.

PAIRING SUGGESTIONS:
- Mashed potatoes or cauliflower mash
- Steamed green beans or glazed carrots

Chicken Reuben Roll-Ups

Servings: 2 | Prep Time: 15 minutes | Baking Time: 20 minutes

INGREDIENTS:
For Chicken Roll-Ups:
- 2 boneless, skinless chicken breasts
- Salt and black pepper, to taste
- 1 tablespoon olive oil
- 1/2 cup sauerkraut, drained
- 1/2 cup Swiss cheese, shredded
- 1/4 cup Russian dressing

For Russian Dressing:
- 1/2 cup mayonnaise
- 2 tablespoons ketchup
- 1 tablespoon sweet pickle relish
- 1 teaspoon Dijon mustard
- Salt and black pepper, to taste

INSTRUCTIONS:
1. *Preheat the Oven:*
   - Preheat your oven to 375°F (190°C).
2. *Season and Sear Chicken:*
   - Season chicken breasts with salt and black pepper.
   - In an oven-safe skillet, heat olive oil over medium-high heat.
   - Sear chicken breasts for 2-3 minutes on each side until browned.
3. *Prepare Russian Dressing:*
   - In a bowl, mix together mayonnaise, ketchup, sweet pickle relish, Dijon mustard, salt, and black pepper. Set aside.
4. *Assemble Roll-Ups:*
   - Spread sauerkraut evenly over each seared chicken breast.
   - Sprinkle Swiss cheese over the sauerkraut.
   - Roll up each chicken breast tightly and secure with toothpicks.
5. *Bake in the Oven:*
   - Place the chicken roll-ups back into the skillet.
   - Bake in the preheated oven for 20 minutes or until the chicken is cooked through.
6. *Serve with Russian Dressing:*
   - Remove toothpicks and slice the chicken roll-ups.
   - Drizzle Russian dressing over the top.

EXPERT TIPS & VARIATIONS:
- Add a layer of thinly sliced corned beef for a more traditional Reuben flavor.
- Substitute Swiss cheese with your favorite melty cheese.

PAIRING SUGGESTIONS:
- Rye bread or pumpernickel bread
- Oven-baked sweet potato fries or a side of coleslaw

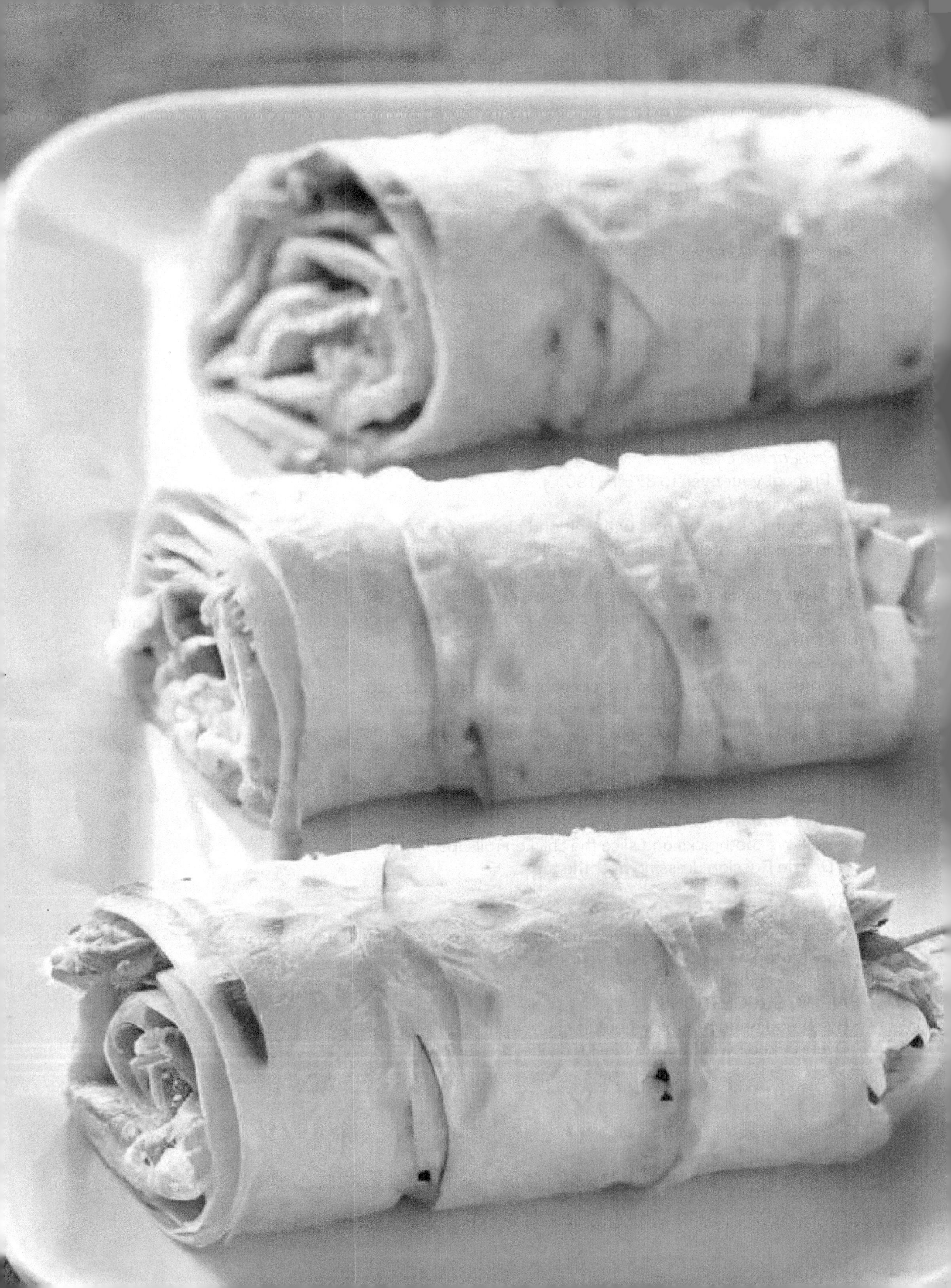

Goat Cheese and Spinach Stuffed Chicken

Servings: 2 | **Prep Time:** 20 minutes | **Baking Time:** 25 minutes

INGREDIENTS:

For Goat Cheese and Spinach Stuffing:
- 1 cup fresh spinach, chopped
- 1/2 cup goat cheese, crumbled
- 2 tablespoons sun-dried tomatoes, finely chopped
- 1 clove garlic, minced
- Salt and black pepper, to taste

For Stuffed Chicken:
- 2 boneless, skinless chicken breasts
- Salt and black pepper, to taste
- 1 tablespoon olive oil
- 1 teaspoon dried thyme
- 1 teaspoon paprika
- Toothpicks or kitchen twine

INSTRUCTIONS:

1. *Preheat the Oven:*
   - Preheat your oven to 375°F (190°C).
2. *Prepare Goat Cheese and Spinach Stuffing:*
   - In a bowl, mix together chopped spinach, crumbled goat cheese, sun-dried tomatoes, minced garlic, salt, and black pepper.
3. *Butterfly and Season Chicken Breasts:*
   - Butterfly each chicken breast by slicing horizontally, creating a pocket.
   - Season the inside of the pocket with salt, black pepper, dried thyme, and paprika.
4. *Stuff Chicken Breasts:*
   - Stuff each chicken breast pocket with the goat cheese and spinach mixture.
   - Secure the openings with toothpicks or tie with kitchen twine.
5. *Sear and Bake:*
   - In an oven-safe skillet, heat olive oil over medium-high heat.
   - Sear the stuffed chicken breasts for 2-3 minutes on each side until browned.
   - Transfer the skillet to the preheated oven and bake for 20-25 minutes or until the chicken is cooked through.
6. *Serve and Enjoy:*
   - Remove toothpicks or twine before serving.
   - Plate the stuffed chicken breasts and drizzle with any juices from the skillet.

EXPERT TIPS & VARIATIONS:
- Add a pinch of red pepper flakes to the stuffing for a hint of heat.
- Incorporate chopped fresh basil or rosemary into the goat cheese mixture for extra flavor.

PAIRING SUGGESTIONS:
- Quinoa or cauliflower rice
- Roasted vegetables or a side of sautéed asparagus

Corsican Chicken

Servings: 2 | Prep Time: 20 minutes | Cooking Time: 25 minutes

INGREDIENTS:

For Chicken Marinade:
- 2 boneless, skinless chicken breasts
- Salt and black pepper, to taste
- 2 tablespoons olive oil
- 1 tablespoon Dijon mustard
- 1 tablespoon honey
- 1 teaspoon dried oregano
- 1 teaspoon paprika
- 2 cloves garlic, minced

For Corsican Tomato Sauce:
- 1 can (14 oz) crushed tomatoes
- 1/4 cup black olives, sliced
- 2 tablespoons capers, drained
- 2 tablespoons fresh basil, chopped
- Salt and black pepper, to taste

INSTRUCTIONS:

1. *Marinate Chicken:*
   - In a bowl, mix together olive oil, Dijon mustard, honey, dried oregano, paprika, minced garlic, salt, and black pepper.
   - Coat chicken breasts in the marinade and let them marinate for at least 15 minutes.
2. *Sear Chicken:*
   - In an oven-safe skillet, heat olive oil over medium-high heat.
   - Sear the marinated chicken breasts for 2-3 minutes on each side until golden brown.
3. *Prepare Corsican Tomato Sauce:*
   - In the same skillet, add crushed tomatoes, black olives, capers, chopped fresh basil, salt, and black pepper.
   - Simmer for 10-15 minutes, allowing the flavors to meld.
4. *Finish in the Oven:*
   - Preheat your oven to 375°F (190°C).
   - Transfer the skillet to the oven and bake for an additional 10 minutes or until the chicken is cooked through.
5. *Serve:*
   - Plate the Corsican Chicken, spooning the tomato sauce over the top.

EXPERT TIPS & VARIATIONS:
- For a spicy kick, add a pinch of red pepper flakes to the marinade.
- Include a splash of white wine to the tomato sauce for a sophisticated flavor.

PAIRING SUGGESTIONS:
- Creamy polenta or mashed cauliflower
- Grilled zucchini or a side of roasted bell peppers

Spinach and Feta Stuffed Chicken

Servings: 2 | **Prep Time:** 20 minutes | **Baking Time:** 25 minutes

INGREDIENTS:

For Spinach and Feta Stuffing:
- 1 cup fresh spinach, chopped
- 1/2 cup feta cheese, crumbled
- 2 tablespoons sun-dried tomatoes, finely chopped
- 1 clove garlic, minced
- Salt and black pepper, to taste

For Stuffed Chicken:
- 2 boneless, skinless chicken breasts
- Salt and black pepper, to taste
- 1 tablespoon olive oil
- 1 teaspoon dried oregano
- 1 teaspoon paprika
- Toothpicks or kitchen twine

INSTRUCTIONS:

1. *Preheat the Oven:*
   - Preheat your oven to 375°F (190°C).
2. *Prepare Spinach and Feta Stuffing:*
   - In a bowl, combine chopped spinach, crumbled feta cheese, sun-dried tomatoes, minced garlic, salt, and black pepper.
3. *Butterfly and Season Chicken Breasts:*
   - Butterfly each chicken breast by slicing horizontally, creating a pocket.
   - Season the inside of the pocket with salt, black pepper, dried oregano, and paprika.
4. *Stuff Chicken Breasts:*
   - Stuff each chicken breast pocket with the spinach and feta mixture.
   - Secure the openings with toothpicks or tie with kitchen twine.
5. *Sear and Bake:*
   - In an oven-safe skillet, heat olive oil over medium-high heat.
   - Sear the stuffed chicken breasts for 2-3 minutes on each side until browned.
   - Transfer the skillet to the preheated oven and bake for 20-25 minutes or until the chicken is cooked through.
6. *Serve and Enjoy:*
   - Remove toothpicks or twine before serving.
   - Plate the stuffed chicken breasts and drizzle with any juices from the skillet.

EXPERT TIPS & VARIATIONS:
- Include chopped Kalamata olives for a Mediterranean twist.
- Add a squeeze of lemon juice over the stuffed chicken before serving for a burst of freshness.

PAIRING SUGGESTIONS:
- Quinoa or couscous
- Roasted vegetables or a side salad

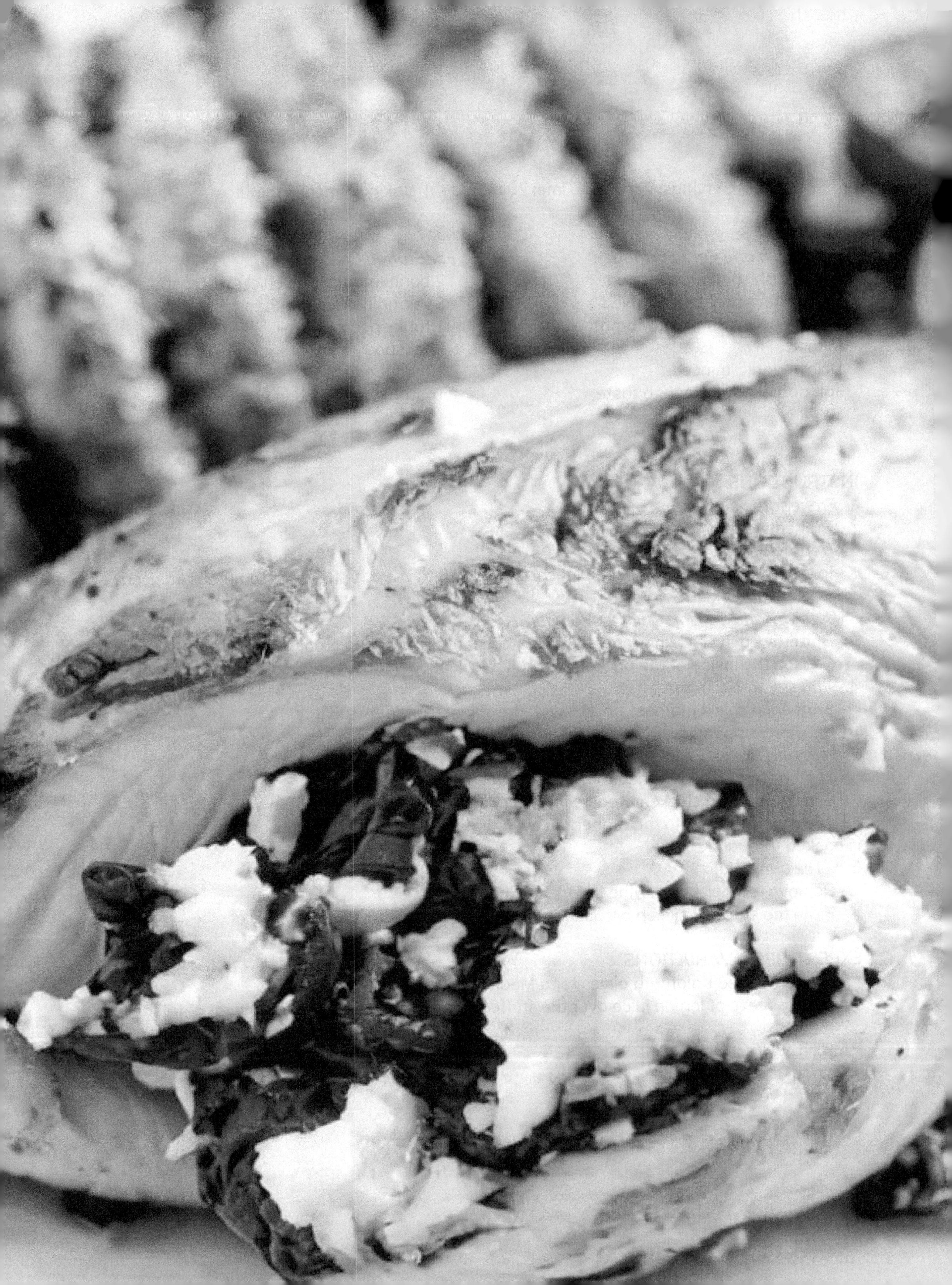

Italian Chicken Skillet

Servings: 2 | Prep Time: 15 minutes | Cooking Time: 25 minutes

INGREDIENTS:
- 2 boneless, skinless chicken breasts
- Salt and black pepper, to taste
- 2 tablespoons olive oil
- 2 cloves garlic, minced
- 1 can (14 oz) diced tomatoes, undrained
- 1 teaspoon dried basil
- 1 teaspoon dried oregano
- 1/2 teaspoon dried thyme
- 1/4 teaspoon red pepper flakes (optional)
- 1/2 cup black olives, sliced
- 1/4 cup fresh basil, chopped, for garnish
- Grated Parmesan cheese, for serving

INSTRUCTIONS:
1. *Season and Sear Chicken:*
   - Season chicken breasts with salt and black pepper.
   - In an oven-safe skillet, heat olive oil over medium-high heat.
   - Sear chicken breasts for 2-3 minutes on each side until browned.
2. *Add Aromatics and Tomatoes:*
   - Add minced garlic to the skillet and sauté for 1 minute.
   - Pour in diced tomatoes with their juice.
3. *Season and Simmer:*
   - Stir in dried basil, dried oregano, dried thyme, and red pepper flakes (if using).
   - Allow the mixture to simmer for 15-20 minutes until the chicken is cooked through.
4. *Add Olives and Finish:*
   - Stir in sliced black olives during the last 5 minutes of cooking.
   - Adjust seasoning if necessary.
5. *Serve and Garnish:*
   - Plate the Italian chicken skillet, spooning tomatoes and olives over the top.
   - Garnish with fresh basil and grated Parmesan cheese.

EXPERT TIPS & VARIATIONS:
- Include a splash of balsamic vinegar for a touch of acidity.
- Add a handful of baby spinach or arugula for extra freshness.

PAIRING SUGGESTIONS:
- Garlic bread or a side of crusty Italian bread
- Pasta or zucchini noodles

Chicken Parmesan

Servings: 2 | **Prep Time:** 20 minutes | **Baking Time:** 25 minutes

INGREDIENTS:

For Breaded Chicken:
- 2 boneless, skinless chicken breasts
- Salt and black pepper, to taste
- 1 cup breadcrumbs
- 1/2 cup grated Parmesan cheese
- 2 large eggs, beaten
- 1 cup marinara sauce

For Tomato Sauce:
- 1 can (14 oz) crushed tomatoes
- 2 cloves garlic, minced
- 1 teaspoon dried oregano
- 1 teaspoon dried basil
- Salt and black pepper, to taste
- 1 tablespoon olive oil

For Cheese Topping:
- 1 cup shredded mozzarella cheese
- 1/4 cup grated Parmesan cheese
- Fresh basil leaves, for garnish

INSTRUCTIONS:

1. *Preheat the Oven:*
   - Preheat your oven to 400°F (200°C).
2. *Season and Bread Chicken:*
   - Season chicken breasts with salt and black pepper.
   - In one bowl, combine breadcrumbs and grated Parmesan cheese.
   - Dip each chicken breast into beaten eggs, then coat with the breadcrumb mixture.
3. *Sear and Prepare Tomato Sauce:*
   - In an oven-safe skillet, heat olive oil over medium-high heat.
   - Sear the breaded chicken breasts for 2-3 minutes on each side until golden brown.
   - In a separate saucepan, combine crushed tomatoes, minced garlic, dried oregano, dried basil, salt, and black pepper. Simmer for 10-15 minutes.
4. *Top with Sauce and Cheese:*
   - Spoon marinara sauce over each chicken breast in the skillet.
   - Sprinkle shredded mozzarella and grated Parmesan over the top.
5. *Bake in the Oven:*
   - Transfer the skillet to the preheated oven and bake for 20-25 minutes until the cheese is melted and bubbly.
6. *Serve and Garnish:*
   - Garnish with fresh basil leaves before serving.

EXPERT TIPS & VARIATIONS:
- Add a pinch of red pepper flakes to the tomato sauce for a hint of heat.
- Mix chopped fresh parsley into the breadcrumb mixture for added freshness.

PAIRING SUGGESTIONS:
- Spaghetti or zucchini noodles
- Caesar salad or a side of roasted vegetables

Asparagus-Stuffed Air Fryer Chicken Rolls

Servings: 2 | Prep Time: 20 minutes | Air Frying Time: 20 minutes

INGREDIENTS:

For Asparagus Stuffing:
- 1/2 bunch asparagus, trimmed
- 1 tablespoon olive oil
- 1 clove garlic, minced
- Salt and black pepper, to taste
- Zest of 1 lemon

For Chicken Rolls:
- 2 boneless, skinless chicken breasts
- Salt and black pepper, to taste
- 1 tablespoon Dijon mustard
- 2 tablespoons cream cheese
- 2 tablespoons breadcrumbs
- 1 tablespoon Parmesan cheese, grated
- 1 tablespoon olive oil

INSTRUCTIONS:

1. *Preheat the Air Fryer:*
   - Preheat your air fryer to 375°F (190°C).
2. *Prepare Asparagus Stuffing:*
   - In a bowl, toss trimmed asparagus with olive oil, minced garlic, salt, black pepper, and lemon zest.
3. *Butterfly and Season Chicken Breasts:*
   - Butterfly each chicken breast by slicing horizontally, creating a pocket.
   - Season the inside with salt and black pepper.
4. *Assemble Chicken Rolls:*
   - Spread Dijon mustard inside each chicken breast.
   - Place a layer of cream cheese, followed by breadcrumbs, Parmesan cheese, and the asparagus mixture. Roll up each chicken breast and secure with toothpicks.
5. *Air Fry Chicken Rolls:*
   - Brush the outside of each chicken roll with olive oil.
   - Place the rolls in the air fryer basket and air fry for 18-20 minutes until the chicken is cooked through and golden brown.
6. *Serve and Enjoy:*
   - Remove toothpicks before serving.
   - Plate the chicken rolls and drizzle with any juices from the air fryer.

EXPERT TIPS & VARIATIONS:
- Add a sprinkle of smoked paprika or your favorite herbs to the breadcrumb mixture.
- Experiment with different cheeses like feta or goat cheese for varied flavors.

PAIRING SUGGESTIONS:
- Quinoa or couscous
- Roasted cherry tomatoes or a side of sautéed spinach

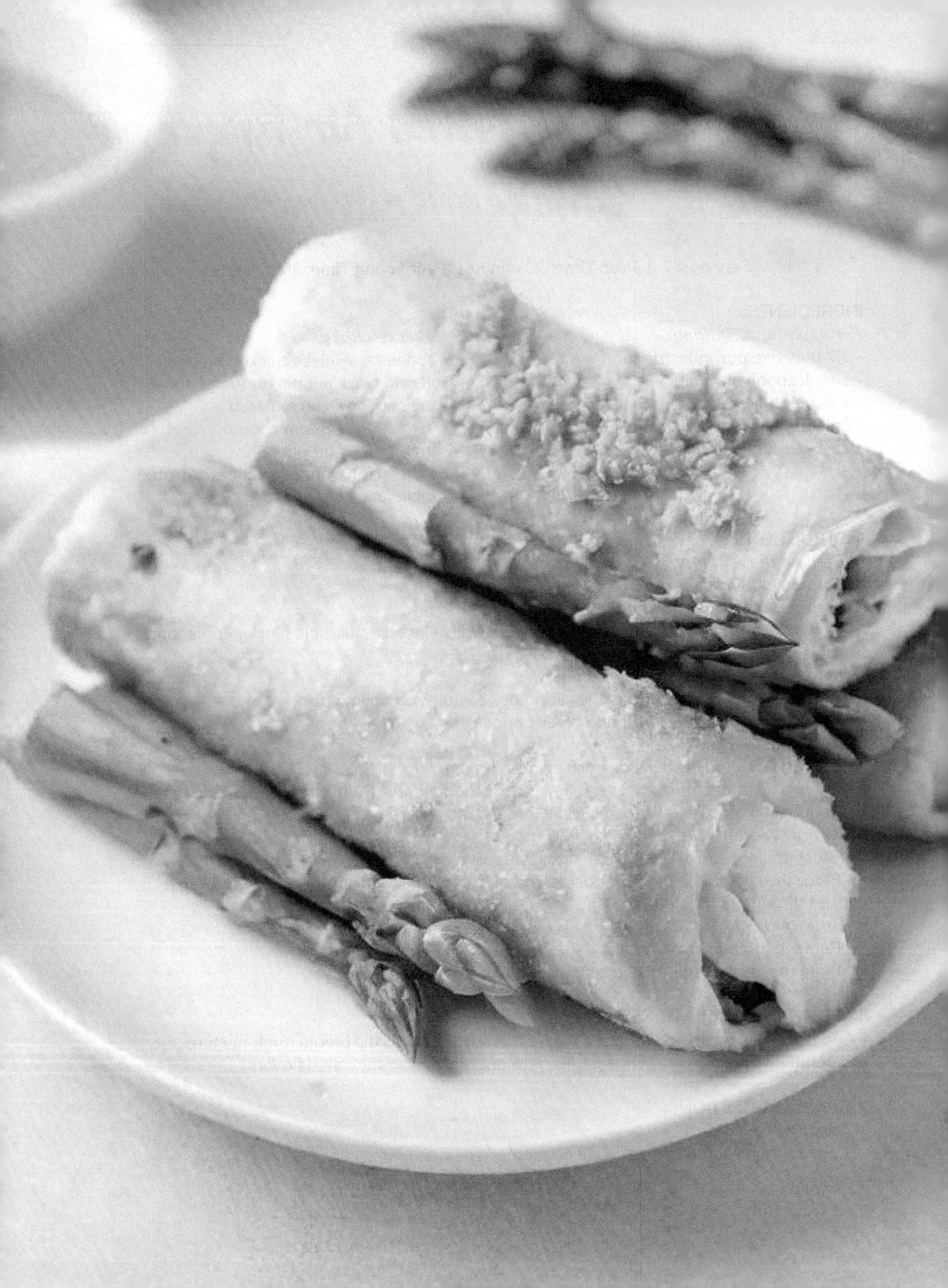

Herb-Stuffed Cornish Hen

Servings: 2 | **Prep Time:** 25 minutes | **Roasting Time:** 1 hour

INGREDIENTS:

For Herb Stuffing:
- 1 cup fresh breadcrumbs
- 2 tablespoons fresh parsley, chopped
- 1 tablespoon fresh thyme leaves
- 1 tablespoon fresh rosemary, chopped
- 1 tablespoon fresh sage, chopped
- 2 cloves garlic, minced
- 2 tablespoons olive oil
- Salt and black pepper, to taste

For Cornish Hen:
- 2 Cornish hens
- Salt and black pepper, to taste
- 2 tablespoons butter, melted
- 1 lemon, sliced
- Fresh herbs for garnish (optional)

INSTRUCTIONS:

1. *Preheat the Oven:*
   - Preheat your oven to 375°F (190°C).
2. *Prepare Herb Stuffing:*
   - In a bowl, mix fresh breadcrumbs, chopped parsley, thyme leaves, rosemary, sage, minced garlic, olive oil, salt, and black pepper.
3. *Season and Stuff Cornish Hen:*
   - Season the Cornish hens with salt and black pepper, inside and out.
   - Stuff each hen with the herb stuffing mixture.
4. *Truss and Brush with Butter:*
   - Truss the Cornish hens by tying the legs together with kitchen twine.
   - Brush the hens with melted butter for a golden finish.
5. *Roast in the Oven:*
   - Place the Cornish hens on a roasting pan or baking sheet.
   - Roast in the preheated oven for 50-60 minutes or until the internal temperature reaches 165°F (74°C).
6. *Garnish and Serve:*
   - Garnish with fresh herbs and lemon slices.
   - Let the hens rest for a few minutes before serving.

EXPERT TIPS & VARIATIONS:
- Include chopped nuts, like pine nuts or almonds, to the herb stuffing for added texture.
- Baste the hens with their juices during roasting for extra flavor.

PAIRING SUGGESTIONS:
- Wild rice or roasted baby potatoes
- Steamed asparagus or honey-glazed carrots

Chicken Scampi

Servings: 2 | **Prep Time:** 15 minutes | **Cooking Time:** 15 minutes

INGREDIENTS:
- 2 boneless, skinless chicken breasts, thinly sliced
- Salt and black pepper, to taste
- 4 tablespoons unsalted butter
- 4 cloves garlic, minced
- 1/4 teaspoon red pepper flakes (optional)
- 1/2 cup dry white wine
- 1 cup cherry tomatoes, halved
- Zest of 1 lemon
- Juice of 1 lemon
- 1/4 cup fresh parsley, chopped
- 8 oz linguine or your preferred pasta, cooked

INSTRUCTIONS:
1. *Season and Sauté Chicken:*
    - Season thinly sliced chicken breasts with salt and black pepper.
    - In a skillet, melt 2 tablespoons of butter over medium-high heat.
    - Sauté the chicken until golden brown on both sides. Remove and set aside.
2. *Prepare Scampi Sauce:*
    - In the same skillet, add the remaining 2 tablespoons of butter.
    - Add minced garlic and red pepper flakes (if using). Sauté until fragrant.
3. *Deglaze with Wine:*
    - Pour in the dry white wine, scraping any browned bits from the bottom of the skillet.
4. *Combine Ingredients:*
    - Return the cooked chicken to the skillet.
    - Add halved cherry tomatoes, lemon zest, and lemon juice. Cook for 3-4 minutes until tomatoes are softened.
5. *Finish and Garnish:*
    - Toss in cooked pasta and fresh parsley.
    - Stir until everything is well coated and heated through.
6. *Serve and Enjoy:*
    - Plate the Chicken Scampi, ensuring each serving has a good mix of chicken, tomatoes, and pasta.

EXPERT TIPS & VARIATIONS:
- Add a handful of baby spinach or arugula for extra freshness.
- Substitute the linguine with zucchini noodles for a low-carb option.

PAIRING SUGGESTIONS:
- Garlic bread or a side of crusty Italian bread
- Caesar salad or a side of roasted vegetables

Pressure Cooked Chicken Paprika

Servings: 2 | **Prep Time:** 15 minutes | **Pressure Cooking Time:** 15 minutes

INGREDIENTS:
- 2 boneless, skinless chicken breasts, cut into cubes
- Salt and black pepper, to taste
- 2 tablespoons olive oil
- 1 onion, finely chopped
- 2 cloves garlic, minced
- 1 tablespoon sweet paprika
- 1 teaspoon smoked paprika
- 1/2 teaspoon caraway seeds
- 1 bell pepper, sliced
- 1 cup chicken broth
- 1/2 cup sour cream
- Fresh parsley, chopped, for garnish
- Cooked rice or egg noodles, for serving

INSTRUCTIONS:
1. *Season and Sauté Chicken:*
   - Season chicken cubes with salt and black pepper.
   - In the pressure cooker, heat olive oil and sauté chicken until browned on all sides.
2. *Sauté Aromatics:*
   - Add chopped onion and minced garlic to the pressure cooker. Sauté until softened.
3. *Add Paprika and Caraway Seeds:*
   - Stir in sweet paprika, smoked paprika, and caraway seeds. Cook for an additional minute to release flavors.
4. *Add Bell Pepper and Broth:*
   - Add sliced bell pepper to the pressure cooker.
   - Pour in chicken broth and deglaze the bottom of the cooker.
5. *Pressure Cook:*
   - Secure the lid and pressure cook for 15 minutes.
6. *Release Pressure and Finish:*
   - Quick-release the pressure and open the cooker.
   - Stir in sour cream until well combined.
7. *Serve and Garnish:*
   - Serve the Chicken Paprika over cooked rice or egg noodles.
   - Garnish with chopped fresh parsley.

EXPERT TIPS & VARIATIONS:
- Add a touch of cayenne pepper for a spicier version.
- Include mushrooms for an extra depth of flavor.

PAIRING SUGGESTIONS:
- Mashed potatoes or cauliflower mash
- Steamed broccoli or a side of green beans

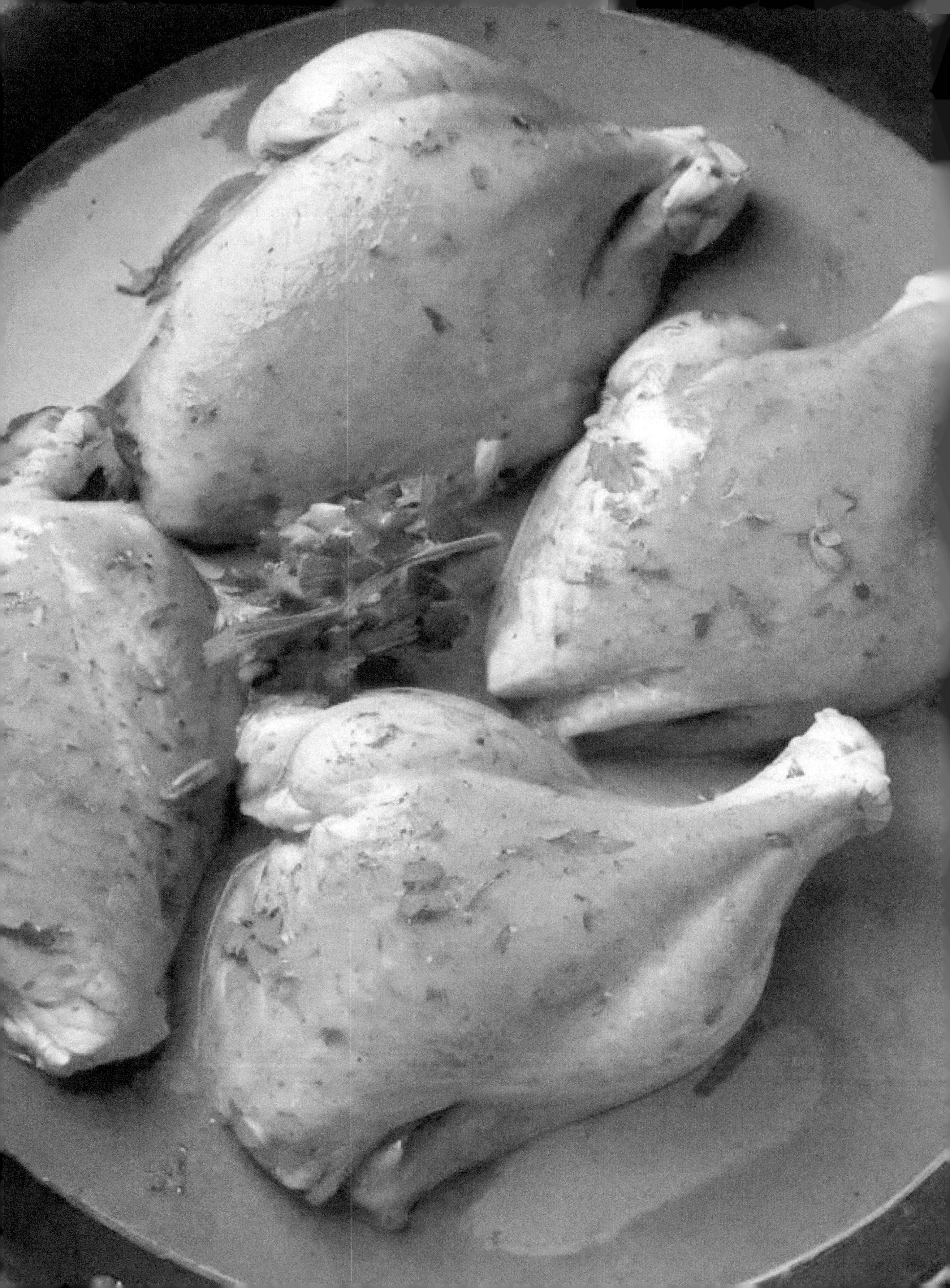

Air Fryer Almond Chicken

Servings: 2 | **Prep Time:** 20 minutes | **Air Frying Time:** 15 minutes

INGREDIENTS:

For Almond Coating:
- 1/2 cup almond flour
- 1/4 cup finely chopped almonds
- 1/2 teaspoon garlic powder
- 1/2 teaspoon onion powder
- Salt and black pepper, to taste

For Chicken:
- 2 boneless, skinless chicken breasts
- Salt and black pepper, to taste
- 2 tablespoons Dijon mustard
- 1 tablespoon olive oil
- Cooking spray (for air frying)

INSTRUCTIONS:

1. *Preheat the Air Fryer:*
   - Preheat your air fryer to 375°F (190°C).
2. *Prepare Almond Coating:*
   - In a bowl, combine almond flour, chopped almonds, garlic powder, onion powder, salt, and black pepper.
3. *Season and Coat Chicken:*
   - Season chicken breasts with salt and black pepper.
   - Brush each chicken breast with Dijon mustard, ensuring it's evenly coated.
   - Press the mustard-coated chicken into the almond coating mixture, making sure to cover all sides.
4. *Air Fry Almond Chicken:*
   - Lightly spray the air fryer basket with cooking spray.
   - Place the coated chicken breasts in the air fryer basket.
   - Air fry for 15 minutes or until the chicken is golden brown and cooked through.
5. *Serve and Enjoy:*
   - Slice the Air Fryer Almond Chicken and serve immediately.

EXPERT TIPS & VARIATIONS:
- Add a pinch of cayenne pepper to the almond coating for a hint of spice.
- Serve with a side of low-carb almond flour-based gravy.

PAIRING SUGGESTIONS:
- Roasted Brussels sprouts or a side of sautéed spinach
- Cauliflower rice or mashed cauliflower

SEAFOOD DISHES

Walnut and Oat-Crusted Salmon

Servings: 2 | Prep Time: 15 minutes | Baking Time: 15 minutes

INGREDIENTS:
For Walnut and Oat Crust:
- 1/2 cup rolled oats
- 1/4 cup walnuts, finely chopped
- 1 tablespoon Dijon mustard
- 1 tablespoon honey
- 1 tablespoon olive oil
- Salt and black pepper, to taste

For Salmon:
- 2 salmon fillets, skin-on
- Salt and black pepper, to taste
- Lemon wedges, for serving

INSTRUCTIONS:
1. *Preheat the Oven:*
   - Preheat your oven to 400°F (200°C).
2. *Prepare Walnut and Oat Crust:*
   - In a bowl, combine rolled oats, finely chopped walnuts, Dijon mustard, honey, olive oil, salt, and black pepper. Mix until well combined.
3. *Season and Coat Salmon:*
   - Pat dry the salmon fillets with a paper towel.
   - Season both sides with salt and black pepper.
   - Press the walnut and oat crust mixture onto the top of each salmon fillet.
4. *Bake the Salmon:*
   - Place the coated salmon fillets on a baking sheet lined with parchment paper.
   - Bake in the preheated oven for 15 minutes or until the salmon is cooked through and the crust is golden brown.
5. *Serve and Enjoy:*
   - Serve the Walnut and Oat-Crusted Salmon with lemon wedges on the side.

EXPERT TIPS & VARIATIONS:
- Add a sprinkle of fresh dill or parsley to the crust for extra freshness.
- Drizzle a bit of balsamic glaze over the salmon before serving.

PAIRING SUGGESTIONS:
- Quinoa or wild rice
- Steamed asparagus or a side of roasted vegetables

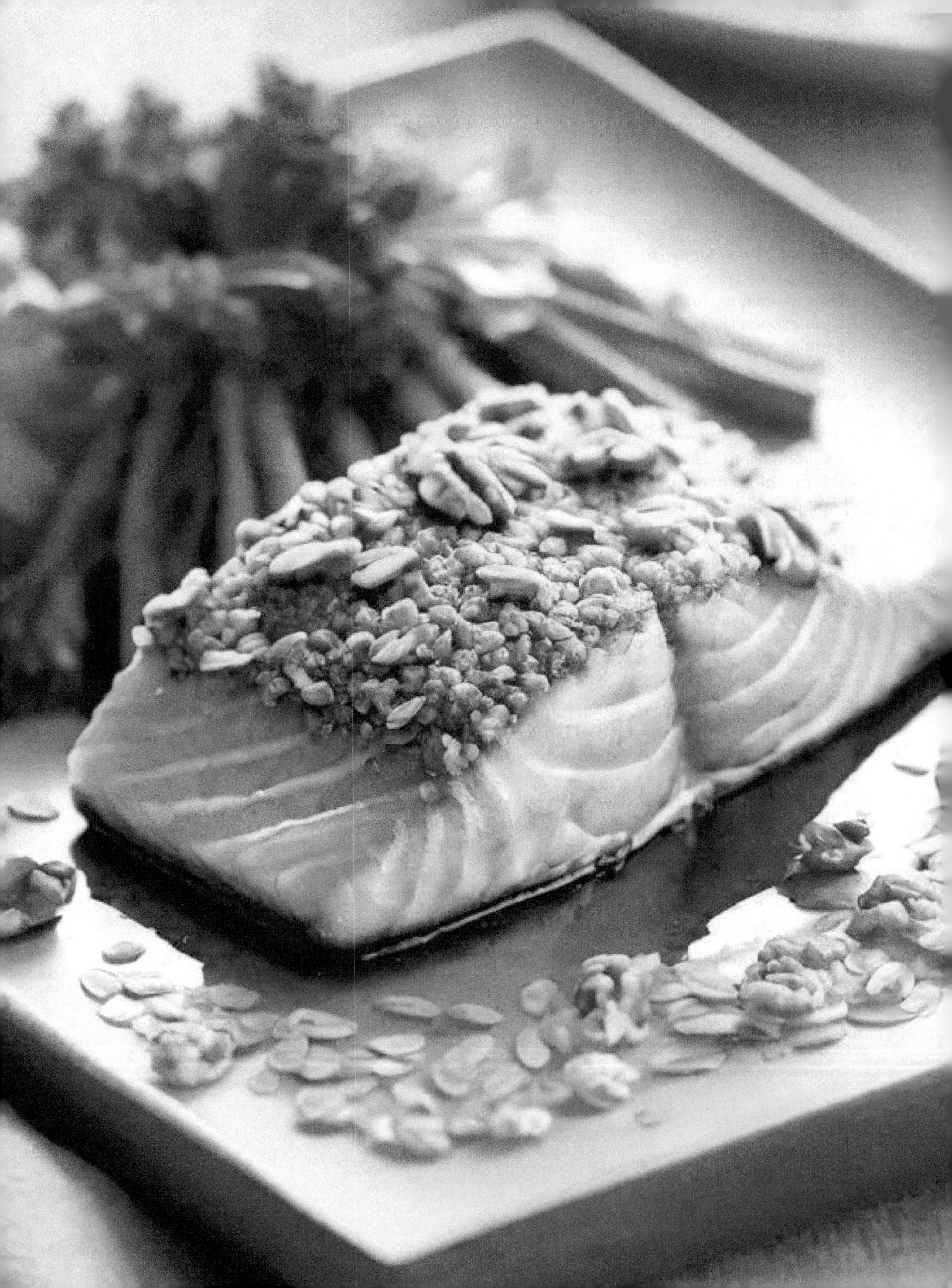

Air Fryer Scallops

Servings: 2 | **Prep Time:** 10 minutes | **Air Frying Time:** 6 minutes

INGREDIENTS:
- 1/2 pound large sea scallops, patted dry
- 1 tablespoon olive oil
- 1 tablespoon melted butter
- 1 clove garlic, minced
- Zest of 1 lemon
- Salt and black pepper, to taste
- Fresh parsley, chopped, for garnish
- Lemon wedges, for serving

INSTRUCTIONS:
1. *Preheat the Air Fryer:*
   - Preheat your air fryer to 400°F (200°C).
2. *Prepare Scallops:*
   - In a bowl, toss the sea scallops with olive oil, melted butter, minced garlic, lemon zest, salt, and black pepper.
3. *Air Fry the Scallops:*
   - Place the seasoned scallops in a single layer in the air fryer basket.
   - Air fry for 6 minutes, turning once halfway through, or until the scallops are opaque and lightly browned.
4. *Serve and Garnish:*
   - Plate the Air Fryer Scallops, garnishing with fresh chopped parsley.
   - Serve with lemon wedges on the side.

EXPERT TIPS & VARIATIONS:
- Add a pinch of smoked paprika or cayenne pepper for a hint of heat.
- Serve over a bed of mixed greens or with a light lemon vinaigrette for a refreshing touch.

PAIRING SUGGESTIONS:
- Cauliflower rice or mashed cauliflower
- Sautéed spinach or a side of grilled asparagus

Flavorful Salmon Fillets

Servings: 2 | Prep Time: 15 minutes | Baking Time: 15 minutes

INGREDIENTS:
For Salmon Marinade:
- 2 salmon fillets
- 2 tablespoons olive oil
- 2 tablespoons soy sauce
- 1 tablespoon Dijon mustard
- 1 tablespoon honey
- 2 cloves garlic, minced
- 1 teaspoon fresh ginger, grated
- Zest of 1 lemon
- Salt and black pepper, to taste

INSTRUCTIONS:
1. *Preheat the Oven:*
   - Preheat your oven to 400°F (200°C).
2. *Prepare Salmon Marinade:*
   - In a bowl, whisk together olive oil, soy sauce, Dijon mustard, honey, minced garlic, grated ginger, lemon zest, salt, and black pepper.
3. *Marinate Salmon:*
   - Place the salmon fillets in a shallow dish and pour the marinade over them.
   - Let the salmon marinate for at least 10 minutes, allowing the flavors to infuse.
4. *Bake the Salmon:*
   - Transfer the marinated salmon fillets to a baking sheet lined with parchment paper.
   - Bake in the preheated oven for 15 minutes or until the salmon is cooked through and flakes easily with a fork.
5. *Serve and Enjoy:*
   - Plate the Flavorful Salmon Fillets and drizzle with any remaining marinade.
   - Garnish with fresh herbs or lemon slices, if desired.

EXPERT TIPS & VARIATIONS:
- Add a splash of fresh orange juice to the marinade for a citrusy twist.
- Sprinkle sesame seeds or chopped green onions over the salmon before serving.

PAIRING SUGGESTIONS:
- Quinoa or couscous
- Steamed broccoli or a side of roasted Brussels sprouts

Seared Scallops with Citrus Herbed Sauce

Servings: 2 | **Prep Time:** 15 minutes | **Cooking Time:** 10 minutes

INGREDIENTS:
For Seared Scallops:
- 1/2 pound large sea scallops, patted dry
- Salt and black pepper, to taste
- 1 tablespoon olive oil
- 1 tablespoon unsalted butter

For Citrus Herbed Sauce:
- Juice of 1 lemon
- Zest of 1 lemon
- 1 tablespoon orange juice
- 1 tablespoon fresh parsley, chopped
- 1 tablespoon fresh chives, chopped
- 1 clove garlic, minced
- 2 tablespoons white wine (optional)
- Salt and black pepper, to taste

INSTRUCTIONS:
1. *Season and Sear Scallops:*
   - Season the sea scallops with salt and black pepper.
   - In a skillet, heat olive oil and butter over medium-high heat.
   - Sear the scallops for 2-3 minutes on each side until golden brown. Ensure not to overcrowd the pan.
2. *Prepare Citrus Herbed Sauce:*
   - In a small bowl, whisk together lemon juice, lemon zest, orange juice, chopped parsley, chopped chives, minced garlic, and white wine (if using).
   - Season the sauce with salt and black pepper to taste.
3. *Finish and Serve:*
   - Pour the citrus herbed sauce over the seared scallops in the skillet.
   - Gently toss the scallops in the sauce until well coated.
4. *Plate and Enjoy:*
   - Plate the Seared Scallops with Citrus Herbed Sauce.
   - Garnish with additional fresh herbs or lemon slices if desired.

EXPERT TIPS & VARIATIONS:
- Add a pinch of red pepper flakes to the sauce for a touch of heat.
- Substitute white wine with chicken or vegetable broth if you prefer a non-alcoholic version.

PAIRING SUGGESTIONS:
- Garlic butter rice or cauliflower rice
- Sautéed spinach or a side of grilled asparagus

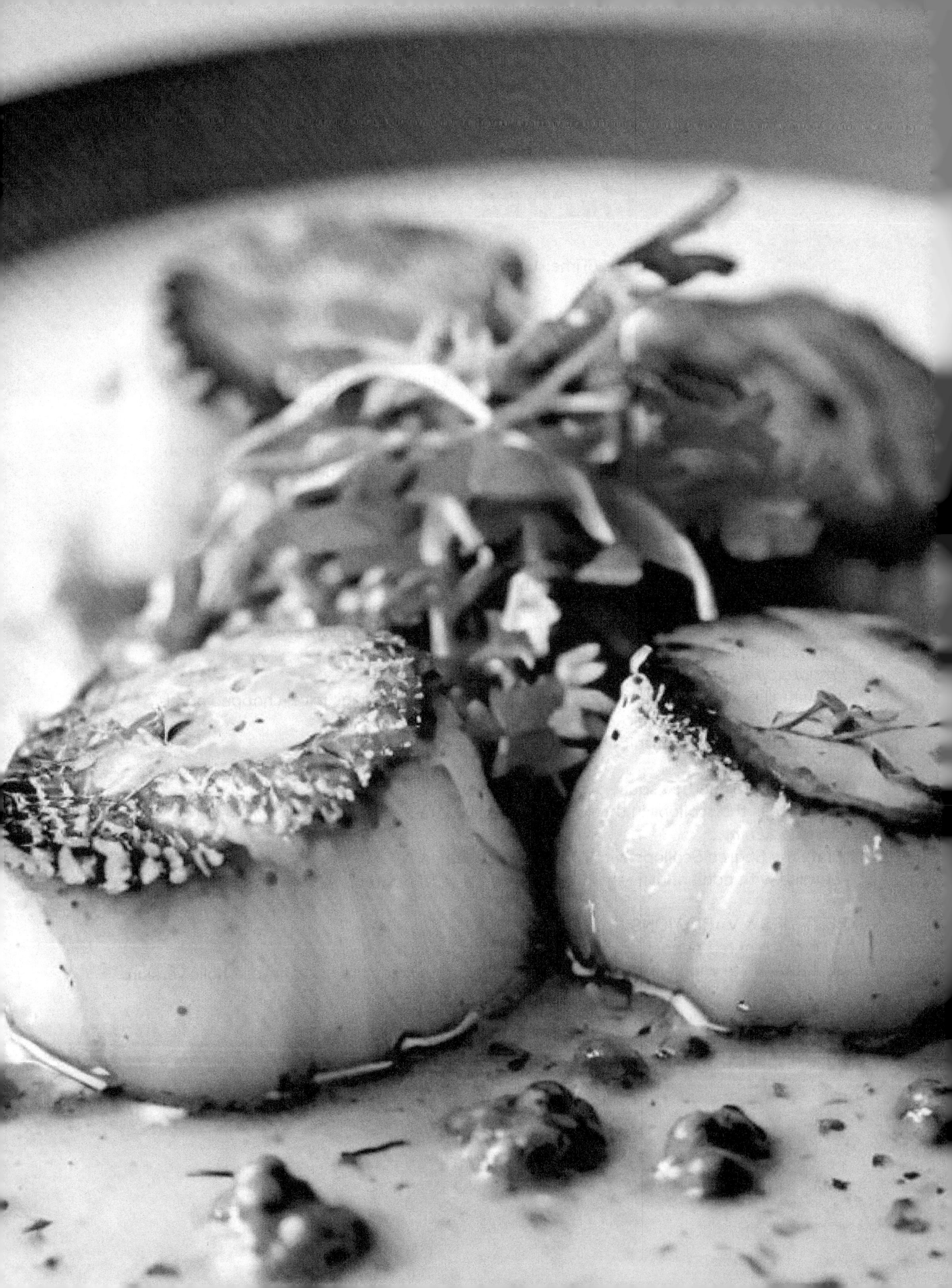

Garlic Lemon Shrimp

Servings: 2 | Prep Time: 10 minutes | Cooking Time: 5 minutes

INGREDIENTS:
- 1/2 pound large shrimp, peeled and deveined
- Salt and black pepper, to taste
- 2 tablespoons olive oil
- 4 cloves garlic, minced
- Zest of 1 lemon
- Juice of 1 lemon
- 2 tablespoons fresh parsley, chopped
- Red pepper flakes, to taste (optional)

INSTRUCTIONS:
1. *Season and Prepare Shrimp:*
   - Season the peeled and deveined shrimp with salt and black pepper.
2. *Sauté Shrimp:*
   - In a skillet, heat olive oil over medium-high heat.
   - Add minced garlic and sauté for about 1 minute until fragrant.
3. *Cook Shrimp:*
   - Add the seasoned shrimp to the skillet.
   - Cook for 2-3 minutes on each side until they turn pink and opaque.
4. *Add Lemon Zest and Juice:*
   - Sprinkle lemon zest over the shrimp.
   - Squeeze fresh lemon juice into the skillet, ensuring to catch any seeds.
5. *Finish and Garnish:*
   - Toss the shrimp in the garlic lemon sauce.
   - Sprinkle with chopped fresh parsley and red pepper flakes if desired.
6. *Serve and Enjoy:*
   - Plate the Garlic Lemon Shrimp and drizzle any remaining sauce over them.

EXPERT TIPS & VARIATIONS:
- For an extra kick, add a splash of white wine or a pinch of cayenne pepper.
- Serve the shrimp over a bed of cooked linguine or zucchini noodles.

PAIRING SUGGESTIONS:
- Garlic butter rice or crusty bread
- Roasted vegetables or a side of sautéed spinach

Lobster Mac 'n' Cheese

Servings: 2 | **Prep Time:** 20 minutes | **Cooking Time:** 20 minutes

INGREDIENTS:
- 8 oz elbow macaroni
- 1 lobster tail, meat removed and chopped
- 2 tablespoons unsalted butter
- 2 tablespoons all-purpose flour
- 1.5 cups whole milk
- 1.5 cups sharp cheddar cheese, shredded
- 1/2 cup Gruyère cheese, shredded
- Salt and black pepper, to taste
- 1/4 teaspoon paprika
- 1/4 cup breadcrumbs
- Fresh chives, chopped, for garnish

INSTRUCTIONS:
1. *Cook Elbow Macaroni:*
   - Cook the elbow macaroni. Drain and set aside.
2. *Prepare Lobster:*
   - In a separate pot, steam or boil the lobster tail until the meat is cooked. Remove the meat and chop it into bite-sized pieces.
3. *Make Cheese Sauce:*
   - In a saucepan, melt butter over medium heat.
   - Add flour, whisking continuously to create a roux.
   - Gradually pour in the milk while whisking to avoid lumps.
   - Add shredded cheddar and Gruyère cheeses, stirring until smooth.
   - Season with salt, black pepper, and paprika.
4. *Combine Lobster and Macaroni:*
   - Fold the chopped lobster meat and cooked macaroni into the cheese sauce until well coated.
5. *Bake Lobster Mac 'n' Cheese:*
   - Transfer the mixture to a baking dish.
   - Sprinkle breadcrumbs over the top.
   - Bake in a preheated oven at 375°F (190°C) for 15-20 minutes or until the top is golden brown and the cheese is bubbly.
6. *Garnish and Serve:*
   - Remove from the oven and let it cool slightly.
   - Garnish with chopped fresh chives before serving.

EXPERT TIPS & VARIATIONS:
- Add a pinch of nutmeg to the cheese sauce for extra depth of flavor.
- Incorporate cooked bacon bits for a smoky twist.

PAIRING SUGGESTIONS:
- Caesar salad or a side of roasted vegetables
- Crusty French bread or garlic bread

Pan-Seared Salmon with Lemon Garlic Butter Sauce

Servings: 2 | **Prep Time:** 10 minutes | **Cooking Time:** 10 minutes

INGREDIENTS:
- 2 salmon fillets
- Salt and black pepper, to taste
- 2 tablespoons olive oil
- 2 tablespoons unsalted butter
- 3 cloves garlic, minced
- Zest of 1 lemon
- Juice of 1 lemon
- 2 tablespoons fresh parsley, chopped

INSTRUCTIONS:
1. *Season Salmon:*
   - Pat dry the salmon fillets and season them with salt and black pepper.
2. *Pan-Sear Salmon:*
   - In a skillet, heat olive oil over medium-high heat.
   - Place the salmon fillets in the skillet, skin side down. Sear for 3-4 minutes until the skin is crispy.
3. *Flip and Cook:*
   - Flip the salmon fillets and cook for an additional 3-4 minutes until the salmon is cooked through. The internal temperature should reach 145°F (63°C).
4. *Prepare Lemon Garlic Butter Sauce:*
   - In the same skillet, add unsalted butter and minced garlic. Sauté for 1-2 minutes until the garlic is fragrant.
5. *Add Lemon Zest and Juice:*
   - Stir in lemon zest and squeeze fresh lemon juice into the skillet. Mix well.
6. *Finish and Garnish:*
   - Pour the lemon garlic butter sauce over the pan-seared salmon.
   - Garnish with chopped fresh parsley.
7. *Serve and Enjoy:*
   - Plate the Pan-Seared Salmon with Lemon Garlic Butter Sauce. Spoon some of the sauce over each fillet.

EXPERT TIPS & VARIATIONS:
- Add a splash of white wine or chicken broth to the sauce for depth of flavor.
- Sprinkle a pinch of red pepper flakes for a subtle heat.

PAIRING SUGGESTIONS:
- Garlic butter rice or mashed potatoes
- Roasted asparagus or a side of sautéed spinach

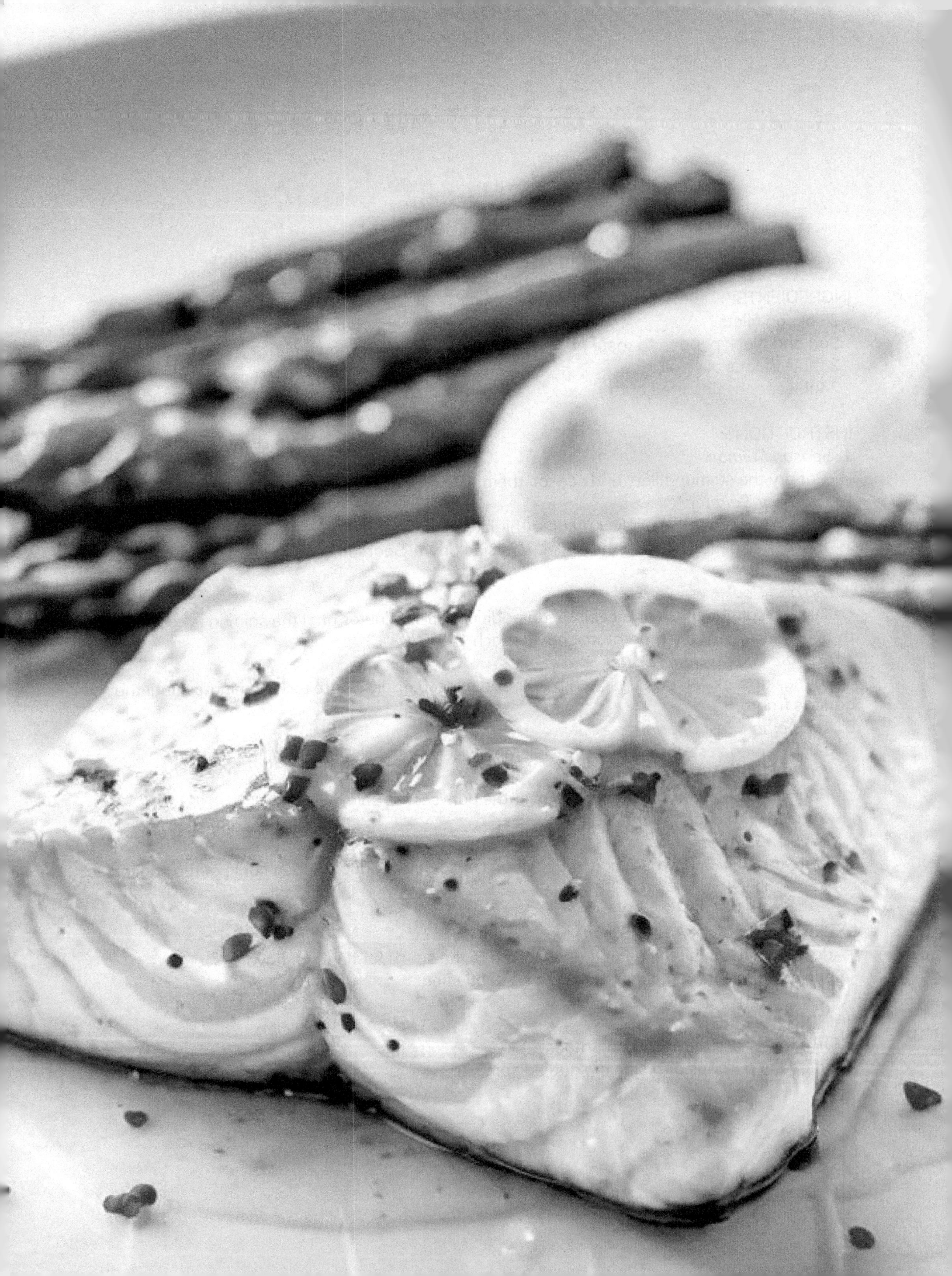

Asparagus and Shrimp with Angel Hair

Servings: 2 | Prep Time: 15 minutes | Cooking Time: 15 minutes

INGREDIENTS:
- 8 oz angel hair pasta
- 1/2 pound large shrimp, peeled and deveined
- Salt and black pepper, to taste
- 2 tablespoons olive oil
- 3 cloves garlic, minced
- 1 bunch asparagus, trimmed and cut into bite-sized pieces
- Zest of 1 lemon
- Juice of 1 lemon
- 1/4 cup fresh basil, chopped
- Grated Parmesan cheese, for serving

INSTRUCTIONS:
1. *Cook Angel Hair Pasta:*
   - Cook the angel hair pasta. Drain and set aside.
2. *Season and Sauté Shrimp:*
   - Season the peeled and deveined shrimp with salt and black pepper.
   - In a large skillet, heat olive oil over medium-high heat. Add minced garlic and sauté for about 1 minute.
3. *Cook Shrimp and Asparagus:*
   - Add the seasoned shrimp to the skillet and cook for 2-3 minutes on each side until pink and opaque.
   - Add asparagus pieces to the skillet and cook for an additional 3-4 minutes until asparagus is tender-crisp.
4. *Combine Pasta and Shrimp Mixture:*
   - Toss the cooked angel hair pasta into the skillet with shrimp and asparagus.
   - Mix well to combine.
5. *Add Lemon Zest and Juice:*
   - Sprinkle lemon zest over the pasta and squeeze fresh lemon juice. Toss to coat evenly.
6. *Finish and Garnish:*
   - Stir in fresh chopped basil.
   - Serve garnished with grated Parmesan cheese.

EXPERT TIPS & VARIATIONS:
- Include cherry tomatoes or sun-dried tomatoes for extra flavor.
- Drizzle with a bit of balsamic glaze before serving.

PAIRING SUGGESTIONS:
- Garlic bread or a side of crusty Italian bread
- Caesar salad or a side of roasted vegetables

Salmon with Spinach Sauce

Servings: 2 | Prep Time: 15 minutes | Cooking Time: 15 minutes

INGREDIENTS:
- 2 salmon fillets
- Salt and black pepper, to taste
- 2 tablespoons olive oil
- 3 cloves garlic, minced
- 4 cups fresh baby spinach
- 1/2 cup heavy cream
- 1/4 cup grated Parmesan cheese
- Zest of 1 lemon
- Juice of 1 lemon
- 1/4 teaspoon nutmeg (optional)

INSTRUCTIONS:
1. *Season Salmon:*
   - Pat dry the salmon fillets and season with salt and black pepper.
2. *Pan-Sear Salmon:*
   - In a skillet, heat olive oil over medium-high heat.
   - Place the salmon fillets in the skillet, skin side down. Sear for 3-4 minutes until the skin is crispy.
3. *Flip and Cook:*
   - Flip the salmon fillets and cook for an additional 3-4 minutes until the salmon is cooked through. The internal temperature should reach 145°F (63°C).
4. *Prepare Spinach Sauce:*
   - In the same skillet, add minced garlic and sauté for 1 minute.
   - Add fresh baby spinach to the skillet and cook until wilted.
5. *Add Cream and Cheese:*
   - Pour in heavy cream and stir in grated Parmesan cheese. Simmer for 2-3 minutes until the sauce thickens.
6. *Add Lemon Zest and Juice:*
   - Stir in lemon zest and squeeze fresh lemon juice into the sauce. Mix well.
7. *Finish and Garnish:*
   - If using, sprinkle nutmeg into the sauce.
   - Pour the spinach sauce over the pan-seared salmon.
8. *Serve and Enjoy:*
   - Plate the Salmon with Spinach Sauce. Drizzle extra sauce over each fillet.

EXPERT TIPS & VARIATIONS:
- Include a handful of cherry tomatoes for a burst of freshness in the sauce.
- Substitute heavy cream with coconut milk for a dairy-free version.

PAIRING SUGGESTIONS:
- Quinoa or wild rice
- Sautéed asparagus or a side of roasted Brussels sprouts

Air Fryer Tilapia

Servings: 2 | **Prep Time:** 10 minutes | **Air Frying Time:** 12 minutes

INGREDIENTS:
- 2 tilapia fillets
- 2 tablespoons olive oil
- 1 teaspoon paprika
- 1/2 teaspoon garlic powder
- 1/2 teaspoon onion powder
- 1/2 teaspoon dried thyme
- Salt and black pepper, to taste
- Lemon wedges, for serving

INSTRUCTIONS:
1. *Preheat the Air Fryer:*
   - Preheat your air fryer to 400°F (200°C).
2. *Prepare Tilapia:*
   - Pat dry the tilapia fillets with a paper towel.
   - In a bowl, mix olive oil, paprika, garlic powder, onion powder, dried thyme, salt, and black pepper.
3. *Coat Tilapia:*
   - Brush the tilapia fillets with the spice mixture, ensuring both sides are well coated.
4. *Air Fry Tilapia:*
   - Place the seasoned tilapia fillets in the air fryer basket.
   - Air fry for 12 minutes or until the tilapia is golden brown and flakes easily with a fork.
5. *Serve and Enjoy:*
   - Plate the Air Fryer Tilapia and serve with lemon wedges on the side.

EXPERT TIPS & VARIATIONS:
- Add a pinch of cayenne pepper for a hint of heat.
- Serve with a side of tartar sauce or a squeeze of fresh lemon juice.

PAIRING SUGGESTIONS:
- Quinoa or couscous
- Steamed broccoli or a side of mixed greens

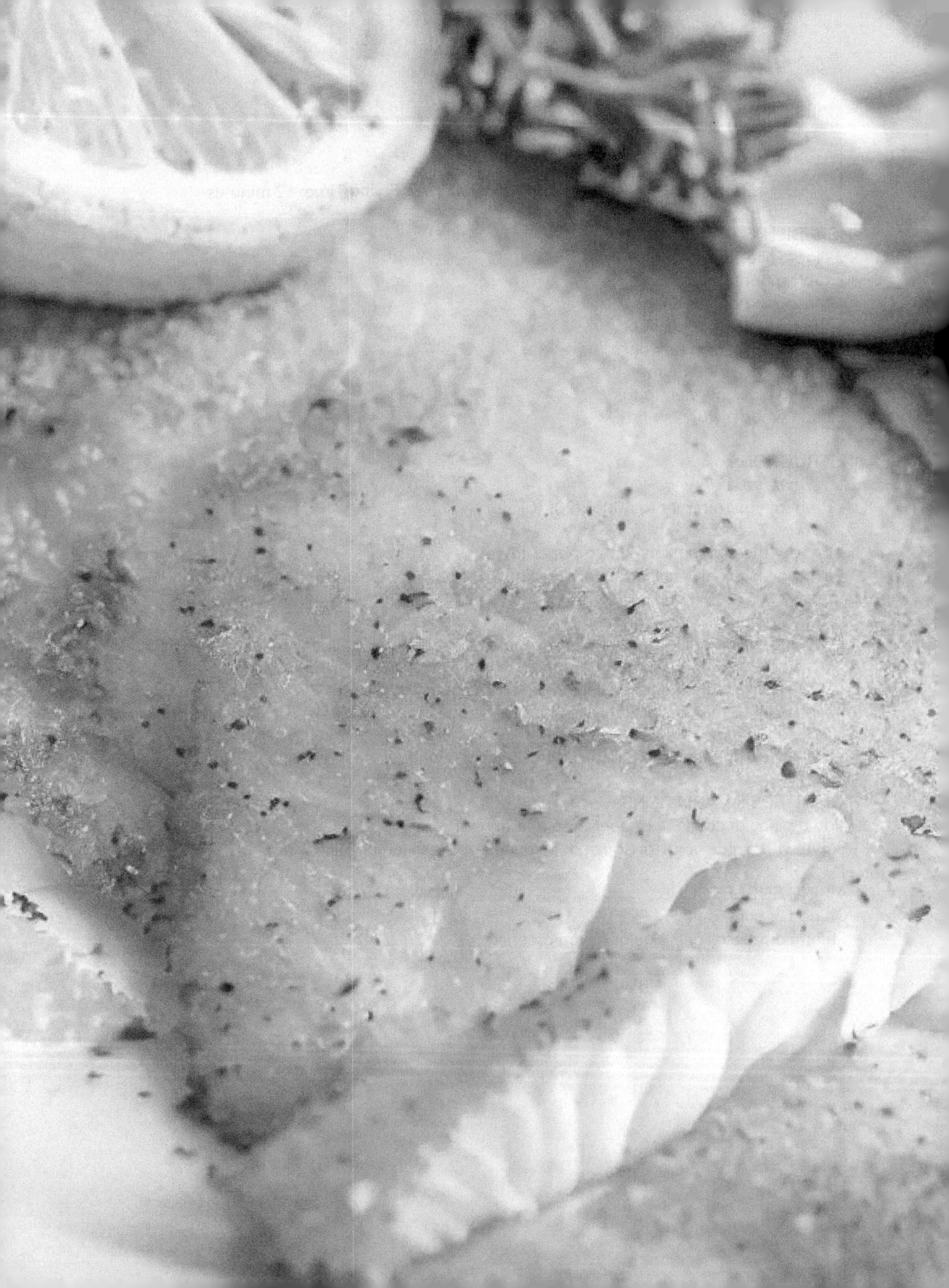

Balsamic Salmon and Spinach Salad

Servings: 2 | Prep Time: 15 minutes | Cooking Time: 15 minutes

INGREDIENTS:

For Balsamic Glazed Salmon:
- 2 salmon fillets
- Salt and black pepper, to taste
- 2 tablespoons olive oil
- 3 tablespoons balsamic glaze

For Spinach Salad:
- 4 cups fresh baby spinach
- 1 cup cherry tomatoes, halved
- 1/2 cucumber, thinly sliced
- 1/4 cup red onion, thinly sliced
- 1/4 cup feta cheese, crumbled

For Salad Dressing:
- 2 tablespoons extra virgin olive oil
- 1 tablespoon balsamic vinegar
- 1 teaspoon Dijon mustard
- Salt and black pepper, to taste

INSTRUCTIONS:

1. *Prepare Balsamic Glazed Salmon:*
   - Season salmon fillets with salt and black pepper.
   - In a skillet, heat olive oil over medium-high heat.
   - Sear salmon for 3-4 minutes on each side until cooked through.
   - Brush balsamic glaze over the salmon in the last minute of cooking.
2. *Make Salad Dressing:*
   - In a small bowl, whisk together extra virgin olive oil, balsamic vinegar, Dijon mustard, salt, and black pepper.
3. *Assemble Spinach Salad:*
   - In a large bowl, combine fresh baby spinach, cherry tomatoes, cucumber slices, red onion, and crumbled feta cheese.
4. *Plate and Serve:*
   - Divide the spinach salad between two plates.
   - Top each salad with a balsamic glazed salmon fillet.
5. *Drizzle Dressing and Enjoy:*
   - Drizzle the balsamic dressing over the salad and salmon.
   - Serve immediately.

EXPERT TIPS & VARIATIONS:
- Add toasted pine nuts or walnuts for crunch.
- Toss in sliced strawberries for a touch of sweetness.

PAIRING SUGGESTIONS:
- Crusty bread or garlic bread
- Quinoa or couscous on the side

Sun-Dried Tomatoes Seafood Linguine

Servings: 2 | **Prep Time:** 20 minutes | **Cooking Time:** 15 minutes

INGREDIENTS:
- 8 oz linguine pasta
- 1/2 pound mixed seafood (shrimp, scallops, mussels)
- 3 tablespoons sun-dried tomatoes, chopped
- 2 tablespoons olive oil
- 3 cloves garlic, minced
- 1/4 teaspoon red pepper flakes (adjust to taste)
- 1/2 cup cherry tomatoes, halved
- 1/4 cup Kalamata olives, sliced
- 1/4 cup fresh parsley, chopped
- Zest of 1 lemon
- Juice of 1 lemon
- Salt and black pepper, to taste
- Grated Parmesan cheese, for serving

INSTRUCTIONS:
1. *Cook Linguine:*
   - Cook the linguine pasta. Drain and set aside.
2. *Prepare Seafood:*
   - In a large skillet, heat olive oil over medium-high heat.
   - Add minced garlic and red pepper flakes. Sauté for 1-2 minutes until garlic is fragrant.
   - Add the mixed seafood and cook until fully cooked.
3. *Combine Ingredients:*
   - Stir in sun-dried tomatoes, cherry tomatoes, Kalamata olives, and chopped fresh parsley.
4. *Add Lemon Zest and Juice:*
   - Sprinkle lemon zest over the seafood mixture.
   - Squeeze fresh lemon juice into the skillet. Mix well.
5. *Toss with Linguine:*
   - Add the cooked linguine to the skillet. Toss until the linguine is well-coated in the seafood and tomato mixture.
6. *Season and Serve:*
   - Season with salt and black pepper to taste.
   - Plate the Sun-Dried Tomatoes Seafood Linguine and garnish with grated Parmesan cheese.

EXPERT TIPS & VARIATIONS:
- Use a combination of fresh and dried herbs for added depth of flavor.
- Include a splash of white wine or chicken broth when cooking the seafood for extra richness.

PAIRING SUGGESTIONS:
- Garlic bread or a side of crusty Italian bread
- Mixed greens or a side of roasted vegetables

Shrimp in Garlic Wine Sauce

Servings: 2 | **Prep Time:** 15 minutes | **Cooking Time:** 10 minutes

INGREDIENTS:
- 1/2 pound large shrimp, peeled and deveined
- Salt and black pepper, to taste
- 2 tablespoons olive oil
- 4 cloves garlic, minced
- 1/2 cup white wine
- 1 tablespoon lemon juice
- 1/4 teaspoon red pepper flakes (adjust to taste)
- 2 tablespoons fresh parsley, chopped
- Zest of 1 lemon
- 2 tablespoons unsalted butter

INSTRUCTIONS:
1. *Season Shrimp:*
   - Season the peeled and deveined shrimp with salt and black pepper.
2. *Sauté Shrimp:*
   - In a skillet, heat olive oil over medium-high heat.
   - Add minced garlic and sauté for about 1 minute until fragrant.
3. *Cook Shrimp:*
   - Add the seasoned shrimp to the skillet.
   - Cook for 2-3 minutes on each side until they turn pink and opaque.
4. *Deglaze with Wine:*
   - Pour in white wine to deglaze the pan, scraping up any browned bits.
   - Allow the wine to simmer for 2-3 minutes to reduce slightly.
5. *Add Lemon Juice and Spices:*
   - Squeeze fresh lemon juice into the skillet.
   - Sprinkle red pepper flakes, chopped fresh parsley, and lemon zest over the shrimp.
6. *Finish with Butter:*
   - Add unsalted butter to the skillet, stirring until it melts and creates a creamy sauce.
7. *Serve and Enjoy:*
   - Plate the Shrimp in Garlic Wine Sauce and spoon some of the sauce over each shrimp.

EXPERT TIPS & VARIATIONS:
- Include a splash of chicken or vegetable broth for additional flavor.
- Serve over cooked pasta, rice, or with crusty bread to soak up the delicious sauce.

PAIRING SUGGESTIONS:
- Garlic butter rice or mashed potatoes
- Sautéed spinach or a side of grilled asparagus

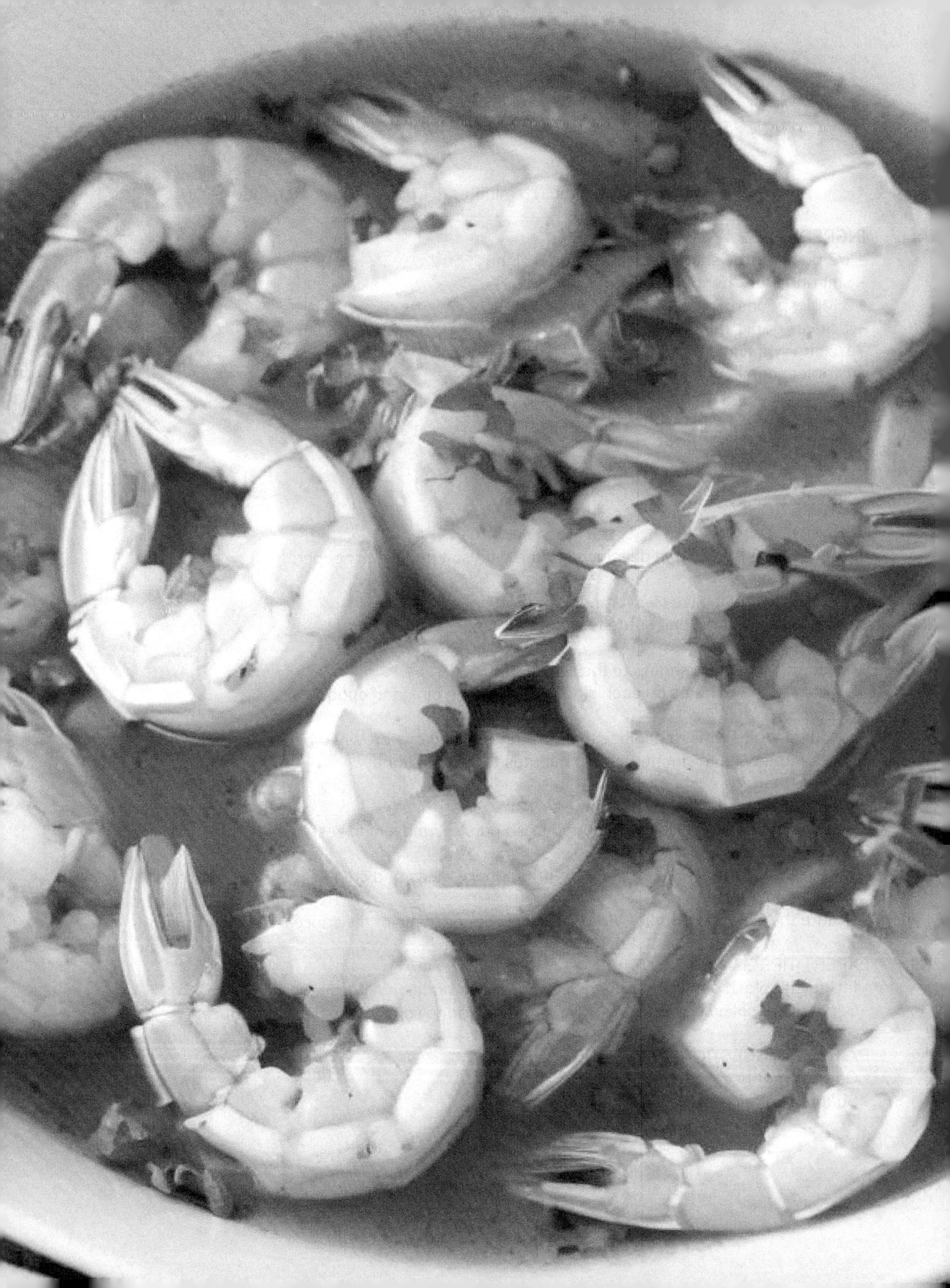

Pan-Seared Scallops with Bacon Cream Sauce

Servings: 2 | **Prep Time:** 15 minutes | **Cooking Time:** 15 minutes

INGREDIENTS:

For Pan-Seared Scallops:
- 1/2 pound large sea scallops, patted dry
- Salt and black pepper, to taste
- 1 tablespoon olive oil
- 1 tablespoon unsalted butter

For Bacon Cream Sauce:
- 4 slices bacon, diced
- 1/4 cup shallots, finely chopped
- 1/2 cup heavy cream
- 1/4 cup chicken broth
- 1 tablespoon Dijon mustard
- Salt and black pepper, to taste
- Fresh chives, chopped, for garnish

INSTRUCTIONS:

1. *Season and Sear Scallops:*
   - Season the sea scallops with salt and black pepper.
   - In a skillet, heat olive oil and butter over medium-high heat.
   - Sear the scallops for 2-3 minutes on each side until golden brown. Ensure not to overcrowd the pan.
2. *Cook Bacon:*
   - In a separate pan, cook diced bacon until crispy. Remove excess fat, leaving about 1 tablespoon in the pan.
3. *Sauté Shallots:*
   - Add finely chopped shallots to the bacon fat. Sauté until shallots are translucent.
4. *Prepare Bacon Cream Sauce:*
   - Pour in heavy cream and chicken broth, stirring to combine.
   - Stir in Dijon mustard and season with salt and black pepper.
5. *Combine Scallops and Sauce:*
   - Place the seared scallops into the bacon cream sauce, ensuring they are well-coated.
6. *Finish and Garnish:*
   - Allow the sauce to simmer for a few minutes until it thickens slightly.
   - Garnish with chopped fresh chives.
   - Plate the Pan-Seared Scallops with Bacon Cream Sauce, spooning extra sauce over each scallop.

EXPERT TIPS & VARIATIONS:
- Add a splash of white wine to the sauce for additional depth.
- Serve over a bed of cauliflower mash or creamy polenta.

PAIRING SUGGESTIONS:
- Garlic butter rice or mashed cauliflower
- Sautéed spinach or a side of roasted Brussels sprouts

Butter-Poached Lobster

Servings: 2 | **Prep Time:** 15 minutes | **Cooking Time:** 15 minutes

INGREDIENTS:
- 2 lobster tails, shells removed and deveined
- Salt and white pepper, to taste
- 1 cup unsalted butter
- 4 cloves garlic, minced
- Zest of 1 lemon
- 2 tablespoons fresh parsley, chopped
- Lemon wedges, for serving

INSTRUCTIONS:
1. *Prepare Lobster Tails:*
   - Remove the shells from the lobster tails and devein them.
   - Season the lobster tails with salt and white pepper.
2. *Butter Poaching:*
   - In a saucepan over low heat, melt the unsalted butter.
   - Add minced garlic to the melted butter and let it infuse for a couple of minutes.
3. *Poach Lobster:*
   - Gently place the seasoned lobster tails into the butter.
   - Poach the lobster tails in the butter over low heat for about 8-10 minutes or until the lobster is opaque and cooked through.
4. *Add Lemon Zest and Parsley:*
   - Sprinkle lemon zest and chopped fresh parsley over the butter-poached lobster tails.
5. *Serve and Enjoy:*
   - Plate the Butter-Poached Lobster and spoon some of the garlic butter over each tail.
   - Serve with lemon wedges on the side.

EXPERT TIPS & VARIATIONS:
- Add a pinch of red pepper flakes for a hint of heat.
- Drizzle extra melted garlic butter over the lobster before serving.

PAIRING SUGGESTIONS:
- Garlic butter rice or a side of crusty bread
- Roasted vegetables or a simple green salad

VEGAN/VEGETARIAN DISHES

Spinach Lasagna Roll-Ups

Servings: 2 | **Prep Time:** 20 minutes | **Baking Time:** 25 minutes

INGREDIENTS:
- 6 lasagna noodles, cooked al dente
- 1 cup ricotta cheese
- 1 cup frozen chopped spinach, thawed and drained
- 1 cup shredded mozzarella cheese
- 1/2 cup grated Parmesan cheese
- 1 egg, beaten
- 2 cups marinara sauce
- Salt and black pepper, to taste
- 1 teaspoon dried oregano
- Fresh basil, for garnish

INSTRUCTIONS:
1. *Preheat Oven:*
   - Preheat your oven to 375°F (190°C).
2. *Prepare Lasagna Noodles:*
   - Cook the lasagna noodles. Drain and set aside.
3. *Prepare Filling:*
   - In a bowl, combine ricotta cheese, chopped spinach, half of the mozzarella cheese, half of the Parmesan cheese, beaten egg, salt, black pepper, and dried oregano.
4. *Assemble Roll-Ups:*
   - Lay out the cooked lasagna noodles and spread the filling mixture evenly over each noodle.
   - Roll up each noodle and place seam side down in a baking dish.
5. *Top with Marinara Sauce and Cheese:*
   - Pour marinara sauce over the top of the roll-ups.
   - Sprinkle the remaining mozzarella and Parmesan cheese on top.
6. *Bake in the Oven:*
   - Bake in the preheated oven for 25 minutes or until the cheese is melted and bubbly.
7. *Garnish and Serve:*
   - Remove from the oven and let it cool slightly.
   - Garnish with fresh basil before serving.

EXPERT TIPS & VARIATIONS:
- Add cooked and crumbled Italian sausage to the filling for extra flavor.
- Use whole wheat or gluten-free lasagna noodles for a healthier option.

PAIRING SUGGESTIONS:
- Garlic bread or a side of crusty Italian bread
- Mixed greens or a side salad with balsamic vinaigrette

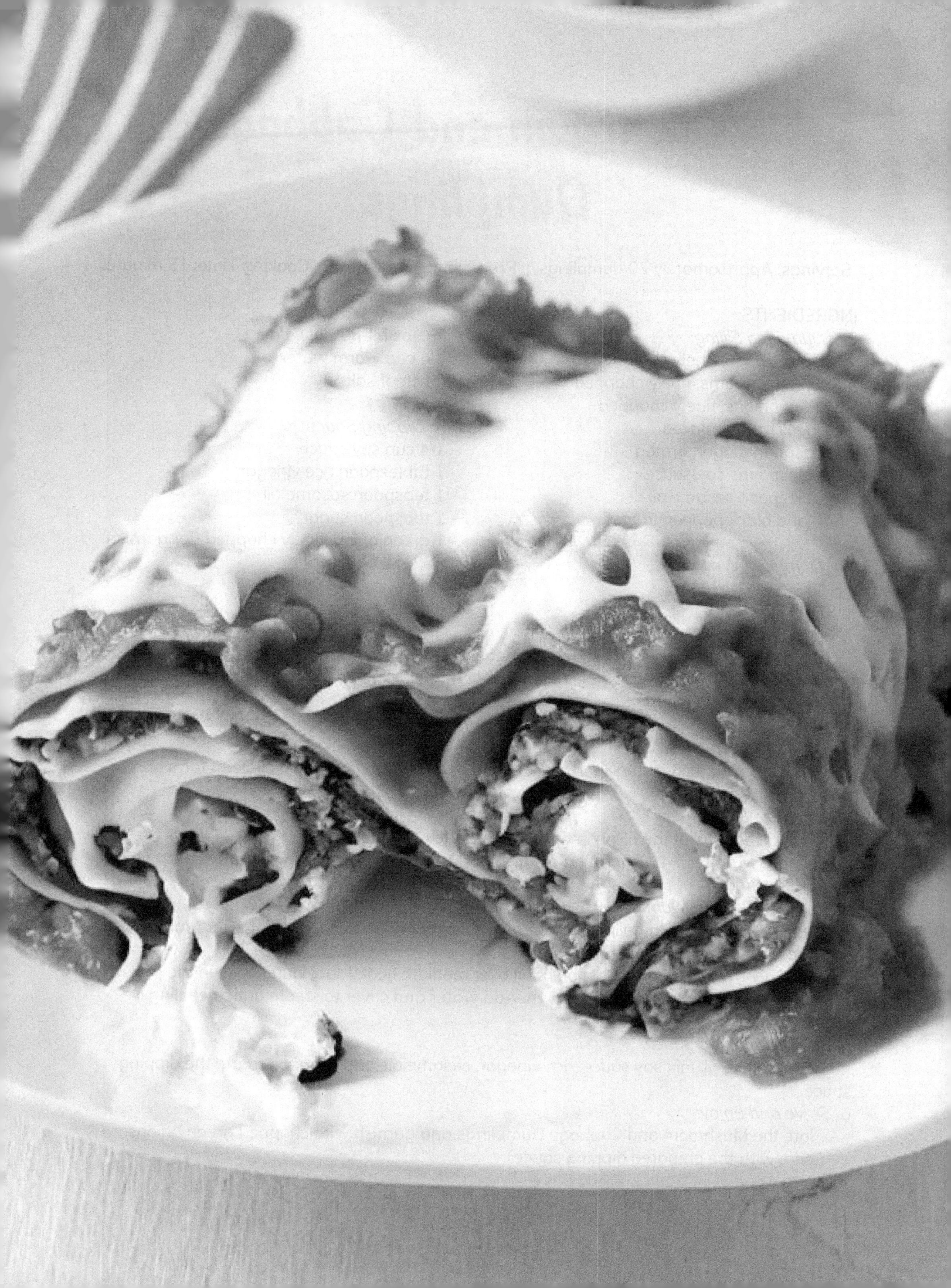

Mushroom and Cabbage Dumplings

Servings: Approximately 20 dumplings | **Prep Time:** 30 minutes | **Cooking Time:** 15 minutes

INGREDIENTS:

For Dumpling Filling:
- 1 cup cabbage, finely shredded
- 1 cup mushrooms, finely chopped
- 2 green onions, finely chopped
- 2 cloves garlic, minced
- 1 teaspoon ginger, grated
- 2 tablespoons soy sauce
- 1 tablespoon sesame oil
- Salt and black pepper, to taste

For Dumpling Wrappers:
- 2 cups all-purpose flour
- 3/4 cup warm water
- Pinch of salt

For Dipping Sauce:
- 1/4 cup soy sauce
- 1 tablespoon rice vinegar
- 1 teaspoon sesame oil
- 1 teaspoon sugar
- 1 green onion, finely chopped (for garnish)

INSTRUCTIONS:

1. *Prepare Dumpling Filling:*
   - In a large bowl, combine shredded cabbage, chopped mushrooms, green onions, minced garlic, grated ginger, soy sauce, sesame oil, salt, and black pepper. Mix well and set aside.
2. *Make Dumpling Wrappers:*
   - In a separate bowl, combine all-purpose flour, warm water, and a pinch of salt. Knead the dough until it forms a smooth ball.
   - Divide the dough into small portions and roll each portion into a thin circle to form dumpling wrappers.
3. *Assemble Dumplings:*
   - Place a spoonful of the filling in the center of each wrapper.
   - Fold the wrapper in half, forming a half-moon shape. Pinch the edges to seal, creating pleats if desired.
4. *Steam or Pan-Fry Dumplings:*
   - *Steaming:* Arrange dumplings in a steamer basket and steam for about 10-12 minutes until the wrappers are cooked.
   - *Pan-Frying:* Heat a pan with a bit of oil over medium heat. Place dumplings in the pan and cook until the bottoms are golden brown. Add water and cover to steam until the filling is cooked.
5. *Prepare Dipping Sauce:*
   - In a small bowl, mix soy sauce, rice vinegar, sesame oil, and sugar to create the dipping sauce.
6. *Serve and Enjoy:*
   - Plate the Mushroom and Cabbage Dumplings and garnish with chopped green onions.
   - Serve with the prepared dipping sauce.

EXPERT TIPS & VARIATIONS:
- Add a bit of minced tofu or cooked glass noodles to the filling for texture variation.
- Experiment with different dipping sauce ingredients like garlic, chili oil, or grated ginger.

PAIRING SUGGESTIONS:
- Steamed jasmine rice or noodles
- Asian-inspired slaw or a side of pickled vegetables

Vegan Broccoli Pesto Pasta with Whipped Tofu Ricotta

Servings: 2 | Prep Time: 15 minutes | Cooking Time: 15 minutes

INGREDIENTS:

For Broccoli Pesto:
- 2 cups broccoli florets, blanched
- 1/2 cup fresh basil leaves
- 1/4 cup nutritional yeast
- 1/4 cup pine nuts
- 2 cloves garlic, minced
- 1/4 cup olive oil
- Salt and black pepper, to taste
- Juice of 1 lemon

For Whipped Tofu Ricotta:
- 1/2 block extra-firm tofu, pressed and crumbled
- 2 tablespoons nutritional yeast
- 1 tablespoon lemon juice
- 1 tablespoon olive oil
- Salt and black pepper, to taste

For Pasta:
- 8 oz vegan pasta of your choice

INSTRUCTIONS:

1. *Prepare Broccoli Pesto:*
   - In a food processor, combine blanched broccoli, fresh basil, nutritional yeast, pine nuts, minced garlic, olive oil, salt, black pepper, and lemon juice. Blend until smooth.
2. *Cook Vegan Pasta:*
   - Cook the vegan pasta. Drain and set aside.
3. *Make Whipped Tofu Ricotta:*
   - In a bowl, mix crumbled tofu, nutritional yeast, lemon juice, olive oil, salt, and black pepper. Whip with a fork until well combined and slightly fluffy.
4. *Combine Pasta and Pesto:*
   - Toss the cooked pasta with the broccoli pesto until well coated.
5. *Plate and Add Whipped Tofu Ricotta:*
   - Plate the Vegan Broccoli Pesto Pasta and dollop whipped tofu ricotta on top.
6. *Garnish and Serve:*
   - Garnish with additional pine nuts, nutritional yeast, or fresh basil.

EXPERT TIPS & VARIATIONS:
- Add a handful of baby spinach to the pesto for extra green goodness.
- Experiment with different nuts in the pesto, such as almonds or walnuts.

PAIRING SUGGESTIONS:
- Garlic bread or a side of crusty baguette
- Roasted vegetables or a simple side salad

Vegan BLT Pizza

Servings: 2 | Prep Time: 20 minutes | Baking Time: 15 minutes

INGREDIENTS:

For Pizza Dough:
- 1 package (2 1/4 teaspoons) active dry yeast
- 1 cup warm water
- 2 1/2 cups all-purpose flour
- 1 tablespoon olive oil
- 1 teaspoon sugar
- 1 teaspoon salt

For Vegan BLT Pizza:

- 1/2 cup vegan mayo
- 1 teaspoon Dijon mustard
- 1 teaspoon maple syrup
- 1 cup cherry tomatoes, halved
- 1 cup lettuce, shredded
- 1/2 cup vegan bacon, cooked and crumbled
- Fresh basil leaves, for garnish
- Salt and black pepper, to taste

INSTRUCTIONS:

1. *Prepare Pizza Dough:*
   - In a bowl, dissolve yeast in warm water with sugar. Let it sit for 5 minutes until frothy.
   - In a large bowl, combine flour and salt. Add the yeast mixture and olive oil. Mix until a dough forms.
   - Knead the dough on a floured surface for 5-7 minutes. Place in an oiled bowl, cover, and let it rise for 1-2 hours.
2. *Roll Out Pizza Dough:*
   - Preheat your oven to 475°F (245°C).
   - Roll out the pizza dough into your desired shape on a floured surface.
3. *Make Vegan BLT Sauce:*
   - In a small bowl, mix vegan mayo, Dijon mustard, and maple syrup to create the sauce.
4. *Assemble Pizza:*
   - Spread the vegan BLT sauce over the rolled-out pizza dough.
   - Top with halved cherry tomatoes, shredded lettuce, and crumbled vegan bacon.
5. *Bake in the Oven:*
   - Transfer the assembled pizza to a baking sheet or pizza stone.
   - Bake for 12-15 minutes or until the crust is golden and the toppings are cooked.
6. *Garnish and Serve:*
   - Remove from the oven and garnish with fresh basil leaves.
   - Sprinkle salt and black pepper to taste.

EXPERT TIPS & VARIATIONS:
- Add avocado slices or vegan cheese for extra creaminess.
- Drizzle balsamic glaze over the pizza before serving for a touch of sweetness.

PAIRING SUGGESTIONS:
- Arugula or mixed greens salad
- Vegan garlic knots or breadsticks

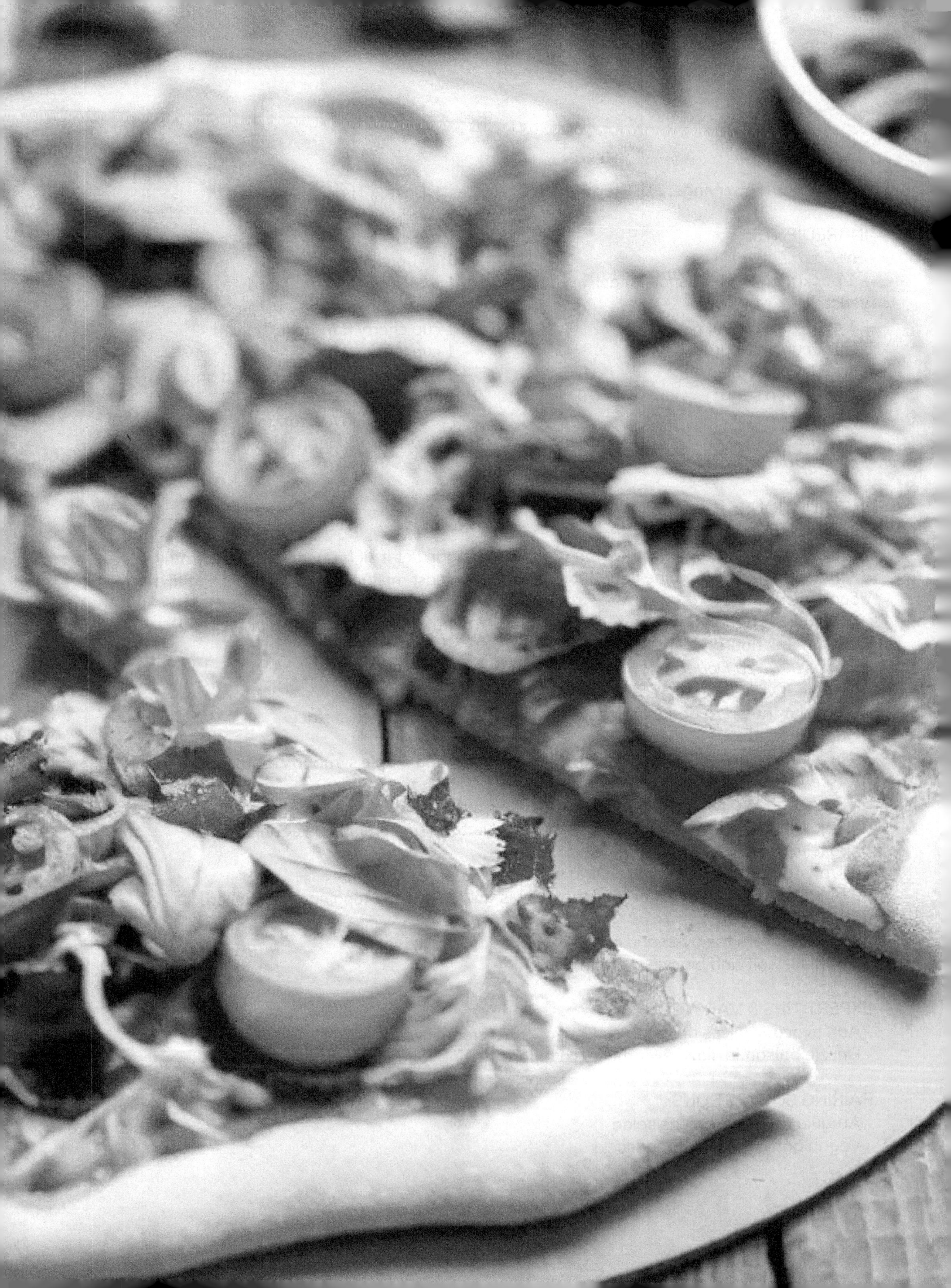

Creamy Vegan Rigatoni with Roasted Cauliflower

Servings: 2 | Prep Time: 20 minutes | Roasting Time: 25 minutes

INGREDIENTS:
- 8 oz rigatoni pasta (vegan, if available)
- 1/2 head cauliflower, cut into florets
- 2 tablespoons olive oil
- Salt and black pepper, to taste
- 1 cup cashews, soaked in hot water for 30 minutes
- 1 cup unsweetened almond milk
- 3 tablespoons nutritional yeast
- 2 cloves garlic, minced
- 1 teaspoon onion powder
- 1 teaspoon lemon juice
- Fresh parsley, chopped, for garnish

INSTRUCTIONS:
1. *Preheat Oven:*
   - Preheat your oven to 425°F (220°C).
2. *Roast Cauliflower:*
   - Toss cauliflower florets with olive oil, salt, and black pepper.
   - Spread them on a baking sheet and roast for 20-25 minutes or until golden and tender.
3. *Cook Rigatoni:*
   - Cook the rigatoni pasta. Drain and set aside.
4. *Prepare Creamy Sauce:*
   - In a blender, combine soaked cashews, almond milk, nutritional yeast, minced garlic, onion powder, and lemon juice. Blend until smooth and creamy.
5. *Combine Rigatoni and Cauliflower:*
   - In a large mixing bowl, toss the cooked rigatoni with the roasted cauliflower.
6. *Pour Creamy Sauce:*
   - Pour the creamy cashew sauce over the rigatoni and cauliflower mixture. Toss until well coated.
7. *Garnish and Serve:*
   - Garnish with chopped fresh parsley.

EXPERT TIPS & VARIATIONS:
- Add sautéed spinach or kale for an extra boost of green goodness.
- Top with vegan Parmesan or a sprinkle of red pepper flakes for added flavor.

PAIRING SUGGESTIONS:
- Garlic bread or a side of crusty baguette
- Mixed greens or a simple side salad

Vegan Teriyaki Oyster Mushrooms

Servings: 2 | **Prep Time:** 15 minutes | **Cooking Time:** 15 minutes

INGREDIENTS:
- 1 pound oyster mushrooms, cleaned and trimmed
- 1/4 cup soy sauce or tamari (for gluten-free option)
- 2 tablespoons maple syrup or agave nectar
- 1 tablespoon rice vinegar
- 1 tablespoon sesame oil
- 2 cloves garlic, minced
- 1 teaspoon ginger, grated
- 1 tablespoon cornstarch mixed with 2 tablespoons water (optional, for thickening)
- Sesame seeds and green onions, for garnish

INSTRUCTIONS:
1. *Prepare Oyster Mushrooms:*
   - Clean and trim the oyster mushrooms, separating them into bite-sized pieces.
2. *Make Teriyaki Sauce:*
   - In a bowl, whisk together soy sauce, maple syrup or agave nectar, rice vinegar, sesame oil, minced garlic, and grated ginger.
3. *Sauté Oyster Mushrooms:*
   - In a pan, heat a bit of oil over medium-high heat.
   - Add oyster mushrooms and sauté for about 5-7 minutes until they start to brown and become tender.
4. *Add Teriyaki Sauce:*
   - Pour the teriyaki sauce over the sautéed oyster mushrooms, stirring to coat evenly.
   - Cook for an additional 5-7 minutes until the mushrooms absorb the flavors.
5. *Optional Thickening:*
   - If desired, mix cornstarch with water to create a slurry. Add to the pan to thicken the sauce.
6. *Garnish and Serve:*
   - Garnish the Vegan Teriyaki Oyster Mushrooms with sesame seeds and chopped green onions.
   - Serve over rice or noodles.

EXPERT TIPS & VARIATIONS:
- Include sliced bell peppers or broccoli for added color and nutrients.
- Adjust the sweetness or saltiness of the teriyaki sauce to your preference.

PAIRING SUGGESTIONS:
- Steamed jasmine rice or soba noodles
- Stir-fried vegetables or a side of edamame

Vegan Lasagna Stuffed Portobello Mushrooms

Servings: 2 | Prep Time: 20 minutes | Baking Time: 25 minutes

INGREDIENTS:
- 4 large portobello mushrooms, stems removed
- 1 cup vegan lasagna filling (pre-cooked)
  - Filling can include vegan ricotta, marinara sauce, spinach, and vegan cheese
- 1 cup marinara sauce
- 1/2 cup vegan mozzarella cheese, shredded
- Fresh basil or parsley, for garnish
- Salt and black pepper, to taste

INSTRUCTIONS:
1. *Preheat Oven:*
   - Preheat your oven to 375°F (190°C).
2. *Prepare Portobello Mushrooms:*
   - Clean the portobello mushrooms and remove the stems. Lightly scrape out the gills to create a hollow space for the filling.
3. *Fill with Lasagna Mixture:*
   - In each mushroom cap, layer a spoonful of marinara sauce, followed by the pre-cooked vegan lasagna filling.
4. *Top with Vegan Mozzarella:*
   - Sprinkle shredded vegan mozzarella cheese over the stuffed mushrooms.
5. *Bake in the Oven:*
   - Place the stuffed portobello mushrooms on a baking sheet.
   - Bake for 20-25 minutes or until the mushrooms are tender, and the cheese is melted and golden.
6. *Garnish and Serve:*
   - Remove from the oven and garnish with fresh basil or parsley.
   - Season with salt and black pepper to taste.

EXPERT TIPS & VARIATIONS:
- Add a layer of sautéed vegetables like zucchini or bell peppers to the lasagna filling.
- Experiment with different vegan cheeses for added variety.

PAIRING SUGGESTIONS:
- Garlic bread or a side of crusty baguette
- Mixed greens or a simple side salad

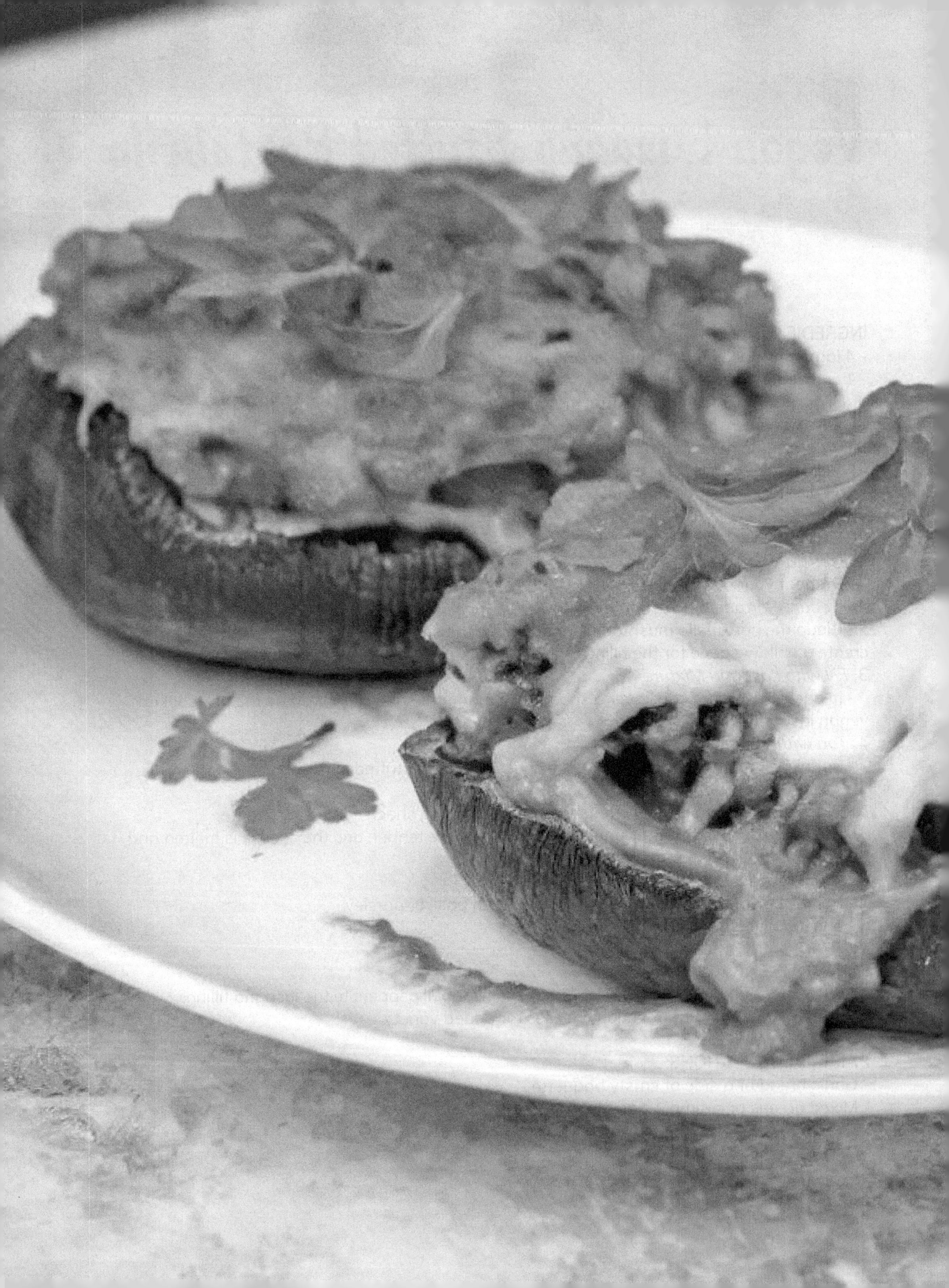

Oyster Mushroom and Jackfruit Vegan Pot Roast

Servings: 2 | Prep Time: 20 minutes | Cooking Time: 1 hour and 30 minutes

INGREDIENTS:
- 1 cup oyster mushrooms, sliced
- 1 cup young jackfruit, shredded
- 1 large onion, diced
- 2 carrots, peeled and sliced
- 2 potatoes, diced
- 3 cloves garlic, minced
- 1 cup vegetable broth
- 1/2 cup red wine (optional)
- 2 tablespoons tomato paste
- 1 tablespoon soy sauce or tamari
- 1 teaspoon dried thyme
- 1 teaspoon dried rosemary
- Salt and black pepper, to taste
- 2 tablespoons olive oil
- Fresh parsley, for garnish

INSTRUCTIONS:
1. *Preheat Oven:*
   - Preheat your oven to 350°F (175°C).
2. *Prepare Vegetables:*
   - Clean and chop the oyster mushrooms, onion, carrots, and potatoes.
3. *Sauté Mushrooms and Jackfruit:*
   - In a large oven-safe pot, heat olive oil over medium heat.
   - Sauté oyster mushrooms and shredded jackfruit until they start to brown.
4. *Add Aromatics and Vegetables:*
   - Add diced onion, minced garlic, carrots, and potatoes to the pot.
   - Cook for a few minutes until the vegetables begin to soften.
5. *Prepare Braising Liquid:*
   - In a bowl, mix vegetable broth, red wine (if using), tomato paste, soy sauce, dried thyme, dried rosemary, salt, and black pepper.
6. *Combine and Braise:*
   - Pour the braising liquid over the vegetables and mushrooms.
   - Bring the pot to a simmer, cover with a lid, and transfer it to the preheated oven.
7. *Roast in the Oven:*
   - Roast for 1 hour and 30 minutes or until the vegetables are tender and the flavors meld.
   - Remove from the oven and garnish with fresh parsley.

EXPERT TIPS & VARIATIONS:
- Add more herbs like sage or bay leaves for additional flavor.
- Include other root vegetables like parsnips or turnips for variety.

PAIRING SUGGESTIONS:
- Mashed potatoes or cauliflower mash
- Steamed green beans or roasted Brussels sprouts

BBQ Vegan Lentil Meatballs

Servings: 2 | **Prep Time:** 20 minutes | **Baking Time:** 25 minutes

INGREDIENTS:

For Lentil Meatballs:
- 1 cup cooked lentils, drained
- 1/2 cup breadcrumbs
- 1/4 cup finely chopped onion
- 2 cloves garlic, minced
- 1 flax egg (1 tablespoon ground flaxseed + 3 tablespoons water)
- 1 tablespoon tomato paste
- 1 teaspoon smoked paprika
- 1 teaspoon dried oregano
- Salt and black pepper, to taste

For BBQ Sauce:
- 1/2 cup barbecue sauce
- 2 tablespoons maple syrup
- 1 tablespoon apple cider vinegar
- 1 teaspoon Dijon mustard

INSTRUCTIONS:

1. *Preheat Oven:*
   - Preheat your oven to 375°F (190°C).
2. *Make Lentil Meatballs:*
   - In a food processor, combine cooked lentils, breadcrumbs, chopped onion, minced garlic, flax egg, tomato paste, smoked paprika, dried oregano, salt, and black pepper.
   - Pulse until the mixture is well combined but still has some texture.
3. *Shape Meatballs:*
   - Form the lentil mixture into small meatballs and place them on a baking sheet lined with parchment paper.
4. *Bake Lentil Meatballs:*
   - Bake in the preheated oven for 20-25 minutes or until the meatballs are golden and firm.
5. *Prepare BBQ Sauce:*
   - In a small saucepan, combine barbecue sauce, maple syrup, apple cider vinegar, and Dijon mustard. Heat over low heat, stirring until well combined.
6. *Coat Meatballs in BBQ Sauce:*
   - Once the meatballs are cooked, transfer them to a bowl and pour the BBQ sauce over, tossing to coat evenly.
7. *Garnish and Serve:*
   - Garnish with chopped fresh parsley or green onions.
   - Serve the BBQ Vegan Lentil Meatballs on a bed of rice or alongside your favorite vegetables.

EXPERT TIPS & VARIATIONS:
- Add a pinch of cayenne pepper to the lentil mixture for a spicy kick.
- Serve the meatballs as sliders with small vegan buns for a fun twist.

PAIRING SUGGESTIONS:
- Coleslaw or a side salad with a tangy vinaigrette
- Baked sweet potato fries or crispy polenta squares

Lemon Millet Rice with Asparagus

Servings: 2 | Prep Time: 15 minutes | Cooking Time: 20 minutes

INGREDIENTS:
- 1 cup millet, rinsed and drained
- 2 cups vegetable broth
- 1 bunch asparagus, trimmed and cut into bite-sized pieces
- 1 lemon, zest and juice
- 2 tablespoons olive oil
- 2 cloves garlic, minced
- 1 teaspoon dried thyme
- Salt and black pepper, to taste
- Fresh parsley, chopped, for garnish

INSTRUCTIONS:
1. *Cook Millet:*
   - In a saucepan, combine millet and vegetable broth. Bring to a boil, then reduce heat, cover, and simmer for 15-20 minutes or until millet is tender and water is absorbed.
2. *Sauté Asparagus:*
   - In a large skillet, heat olive oil over medium heat. Add minced garlic and sauté for a minute until fragrant.
   - Add asparagus pieces to the skillet and cook until they are tender-crisp, about 5-7 minutes.
3. *Combine Millet and Asparagus:*
   - Once the millet is cooked, fluff it with a fork and add it to the skillet with the sautéed asparagus. Mix well.
4. *Add Lemon Zest and Juice:*
   - Zest the lemon and add both the zest and juice to the millet and asparagus mixture. Stir to combine.
5. *Season and Garnish:*
   - Season the Lemon Millet Rice with dried thyme, salt, and black pepper. Adjust seasoning to taste.
   - Garnish with chopped fresh parsley.
6. *Serve and Enjoy:*
   - Plate the Lemon Millet Rice with Asparagus and serve it as a flavorful side dish.

EXPERT TIPS & VARIATIONS:
- Add a handful of pine nuts or sliced almonds for a crunchy texture.
- Include a splash of white wine when sautéing the asparagus for extra depth of flavor.

PAIRING SUGGESTIONS:
- Grilled lemon herb tofu or your favorite plant-based protein
- Mixed greens salad with a light vinaigrette dressing

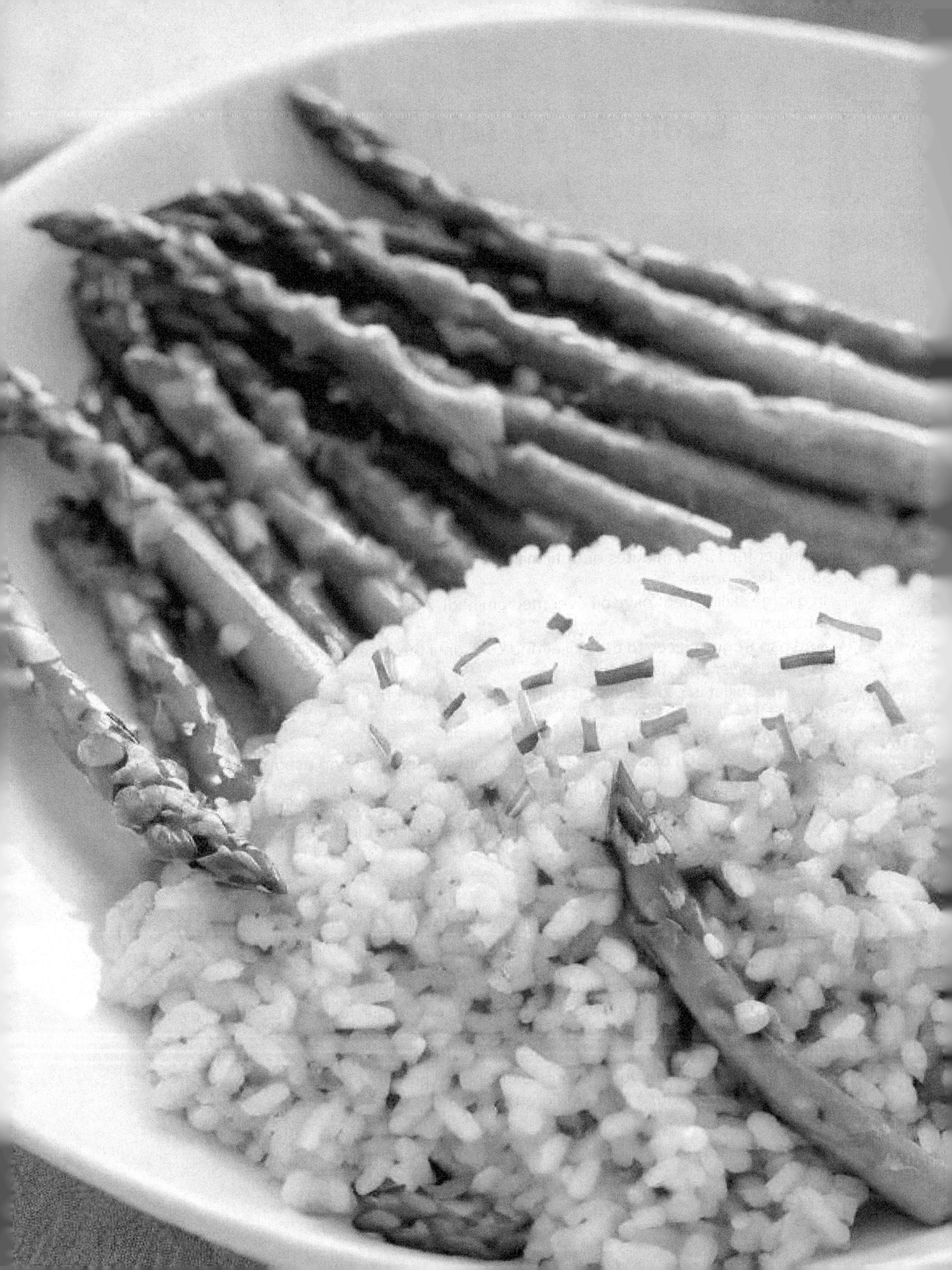

Vegan Sri Lankan Curry

Servings: 2 | **Prep Time:** 20 minutes | **Cooking Time:** 30 minutes

INGREDIENTS:
- 1 cup cauliflower florets
- 1 cup potatoes, diced
- 1 cup carrots, sliced
- 1 cup green beans, chopped
- 1 cup bell peppers, diced
- 1 cup coconut milk
- 2 tablespoons vegetable oil
- 1 onion, finely chopped
- 2 cloves garlic, minced
- 1-inch ginger, grated
- 1-2 green chilies, sliced (adjust to taste)
- 2 tablespoons Sri Lankan curry powder
- 1 teaspoon turmeric powder
- 1 teaspoon cumin seeds
- 1 cinnamon stick
- 4-5 curry leaves
- Salt and black pepper, to taste
- Fresh cilantro, chopped, for garnish

INSTRUCTIONS:
1. *Prepare Vegetables:*
   - Clean and chop cauliflower, potatoes, carrots, green beans, and bell peppers.
2. *Make Sri Lankan Curry Base:*
   - In a large pan, heat vegetable oil over medium heat. Add cumin seeds, cinnamon stick, and curry leaves. Sauté for a minute until fragrant.
   - Add chopped onions, minced garlic, grated ginger, and green chilies. Sauté until the onions are translucent.
3. *Add Curry Powder and Vegetables:*
   - Stir in Sri Lankan curry powder and turmeric powder. Cook for another minute.
   - Add cauliflower, potatoes, carrots, green beans, and bell peppers. Mix well to coat the vegetables with the spices.
4. *Pour Coconut Milk:*
   - Pour in coconut milk, ensuring it covers the vegetables. Bring to a gentle simmer.
5. *Simmer and Season:*
   - Simmer for 20-25 minutes or until the vegetables are tender.
   - Season with salt and black pepper according to taste.
6. *Garnish and Serve:*
   - Remove from heat and garnish with fresh cilantro.
   - Serve the Vegan Sri Lankan Curry over rice or your favorite grain.

EXPERT TIPS & VARIATIONS:
- Adjust the spice level by adding or reducing the amount of green chilies.
- Include protein sources like tofu or chickpeas for a heartier curry.

PAIRING SUGGESTIONS:
- Coconut sambal or chutney on the side
- Roti or naan bread for a traditional touch

Spaghetti Squash Burrito Bowls

Servings: 2 | Prep Time: 20 minutes | Cooking Time: 40 minutes

INGREDIENTS:

For Spaghetti Squash:
- 1 medium-sized spaghetti squash
- 2 tablespoons olive oil
- Salt and black pepper, to taste

For Burrito Bowl Filling:
- 1 cup black beans, cooked and drained
- 1 cup corn kernels, fresh or frozen
- 1 cup cherry tomatoes, halved
- 1 avocado, sliced
- 1/2 cup red onion, finely chopped
- 1/4 cup fresh cilantro, chopped

For Burrito Bowl Sauce:
- 1 lime, juiced
- 2 tablespoons olive oil
- 1 teaspoon ground cumin
- 1 teaspoon chili powder
- Salt and black pepper, to taste

INSTRUCTIONS:

1. *Preheat Oven:*
   - Preheat your oven to 400°F (200°C).
2. *Prepare Spaghetti Squash:*
   - Cut the spaghetti squash in half lengthwise. Scoop out the seeds.
   - Brush each half with olive oil and season with salt and black pepper.
   - Place them face down on a baking sheet and roast in the oven for 30-40 minutes or until the squash is tender.
3. *Scrape Spaghetti Squash Strands:*
   - Allow the roasted spaghetti squash to cool slightly. Use a fork to scrape the flesh, creating spaghetti-like strands. Set aside.
4. *Make Burrito Bowl Sauce:*
   - In a small bowl, whisk together lime juice, olive oil, ground cumin, chili powder, salt, and black pepper to create the sauce.
5. *Assemble Burrito Bowls:*
   - In each bowl, layer the spaghetti squash strands as the base.
   - Top with black beans, corn kernels, cherry tomatoes, avocado slices, and chopped red onion.
6. *Drizzle with Sauce:*
   - Drizzle the prepared burrito bowl sauce over the toppings.
7. *Garnish and Serve:*
   - Garnish with fresh cilantro.
   - Serve the Spaghetti Squash Burrito Bowls with additional lime wedges if desired.

EXPERT TIPS & VARIATIONS:
- Add a plant-based protein like grilled tofu or tempeh.
- Spice it up with sliced jalapeños or a sprinkle of cayenne pepper.

PAIRING SUGGESTIONS:
- Lime wedges and hot sauce on the side
- Serve with a side of Mexican rice or a simple green salad

Vegetarian Sausage Sheet Pan Dinner

Servings: 2 | **Prep Time:** 15 minutes | **Cooking Time:** 25 minutes

INGREDIENTS:
- 4 vegetarian sausages (your choice of flavor)
- 1 cup baby potatoes, halved
- 1 cup Brussels sprouts, trimmed and halved
- 1 cup baby carrots
- 1 bell pepper, sliced
- 2 tablespoons olive oil
- 1 teaspoon dried thyme
- 1 teaspoon smoked paprika
- Salt and black pepper, to taste
- Fresh parsley, chopped, for garnish

INSTRUCTIONS:
1. *Preheat Oven:*
   - Preheat your oven to 425°F (220°C).
2. *Prepare Vegetarian Sausages and Vegetables:*
   - Place vegetarian sausages on a baking sheet. Surround them with halved baby potatoes, Brussels sprouts, baby carrots, and sliced bell pepper.
3. *Drizzle with Olive Oil and Season:*
   - Drizzle olive oil over the sausages and vegetables. Sprinkle with dried thyme, smoked paprika, salt, and black pepper.
4. *Toss and Arrange:*
   - Toss the sausages and vegetables on the sheet pan until well coated in the oil and seasonings. Arrange them in a single layer.
5. *Roast in the Oven:*
   - Roast in the preheated oven for 20-25 minutes or until the sausages are cooked through, and the vegetables are golden and tender. Flip the sausages and stir the vegetables halfway through.
6. *Garnish and Serve:*
   - Remove from the oven and garnish with chopped fresh parsley.
   - Serve the Vegetarian Sausage Sheet Pan Dinner hot.

EXPERT TIPS & VARIATIONS:
- Add a drizzle of balsamic glaze before serving for extra flavor.
- Include other favorite vegetables like cherry tomatoes or zucchini.

PAIRING SUGGESTIONS:
- Mustard or your favorite dipping sauce for the sausages
- Quinoa, couscous, or a side of garlic bread

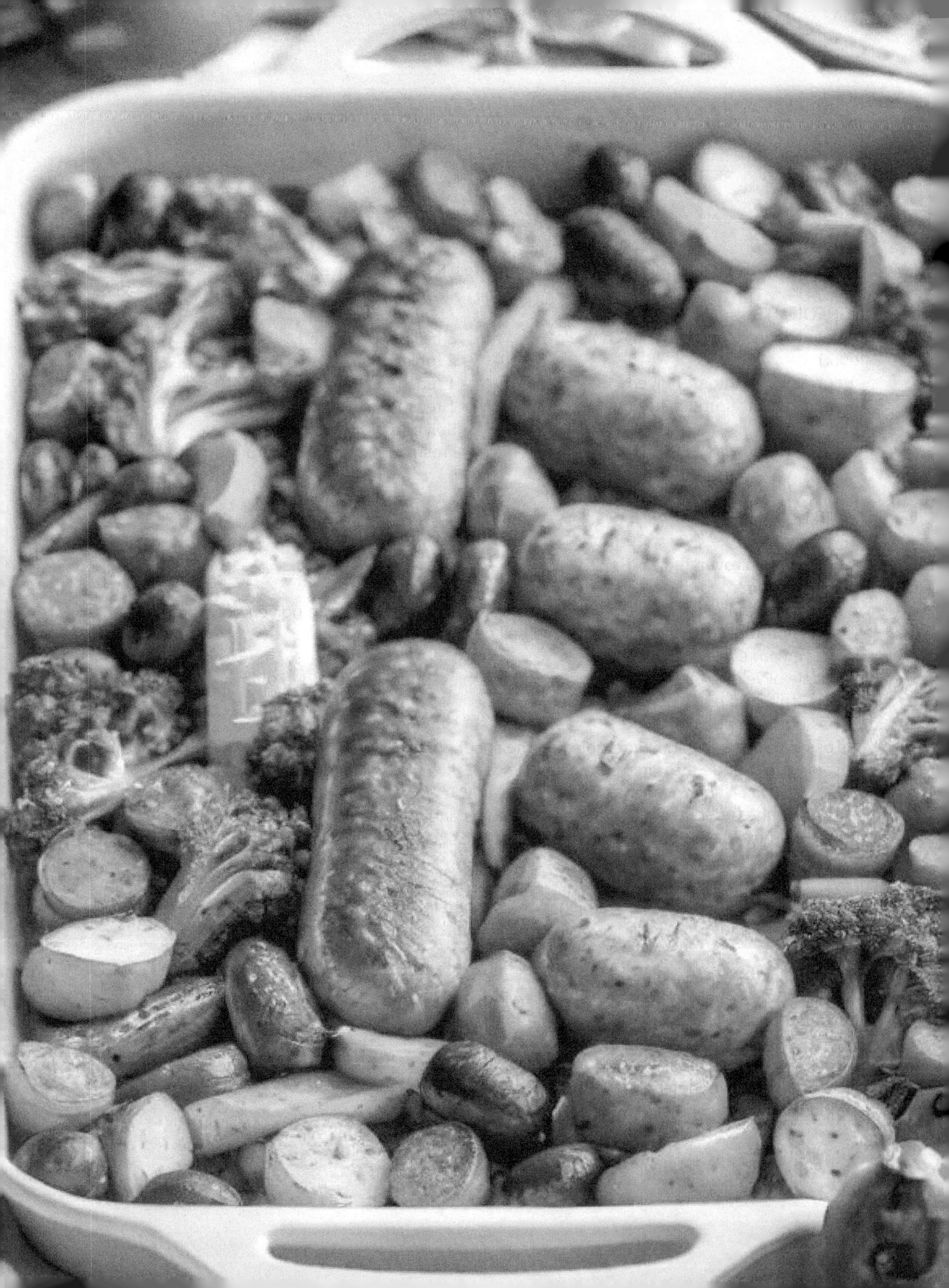

Toaster Oven-Baked Potatoes

Servings: 2 | **Prep Time:** 10 minutes | **Cooking Time:** 30-40 minutes

INGREDIENTS:
- 2 large russet potatoes
- 2 tablespoons olive oil
- 1 teaspoon garlic powder
- 1 teaspoon dried rosemary
- Salt and black pepper, to taste
- Sour cream, chives, or your favorite toppings for serving

INSTRUCTIONS:
1. *Preheat Toaster Oven:*
   - Preheat your toaster oven to 400°F (200°C).
2. *Prepare Potatoes:*
   - Wash and scrub the potatoes thoroughly. Pat them dry with a paper towel.
3. *Coat with Olive Oil and Season:*
   - Rub each potato with olive oil, ensuring they are well coated. Sprinkle garlic powder, dried rosemary, salt, and black pepper evenly over the potatoes.
4. *Bake in the Toaster Oven:*
   - Place the seasoned potatoes directly on the toaster oven rack or on a small baking sheet.
   - Bake for 30-40 minutes or until the potatoes are fork-tender and the skin is crispy.
5. *Check for Doneness:*
   - Check for doneness by inserting a fork into the center of the potatoes. They should be soft and easily pierced.
6. *Garnish and Serve:*
   - Once baked, let the potatoes cool for a few minutes. Cut a slit in the top, fluff the insides with a fork, and add your favorite toppings like sour cream and chives.

EXPERT TIPS & VARIATIONS:
- Experiment with different seasonings like smoked paprika or onion powder.
- For a crispy skin, rub the potatoes with a bit of vegetable oil before seasoning.

PAIRING SUGGESTIONS:
- Grated cheese or vegan cheese for added richness
- Serve alongside a light salad or steamed vegetables

Asparagus Couscous Bowls

Servings: 2 | **Prep Time:** 15 minutes | **Cooking Time:** 15 minutes

INGREDIENTS:
- 1 cup couscous
- 1 bunch asparagus, trimmed and cut into bite-sized pieces
- 1 cup cherry tomatoes, halved
- 1/2 cup feta cheese, crumbled
- 1/4 cup pine nuts, toasted
- 2 tablespoons olive oil
- 1 lemon, zest and juice
- 2 tablespoons fresh basil, chopped
- Salt and black pepper, to taste

INSTRUCTIONS:
1. *Prepare Couscous:*
   - Cook couscous. Fluff it with a fork and set aside.
2. *Sauté Asparagus:*
   - In a skillet, heat olive oil over medium heat. Add asparagus pieces and sauté for 4-5 minutes until they are tender-crisp.
3. *Combine Asparagus and Couscous:*
   - In a large bowl, combine the cooked couscous and sautéed asparagus.
4. *Add Tomatoes, Feta, and Pine Nuts:*
   - Mix in cherry tomatoes, crumbled feta cheese, and toasted pine nuts.
5. *Make Lemon Basil Dressing:*
   - In a small bowl, whisk together olive oil, lemon zest, lemon juice, chopped fresh basil, salt, and black pepper.
6. *Drizzle Dressing and Toss:*
   - Drizzle the lemon basil dressing over the couscous mixture. Toss everything together until well coated.
7. *Garnish and Serve:*
   - Garnish with additional basil leaves or a sprinkle of feta.
   - Serve the Asparagus Couscous Bowls warm or at room temperature.

EXPERT TIPS & VARIATIONS:
- Add grilled chicken or chickpeas for extra protein.
- Include other favorite vegetables like roasted bell peppers or cucumber.

PAIRING SUGGESTIONS:
- A side of tzatziki sauce or hummus
- Grilled pita bread or naan

Vegetable Calzones

Servings: 2 | Prep Time: 20 minutes | Cooking Time: 20 minutes

INGREDIENTS:

For Dough:
- 1 1/2 cups all-purpose flour
- 1 teaspoon active dry yeast
- 1/2 teaspoon sugar
- 1/2 teaspoon salt
- 1/2 cup warm water

For Filling:
- 1 cup part-skim ricotta cheese
- 1 cup shredded mozzarella cheese
- 1 cup mixed vegetables (bell peppers, mushrooms, spinach, etc.), chopped
- 1/4 cup grated Parmesan cheese
- 2 tablespoons olive oil
- 1 teaspoon dried oregano
- Salt and black pepper, to taste

INSTRUCTIONS:

1. *Prepare Dough:*
   - In a bowl, combine warm water, sugar, and yeast. Let it sit for 5 minutes until it becomes frothy.
   - In a large mixing bowl, combine flour and salt. Pour in the yeast mixture and knead until a smooth dough forms. Let it rest for 10-15 minutes.
2. *Preheat Oven:*
   - Preheat your oven to 450°F (230°C).
3. *Make Filling:*
   - In a separate bowl, mix ricotta cheese, mozzarella cheese, mixed vegetables, Parmesan cheese, olive oil, dried oregano, salt, and black pepper.
4. *Divide and Roll Dough:*
   - Divide the dough into two equal portions. Roll each portion into a round disc, approximately 8-10 inches in diameter.
5. *Fill and Seal:*
   - Place half of the filling on one side of each dough disc, leaving a border around the edges. Fold the other half over the filling, creating a half-moon shape. Seal the edges by pressing with a fork.
6. *Bake Calzones:*
   - Place the calzones on a baking sheet lined with parchment paper. Bake in the preheated oven for 18-20 minutes or until golden brown.
   - Allow the calzones to cool for a few minutes before slicing. Serve warm.

EXPERT TIPS & VARIATIONS:
- Customize the filling with your favorite vegetables or add a protein source like diced cooked chicken.
- Brush the calzones with garlic-infused olive oil before baking for extra flavor.

PAIRING SUGGESTIONS:
- Marinara or pesto sauce for dipping
- A crisp mixed greens salad with a balsamic vinaigrette

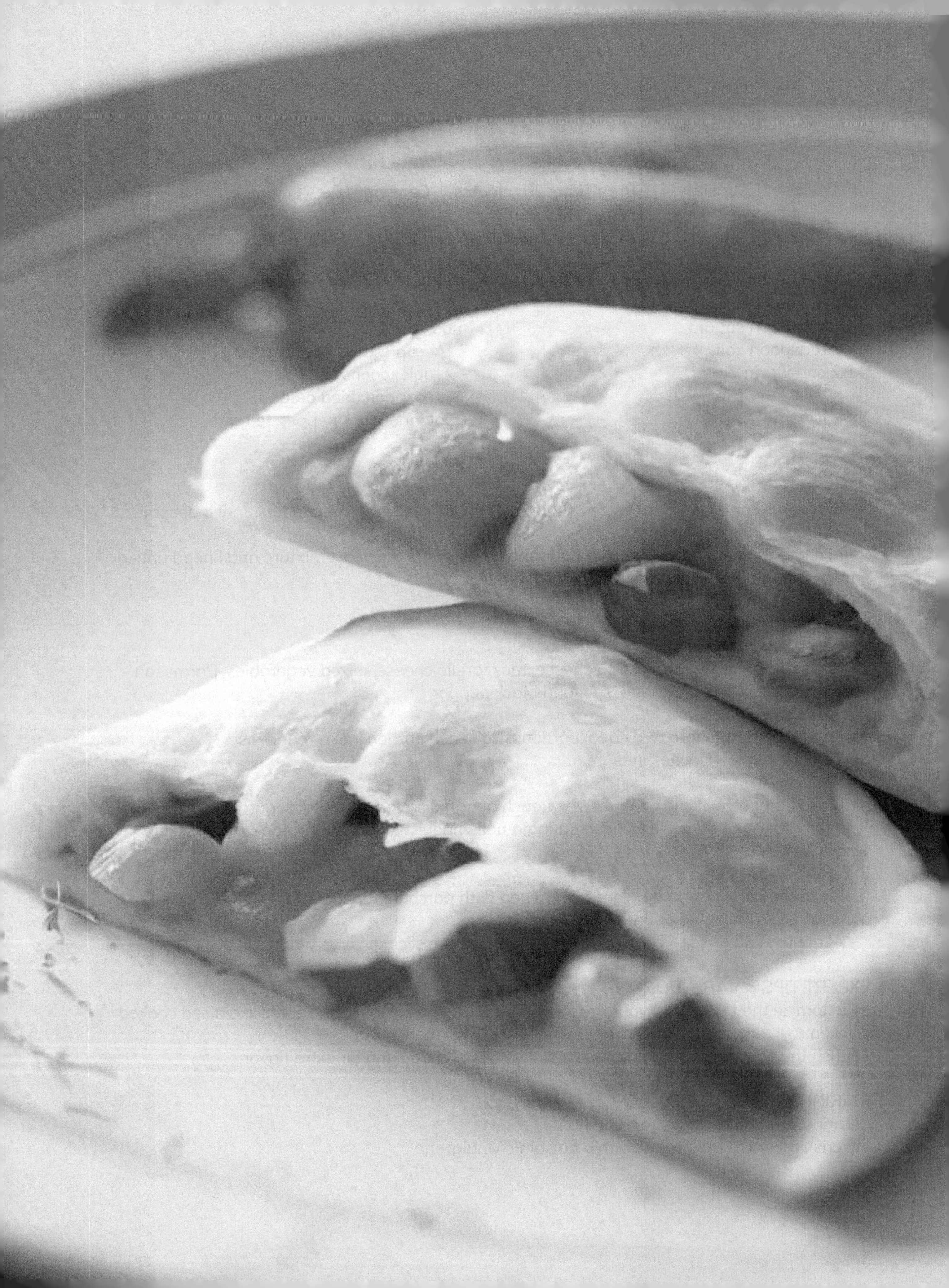

Vegetable Pot Pie

Servings: 2 | **Prep Time:** 20 minutes | **Cooking Time:** 30 minutes

INGREDIENTS:

For Filling:
- 2 tablespoons unsalted butter
- 1/4 cup all-purpose flour
- 1 1/2 cups vegetable broth
- 1 cup milk (plant-based or dairy)
- 1 cup mixed vegetables (carrots, peas, corn, green beans), frozen or fresh
- 1/2 cup mushrooms, sliced
- 1/4 cup onion, finely chopped
- 2 cloves garlic, minced
- 1 teaspoon dried thyme
- Salt and black pepper, to taste

For Crust:
- 1 sheet of puff pastry, thawed if frozen
- 1 egg (optional, for egg wash)

INSTRUCTIONS:

1. *Preheat Oven:*
   - Preheat your oven to 400°F (200°C).
2. *Prepare Filling:*
   - In a large saucepan, melt butter over medium heat. Add chopped onions and minced garlic, sauté until softened.
   - Stir in flour to create a roux. Cook for 2-3 minutes.
   - Gradually whisk in vegetable broth and milk until the mixture thickens.
   - Add mixed vegetables, mushrooms, dried thyme, salt, and black pepper. Simmer for 5-7 minutes until the vegetables are slightly tender.
3. *Assemble Pot Pie:*
   - Pour the vegetable filling into two oven-safe bowls or ramekins.
4. *Roll Out Puff Pastry:*
   - Roll out the puff pastry on a floured surface. Cut rounds slightly larger than the diameter of your bowls.
5. *Cover and Seal:*
   - Place the puff pastry rounds over each bowl, pressing the edges to seal. Cut a small slit in the center to allow steam to escape.
   - Optional: Brush the puff pastry with a beaten egg for a golden finish.
6. *Bake in the Oven:*
   - Place the bowls on a baking sheet and bake in the preheated oven for 20-25 minutes or until the crust is golden and the filling is bubbly.
7. *Cool and Serve:*
   - Allow the Vegetable Pot Pies to cool for a few minutes before serving.

EXPERT TIPS & VARIATIONS:
- Add a splash of white wine to the filling for extra depth of flavor.
- Experiment with herbs like rosemary or sage for a different flavor profile.

PAIRING SUGGESTIONS:
- Mixed green salad with a lemon vinaigrette
- Mashed potatoes or a side of roasted sweet potatoes

PASTA DISHES

Fettuccine Alfredo

Servings: 2 | Prep Time: 10 minutes | Cooking Time: 15 minutes

INGREDIENTS:
- 8 oz fettuccine pasta
- 1/2 cup unsalted butter
- 1 cup heavy cream
- 1 cup Parmesan cheese, grated
- 2 cloves garlic, minced
- Salt and black pepper, to taste
- Fresh parsley, chopped, for garnish

INSTRUCTIONS:
1. *Cook Fettuccine:*
   - Cook the fettuccine pasta in a large pot of salted boiling water. Drain and set aside.
2. *Prepare Alfredo Sauce:*
   - In a saucepan, melt butter over medium heat. Add minced garlic and sauté until fragrant.
   - Pour in the heavy cream and bring it to a simmer. Reduce heat to low.
3. *Add Parmesan Cheese:*
   - Gradually whisk in the grated Parmesan cheese, stirring continuously until the cheese is melted and the sauce is smooth.
4. *Season and Combine:*
   - Season the Alfredo sauce with salt and black pepper to taste. Stir in the cooked fettuccine pasta, coating it evenly with the creamy sauce.
5. *Serve and Garnish:*
   - Plate the Fettuccine Alfredo and garnish with chopped fresh parsley.

EXPERT TIPS & VARIATIONS:
- For added flavor, include a pinch of nutmeg or a dash of white pepper to the Alfredo sauce.
- Toss in cooked chicken, shrimp, or broccoli for a heartier meal.

PAIRING SUGGESTIONS:
- Garlic bread or breadsticks for dipping
- Caesar salad or a side of roasted vegetables

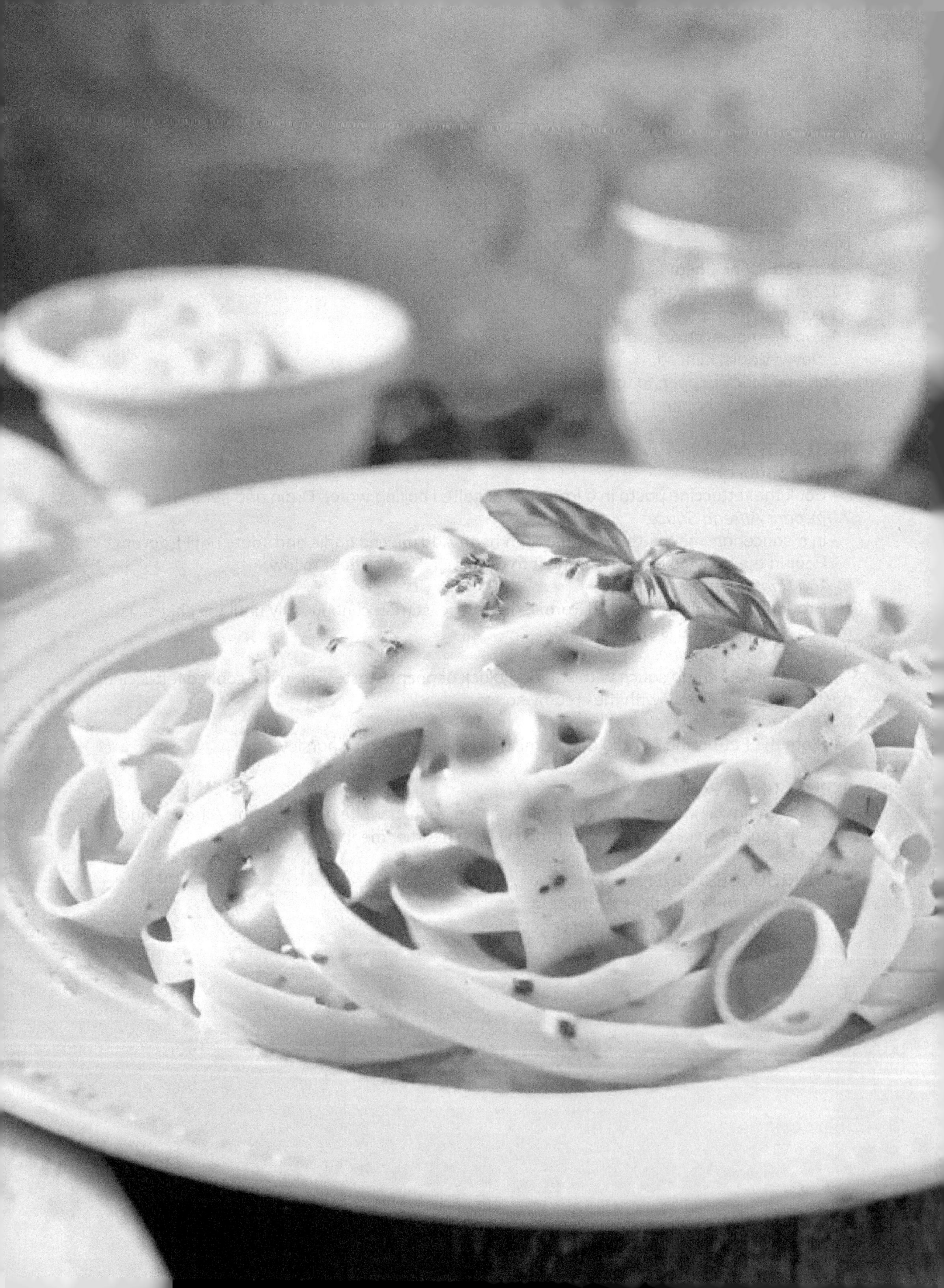

Quick One-Pan Carbonara

Servings: 2 | **Prep Time:** 10 minutes | **Cooking Time:** 15 minutes

INGREDIENTS:
- 8 oz spaghetti or fettuccine pasta
- 2 tablespoons olive oil
- 4 slices bacon, chopped
- 2 cloves garlic, minced
- 2 large eggs
- 1 cup Parmesan cheese, grated
- Salt and black pepper, to taste
- Fresh parsley, chopped, for garnish

INSTRUCTIONS:
1. *Cook Pasta:*
   - Cook the pasta in a large pot of salted boiling water. Drain and set aside.
2. *Sauté Bacon and Garlic:*
   - In a large skillet, heat olive oil over medium heat. Add chopped bacon and sauté until it becomes crispy. Add minced garlic and cook for an additional 1-2 minutes.
3. *Prepare Carbonara Sauce:*
   - In a bowl, whisk together eggs and grated Parmesan cheese until well combined.
4. *Combine Pasta and Sauce:*
   - Add the cooked pasta to the skillet with bacon and garlic. Toss to combine.
5. *Add Carbonara Sauce:*
   - Pour the egg and Parmesan mixture over the pasta. Quickly toss the pasta in the sauce until it coats the noodles evenly. The heat from the pasta will cook the eggs, creating a creamy sauce.
6. *Season and Garnish:*
   - Season the Carbonara with salt and black pepper to taste. Garnish with chopped fresh parsley.

EXPERT TIPS & VARIATIONS:
- For extra creaminess, add a splash of heavy cream to the egg and Parmesan mixture.
- Experiment with pancetta or prosciutto instead of bacon.

PAIRING SUGGESTIONS:
- Caesar salad or a side of roasted vegetables
- Garlic bread or ciabatta for dipping

Sweet Potato Tortellini with Hazelnut Sauce

Servings: 2 | **Prep Time:** 25 minutes | **Cooking Time:** 15 minutes

INGREDIENTS:
For Sweet Potato Tortellini:
- 8 oz sweet potato tortellini
- 1 large sweet potato, peeled and diced
- 1 tablespoon olive oil
- Salt and black pepper, to taste

For Hazelnut Sauce:

- 1/2 cup hazelnuts, toasted and chopped
- 2 tablespoons unsalted butter
- 1/4 cup heavy cream
- 1/4 cup Parmesan cheese, grated
- Salt and black pepper, to taste
- Fresh sage leaves, for garnish

INSTRUCTIONS:
1. *Prepare Sweet Potato Tortellini:*
   - Cook sweet potato tortellini in a large pot of salted boiling water. Drain and set aside.
2. *Roast Sweet Potatoes:*
   - Preheat your oven to 400°F (200°C).
   - Toss diced sweet potatoes with olive oil, salt, and black pepper. Roast in the oven for 15-20 minutes or until tender.
3. *Make Hazelnut Sauce:*
   - In a skillet, melt butter over medium heat. Add chopped hazelnuts and sauté until fragrant.
   - Pour in heavy cream and bring to a simmer. Stir in grated Parmesan cheese until the sauce is smooth. Season with salt and black pepper.
4. *Combine Tortellini and Sweet Potatoes:*
   - Toss the cooked sweet potato tortellini and roasted sweet potatoes in the hazelnut sauce until well coated.
5. *Serve and Garnish:*
   - Plate the Sweet Potato Tortellini with Hazelnut Sauce. Garnish with fresh sage leaves.

EXPERT TIPS & VARIATIONS:
- Add a pinch of nutmeg or cinnamon to the roasted sweet potatoes for extra warmth.
- Top with additional grated Parmesan or shaved Pecorino before serving.

PAIRING SUGGESTIONS:
- A side of sautéed greens or a mixed salad
- Crusty bread or garlic knots for dipping

Four Cheese Stuffed Shells

Servings: 2 | Prep Time: 20 minutes | Cooking Time: 25 minutes

INGREDIENTS:
- 14 jumbo pasta shells
- 1 cup ricotta cheese
- 1/2 cup mozzarella cheese, shredded
- 1/4 cup Parmesan cheese, grated
- 1/4 cup Asiago cheese, grated
- 1 egg, beaten
- 2 cloves garlic, minced
- 1/4 cup fresh basil, chopped
- Salt and black pepper, to taste
- 2 cups marinara sauce
- Fresh parsley, chopped, for garnish

INSTRUCTIONS:
1. *Cook Pasta Shells:*
   - Cook the jumbo pasta shells in a large pot of salted boiling water. Drain and let them cool.
2. *Prepare Filling:*
   - In a bowl, combine ricotta cheese, shredded mozzarella, grated Parmesan, grated Asiago, beaten egg, minced garlic, chopped fresh basil, salt, and black pepper.
3. *Stuff Pasta Shells:*
   - Preheat your oven to 375°F (190°C).
   - Fill each cooked pasta shell with the four cheese mixture.
4. *Assemble in Baking Dish:*
   - Spread a thin layer of marinara sauce in the bottom of a baking dish.
   - Arrange the stuffed pasta shells in the dish.
5. *Bake:*
   - Cover the baking dish with foil and bake in the preheated oven for 20 minutes. Remove the foil and bake for an additional 5 minutes until the cheese is melted and bubbly.
6. *Garnish and Serve:*
   - Garnish the Four Cheese Stuffed Shells with chopped fresh parsley before serving.

EXPERT TIPS & VARIATIONS:
- Add cooked and crumbled Italian sausage to the cheese mixture for added flavor.
- Drizzle extra marinara sauce on top before serving.

PAIRING SUGGESTIONS:
- A side salad with a balsamic vinaigrette
- Garlic bread or a crusty baguette

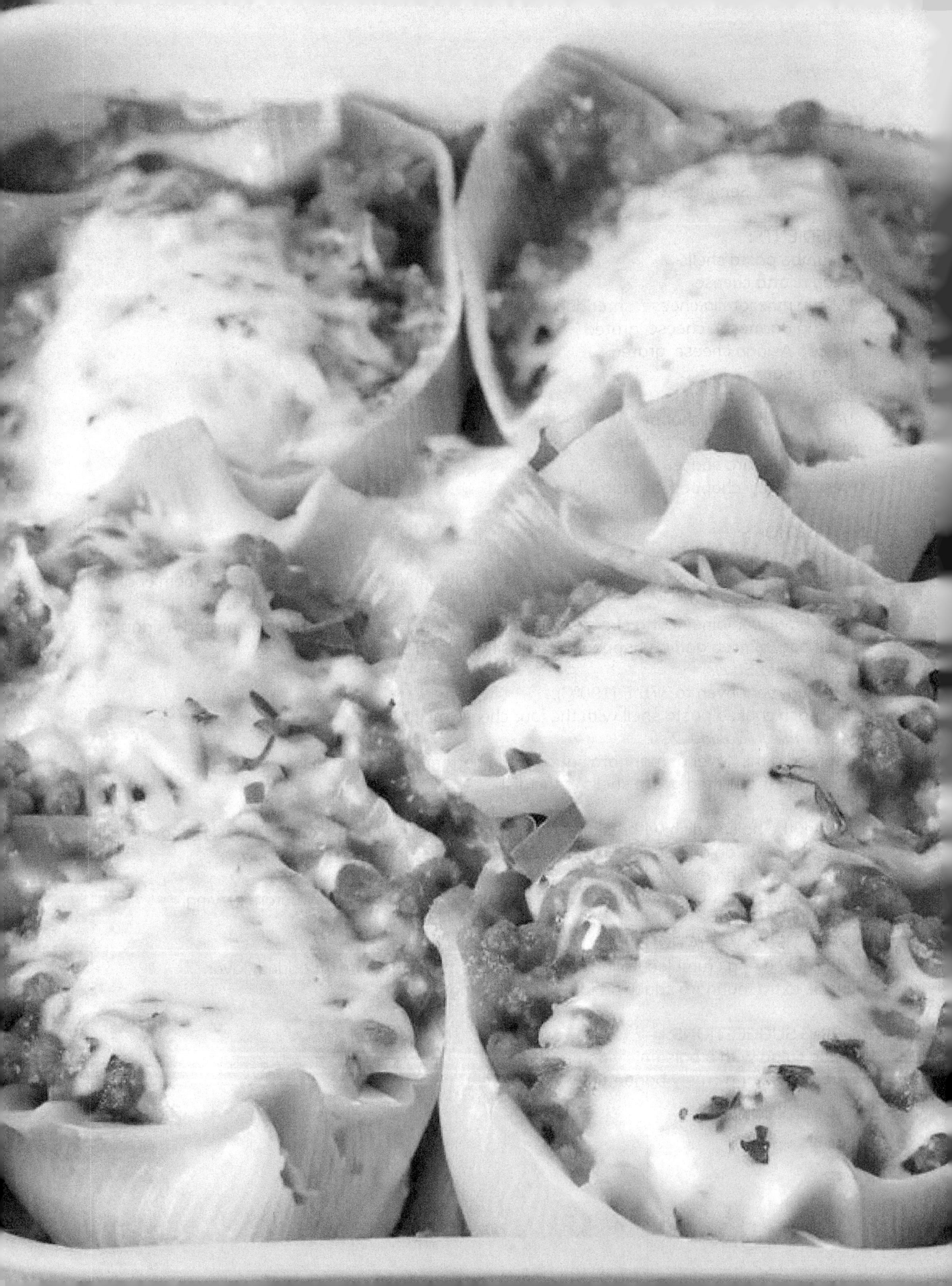

Ricotta Gnocchi with Spinach & Gorgonzola

Servings: 2 | **Prep Time:** 30 minutes | **Cooking Time:** 15 minutes

INGREDIENTS:

For Ricotta Gnocchi:
- 1 cup ricotta cheese
- 1/2 cup grated Parmesan cheese
- 1 large egg
- 1 cup all-purpose flour, plus extra for dusting
- Salt and nutmeg, to taste

For Spinach & Gorgonzola Sauce:
- 2 tablespoons unsalted butter
- 2 cloves garlic, minced
- 2 cups fresh spinach, chopped
- 1/2 cup Gorgonzola cheese, crumbled
- Salt and black pepper, to taste
- Fresh parsley, chopped, for garnish

INSTRUCTIONS:

1. *Prepare Ricotta Gnocchi:*
   - In a bowl, combine ricotta cheese, grated Parmesan, egg, salt, and a pinch of nutmeg. Gradually add flour, mixing until a soft dough forms.
   - On a floured surface, shape the dough into ropes, then cut into bite-sized pieces. Use a fork to create ridges on each piece.
2. *Cook Ricotta Gnocchi:*
   - Boil the gnocchi in salted water until they float to the surface. Remove with a slotted spoon and set aside.
3. *Make Spinach & Gorgonzola Sauce:*
   - In a skillet, melt butter over medium heat. Add minced garlic and sauté until fragrant.
   - Add chopped spinach and cook until wilted. Stir in crumbled Gorgonzola cheese until melted. Season with salt and black pepper.
4. *Combine Gnocchi and Sauce:*
   - Toss the cooked ricotta gnocchi in the spinach and Gorgonzola sauce until well coated.
5. *Serve and Garnish:*
   - Plate the Ricotta Gnocchi with Spinach & Gorgonzola. Garnish with chopped fresh parsley.

EXPERT TIPS & VARIATIONS:
- Add a handful of toasted pine nuts for crunch.
- Experiment with other herbs like sage or thyme in the sauce.

PAIRING SUGGESTIONS:
- A light salad with a lemon vinaigrette
- Crusty bread or garlic knots for soaking up the delicious sauce

Garlic Salmon Linguine

Servings: 2 | **Prep Time:** 15 minutes | **Cooking Time:** 15 minutes

INGREDIENTS:
- 8 oz linguine pasta
- 2 salmon fillets
- 3 tablespoons olive oil
- 4 cloves garlic, minced
- 1/2 teaspoon red pepper flakes (adjust to taste)
- Zest and juice of 1 lemon
- Salt and black pepper, to taste
- 1/4 cup fresh parsley, chopped
- Grated Parmesan cheese, for serving

INSTRUCTIONS:
1. *Cook Linguine:*
   - Cook linguine pasta in a large pot of salted boiling water. Drain and set aside.
2. *Prepare Salmon:*
   - Season salmon fillets with salt and black pepper. In a skillet, heat 2 tablespoons of olive oil over medium heat. Cook salmon fillets for 3-4 minutes per side or until cooked through. Break the salmon into flakes with a fork and set aside.
3. *Make Garlic Sauce:*
   - In the same skillet, add the remaining 1 tablespoon of olive oil. Add minced garlic and red pepper flakes. Sauté until garlic is golden but not burnt.
4. *Combine Pasta and Salmon:*
   - Toss the cooked linguine in the garlic sauce. Add the flaked salmon, lemon zest, and lemon juice. Mix until everything is well combined.
5. *Season and Garnish:*
   - Season with additional salt and black pepper if needed. Garnish with chopped fresh parsley.
6. *Serve and Top with Parmesan:*
   - Plate the Garlic Salmon Linguine and top with grated Parmesan cheese.

EXPERT TIPS & VARIATIONS:
- Add a splash of white wine to the garlic sauce for extra depth.
- Include cherry tomatoes or spinach for a burst of color and freshness.

PAIRING SUGGESTIONS:
- A side of garlic bread or baguette
- Mixed green salad with a balsamic vinaigrette

Shrimp Scampi

Servings: 2 | **Prep Time:** 15 minutes | **Cooking Time:** 10 minutes

INGREDIENTS:
- 8 oz linguine or spaghetti
- 8 oz large shrimp, peeled and deveined
- 4 tablespoons unsalted butter
- 3 tablespoons olive oil
- 4 cloves garlic, minced
- 1/2 teaspoon red pepper flakes (adjust to taste)
- Zest and juice of 1 lemon
- Salt and black pepper, to taste
- 1/4 cup fresh parsley, chopped
- Grated Parmesan cheese, for serving

INSTRUCTIONS:
1. *Cook Pasta:*
   - Cook linguine or spaghetti in a large pot of salted boiling water. Drain and set aside.
2. *Prepare Shrimp:*
   - In a skillet, heat 2 tablespoons of butter and 2 tablespoons of olive oil over medium heat. Add shrimp and cook until they turn pink and opaque, about 2-3 minutes per side. Remove shrimp from the skillet and set aside.
3. *Make Garlic Sauce:*
   - In the same skillet, add the remaining 2 tablespoons of butter and 1 tablespoon of olive oil. Add minced garlic and red pepper flakes. Sauté until garlic is fragrant but not browned.
4. *Combine Pasta and Shrimp:*
   - Toss the cooked pasta in the garlic sauce. Add the cooked shrimp, lemon zest, and lemon juice. Mix until everything is well coated.
5. *Season and Garnish:*
   - Season with salt and black pepper to taste. Garnish with chopped fresh parsley.
6. *Serve and Top with Parmesan:*
   - Plate the Shrimp Scampi and top with grated Parmesan cheese.

EXPERT TIPS & VARIATIONS:
- Add a splash of white wine or chicken broth for extra flavor in the sauce.
- Include cherry tomatoes or spinach for a pop of color and freshness.

PAIRING SUGGESTIONS:
- A side of garlic bread or baguette
- Mixed green salad with a lemon vinaigrette

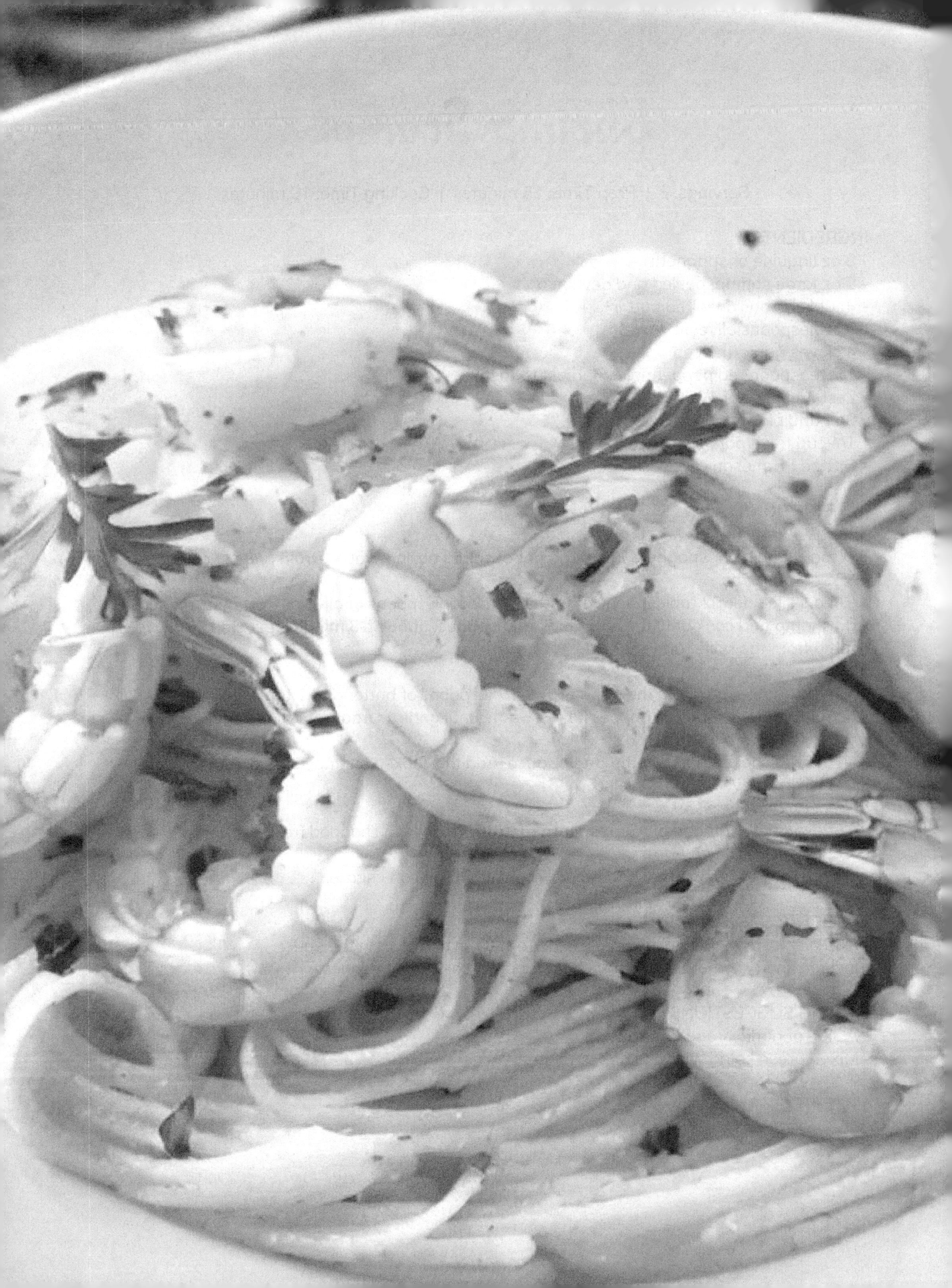

Crab-Stuffed Manicotti

Servings: 2 | Prep Time: 30 minutes | Cooking Time: 25 minutes

INGREDIENTS:
For Crab Filling:
- 1 cup lump crab meat, cooked and shredded
- 1 cup ricotta cheese
- 1/2 cup mozzarella cheese, shredded
- 2 tablespoons Parmesan cheese, grated
- 1 egg
- 2 tablespoons fresh parsley, chopped
- Salt and black pepper, to taste

For Manicotti and Sauce:
- 6 manicotti shells, cooked al dente
- 2 cups marinara sauce
- 1 cup mozzarella cheese, shredded
- Fresh basil, chopped, for garnish

INSTRUCTIONS:
1. *Prepare Crab Filling:*
   - In a bowl, combine lump crab meat, ricotta cheese, mozzarella cheese, Parmesan cheese, egg, chopped fresh parsley, salt, and black pepper. Mix until well combined.
2. *Stuff Manicotti:*
   - Preheat your oven to 375°F (190°C).
   - Carefully stuff each cooked manicotti shell with the crab filling.
3. *Arrange in Baking Dish:*
   - Pour a thin layer of marinara sauce in the bottom of a baking dish. Arrange the stuffed manicotti in the dish.
4. *Top with Sauce and Cheese:*
   - Pour the remaining marinara sauce over the stuffed manicotti. Sprinkle shredded mozzarella cheese on top.
5. *Bake:*
   - Cover the baking dish with foil and bake in the preheated oven for 20 minutes. Remove the foil and bake for an additional 5 minutes or until the cheese is melted and bubbly.
6. *Garnish and Serve:*
   - Garnish the Crab-Stuffed Manicotti with chopped fresh basil before serving.

EXPERT TIPS & VARIATIONS:
- Add a pinch of Old Bay seasoning to the crab filling for a touch of seafood spice.
- Drizzle extra marinara sauce on top or serve with a side of lemon wedges for freshness.

PAIRING SUGGESTIONS:
- Garlic bread or crusty baguette
- A side salad with a balsamic vinaigrette

Creamy Roasted Garlic and Beets Pasta

Servings: 2 | **Prep Time:** 15 minutes | **Cooking Time:** 45 minutes

INGREDIENTS:

For Roasted Garlic and Beets:
- 2 medium beets, peeled and diced
- 1 head of garlic, top trimmed off
- 2 tablespoons olive oil
- Salt and black pepper, to taste

For Creamy Sauce:
- 1 cup heavy cream
- 1/2 cup Parmesan cheese, grated
- 2 tablespoons unsalted butter
- Salt and black pepper, to taste

For Pasta:
- 8 oz fettuccine or your favorite pasta
- Fresh parsley, chopped, for garnish

INSTRUCTIONS:

1. *Roast Garlic and Beets:*
   - Preheat your oven to 400°F (200°C).
   - Place diced beets and the head of garlic on a baking sheet. Drizzle with olive oil and season with salt and black pepper. Roast for 30-35 minutes or until beets are tender and garlic is soft.
2. *Prepare Creamy Sauce:*
   - Squeeze the roasted garlic cloves into a blender. Add heavy cream, Parmesan cheese, and butter. Blend until smooth. Season with salt and black pepper to taste.
3. *Cook Pasta:*
   - Cook fettuccine or your preferred pasta in a large pot of salted boiling water. Drain and set aside.
4. *Combine Pasta and Sauce:*
   - Toss the cooked pasta in the creamy roasted garlic and beet sauce until well coated.
5. *Serve and Garnish:*
   - Plate the Creamy Roasted Garlic and Beets Pasta. Garnish with chopped fresh parsley.

EXPERT TIPS & VARIATIONS:
- Add a splash of balsamic vinegar to the sauce for a hint of acidity.
- Top with roasted walnuts or pine nuts for extra crunch.

PAIRING SUGGESTIONS:
- A side of garlic bread or baguette
- Mixed green salad with a lemon vinaigrette

Roasted Red Pepper Fettuccine with Creamy Feta Sauce

Servings: 2 | Prep Time: 20 minutes | Cooking Time: 25 minutes

INGREDIENTS:

For Roasted Red Pepper Sauce:
- 2 large red bell peppers, roasted and peeled
- 2 cloves garlic, minced
- 2 tablespoons olive oil
- 1/2 cup chicken or vegetable broth
- Salt and black pepper, to taste

For Creamy Feta Sauce:
- 1/2 cup feta cheese, crumbled
- 1/2 cup heavy cream
- 2 tablespoons unsalted butter
- 1/4 cup Parmesan cheese, grated
- Salt and black pepper, to taste

For Fettuccine:
- 8 oz fettuccine pasta
- Fresh basil, chopped, for garnish
- Crushed red pepper flakes (optional, for heat)

INSTRUCTIONS:

1. *Roast Red Peppers:*
   - Preheat your oven to 450°F (230°C). Place red bell peppers on a baking sheet and roast until the skins blister and turn black. Allow them to cool, peel, and remove seeds.
2. *Prepare Roasted Red Pepper Sauce:*
   - In a blender, combine roasted red peppers, minced garlic, olive oil, chicken or vegetable broth, salt, and black pepper. Blend until smooth.
3. *Make Creamy Feta Sauce:*
   - In a saucepan, melt butter over medium heat. Add crumbled feta, heavy cream, and grated Parmesan. Stir until cheeses are melted and the sauce is smooth. Season with salt and black pepper.
4. *Cook Fettuccine:*
   - Cook fettuccine pasta in a large pot of salted boiling water. Drain and set aside.
5. *Combine Pasta and Sauces:*
   - Toss the cooked fettuccine in the roasted red pepper sauce. Then, fold in the creamy feta sauce until well combined.
   - Plate the Roasted Red Pepper Fettuccine with Creamy Feta Sauce. Garnish with chopped fresh basil and optional crushed red pepper flakes.

EXPERT TIPS & VARIATIONS:
- Add grilled chicken or shrimp for a protein boost.
- Enhance the flavor with a dash of balsamic vinegar or a squeeze of lemon.

PAIRING SUGGESTIONS:
- A side of garlic bread or baguette
- Mixed green salad with a balsamic vinaigrette

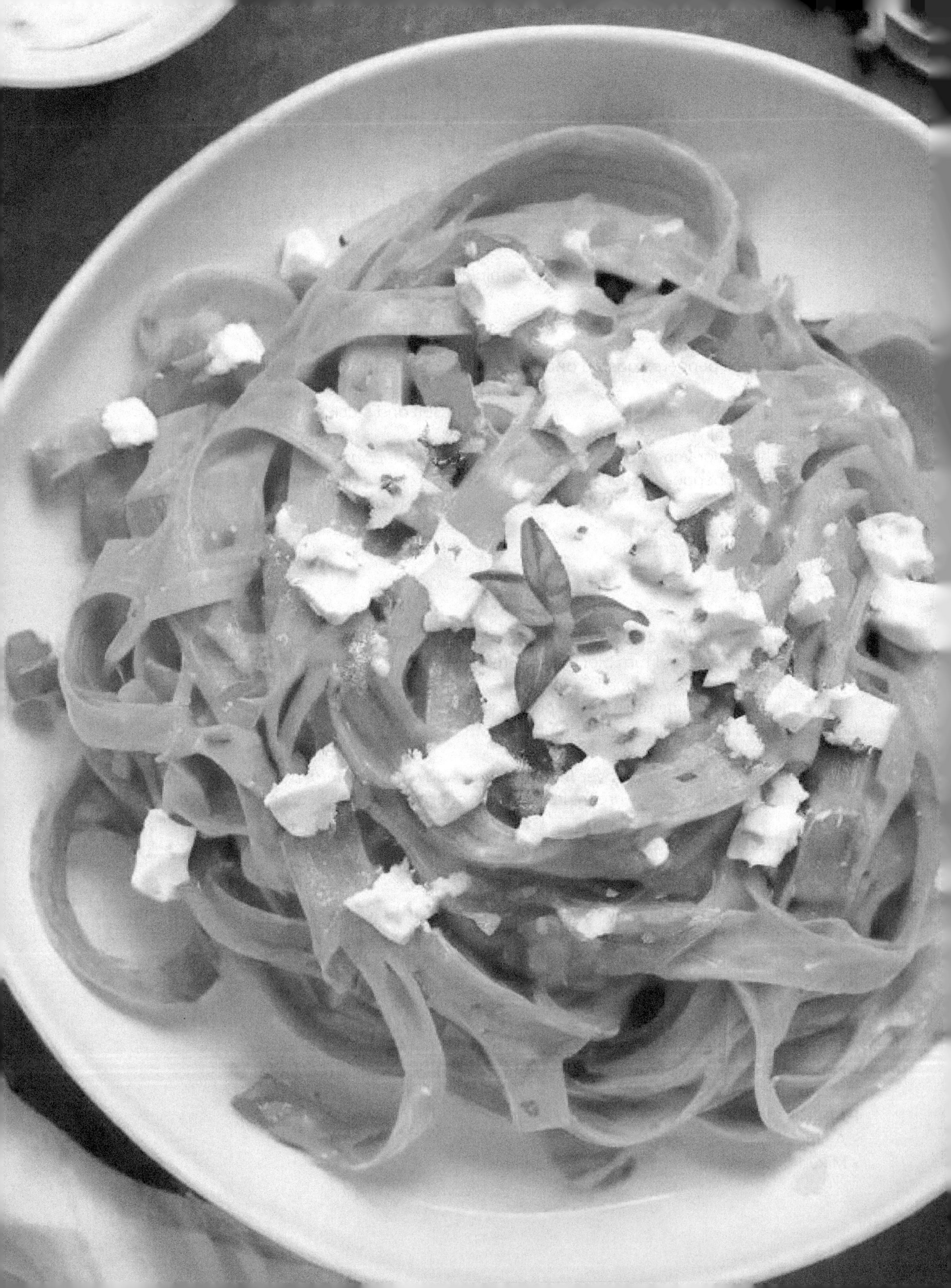

Mozzarella Penne Rosa with Sun-Dried Tomatoes

Servings: 2 | **Prep Time:** 15 minutes | **Cooking Time:** 20 minutes

INGREDIENTS:
- 8 oz penne pasta
- 1 cup sun-dried tomatoes, sliced
- 2 tablespoons olive oil
- 3 cloves garlic, minced
- 1/2 teaspoon red pepper flakes (adjust to taste)
- 1 can (14 oz) diced tomatoes, drained
- 1 cup heavy cream
- 1 cup mozzarella cheese, shredded
- Salt and black pepper, to taste
- Fresh basil, chopped, for garnish
- Grated Parmesan cheese, for serving

INSTRUCTIONS:
1. *Cook Penne Pasta:*
   - Cook penne pasta in a large pot of salted boiling water. Drain and set aside.
2. *Sauté Sun-Dried Tomatoes:*
   - In a skillet, heat olive oil over medium heat. Add sliced sun-dried tomatoes and sauté for 2-3 minutes until they are slightly softened.
3. *Add Garlic and Red Pepper Flakes:*
   - Add minced garlic and red pepper flakes to the skillet. Sauté for an additional 1-2 minutes until garlic is fragrant.
4. *Combine with Diced Tomatoes:*
   - Stir in drained diced tomatoes and cook for 2-3 minutes until heated through.
5. *Make Creamy Sauce:*
   - Pour in heavy cream and bring to a simmer. Add mozzarella cheese and stir until the cheese is melted and the sauce is creamy.
6. *Season and Toss with Pasta:*
   - Season the sauce with salt and black pepper to taste. Toss the cooked penne pasta in the Mozzarella Penne Rosa sauce until well coated.
7. *Garnish and Serve:*
   - Plate the Mozzarella Penne Rosa with Sun-Dried Tomatoes. Garnish with chopped fresh basil and serve with grated Parmesan cheese.

EXPERT TIPS & VARIATIONS:
- Add cooked chicken or shrimp for extra protein.
- Enhance the flavor with a splash of balsamic vinegar or a sprinkle of Italian seasoning.

PAIRING SUGGESTIONS:
- A side of garlic bread or baguette
- Mixed green salad with a balsamic vinaigrette

Thai Red Curry Vegetable Soup

Servings: 2 | **Prep Time:** 15 minutes | **Cooking Time:** 25 minutes

INGREDIENTS:
- 1 tablespoon vegetable oil
- 1 small onion, thinly sliced
- 2 tablespoons Thai red curry paste
- 1 can (14 oz) coconut milk
- 3 cups vegetable broth
- 1 small sweet potato, peeled and diced
- 1 carrot, sliced
- 1 red bell pepper, sliced
- 1 cup broccoli florets
- 1 cup mushrooms, sliced
- 1 tablespoon soy sauce
- 1 tablespoon brown sugar
- Juice of 1 lime
- Fresh cilantro, chopped, for garnish
- Red chili flakes (optional, for heat)

INSTRUCTIONS:
1. *Sauté Vegetables:*
   - In a large pot, heat vegetable oil over medium heat. Add sliced onion and sauté until softened.
2. *Add Thai Red Curry Paste:*
   - Stir in Thai red curry paste and cook for 1-2 minutes until fragrant.
3. *Pour Coconut Milk and Broth:*
   - Pour in coconut milk and vegetable broth. Bring to a simmer.
4. *Add Vegetables:*
   - Add diced sweet potato, sliced carrot, red bell pepper, broccoli florets, and sliced mushrooms to the pot. Simmer until vegetables are tender.
5. *Season:*
   - Stir in soy sauce, brown sugar, and lime juice. Adjust seasoning to taste.
6. *Serve:*
   - Ladle the Thai Red Curry Vegetable Soup into bowls. Garnish with fresh cilantro and, if desired, red chili flakes for extra heat.

EXPERT TIPS & VARIATIONS:
- Customize with your favorite vegetables like baby corn, snow peas, or bok choy.
- For protein, add tofu cubes or cooked shrimp.

PAIRING SUGGESTIONS:
- Jasmine rice or rice noodles on the side
- Thai basil leaves for additional freshness

Creamy Tuscan Chicken Pasta

Servings: 2 | Prep Time: 15 minutes Cooking Time: 20 minutes

INGREDIENTS:
- 8 oz fettuccine pasta
- 2 boneless, skinless chicken breasts
- Salt and black pepper, to taste
- 2 tablespoons olive oil
- 3 cloves garlic, minced
- 1 cup cherry tomatoes, halved
- 1/2 cup sun-dried tomatoes, sliced
- 1 cup spinach leaves
- 1 cup heavy cream
- 1/2 cup Parmesan cheese, grated
- 1 teaspoon dried Italian herbs
- Fresh basil, chopped, for garnish

INSTRUCTIONS:
1. *Cook Fettuccine Pasta:*
   - Cook fettuccine pasta in a large pot of salted boiling water. Drain and set aside.
2. *Season and Cook Chicken:*
   - Season chicken breasts with salt and black pepper. In a skillet, heat olive oil over medium-high heat. Cook chicken for 5-6 minutes per side or until cooked through. Remove from the skillet and let it rest before slicing.
3. *Sauté Garlic and Tomatoes:*
   - In the same skillet, add minced garlic and sauté for 1-2 minutes until fragrant. Add halved cherry tomatoes and sun-dried tomatoes. Cook for an additional 2-3 minutes.
4. *Add Spinach and Cream:*
   - Stir in spinach leaves until wilted. Pour in heavy cream and bring to a simmer.
5. *Combine with Pasta:*
   - Add sliced chicken, grated Parmesan, and dried Italian herbs to the skillet. Toss until the sauce is creamy and ingredients are well combined.
6. *Season and Garnish:*
   - Season with additional salt and black pepper to taste. Garnish with chopped fresh basil.
7. *Serve:*
   - Plate the Creamy Tuscan Chicken Pasta and serve immediately.

EXPERT TIPS & VARIATIONS:
- Add a splash of white wine or chicken broth for extra flavor in the sauce.
- Top with toasted pine nuts or crushed red pepper flakes for additional texture or heat.

PAIRING SUGGESTIONS:
- A side of garlic bread or baguette
- Mixed green salad with a balsamic vinaigrette

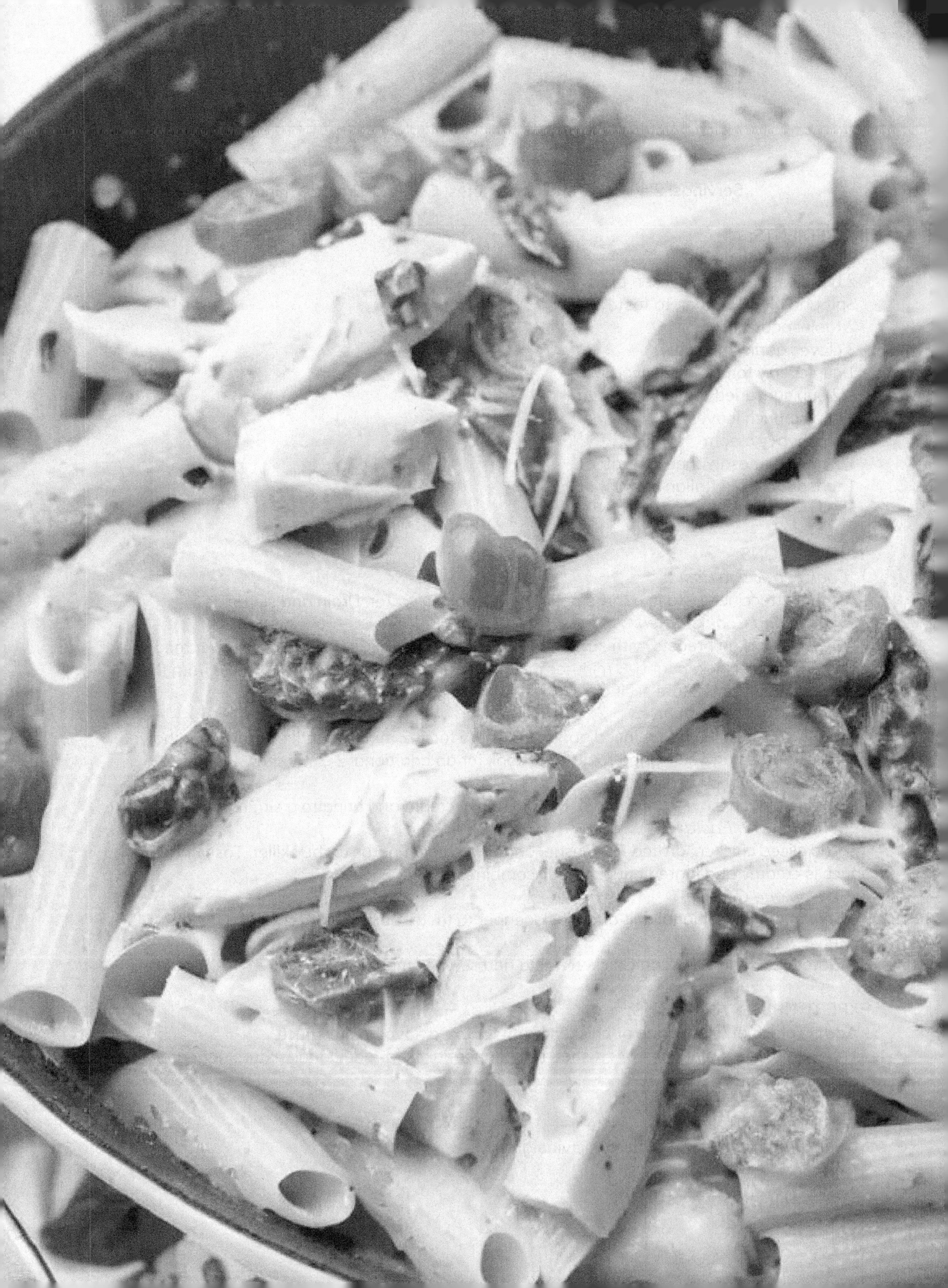

APPETIZERS

Caprese Phyllo Cups

Servings: 2 | Prep Time: 15 minutes | Cooking Time: 10 minutes

INGREDIENTS:
- 6 phyllo cups (store-bought or homemade)
- 1 cup cherry tomatoes, halved
- 1 cup fresh mozzarella pearls or diced mozzarella
- Fresh basil leaves, torn
- Balsamic glaze, for drizzling
- Extra virgin olive oil, for drizzling
- Salt and black pepper, to taste

INSTRUCTIONS:
1. *Prepare Phyllo Cups:*
   - If using store-bought phyllo cups, follow the package instructions for baking. If making homemade, bake according to your recipe.
2. *Assemble Caprese Filling:*
   - In a bowl, combine halved cherry tomatoes and fresh mozzarella pearls. Season with salt and black pepper to taste.
3. *Fill Phyllo Cups:*
   - Fill each phyllo cup with the Caprese filling mixture.
4. *Garnish:*
   - Top each cup with torn fresh basil leaves for a burst of flavor.
5. *Drizzle and Serve:*
   - Drizzle balsamic glaze and extra virgin olive oil over the Caprese Phyllo Cups.
6. *Serve:*
   - Arrange the Caprese Phyllo Cups on a serving plate and enjoy immediately.

EXPERT TIPS & VARIATIONS:
- Add a sprinkle of sea salt or a dash of balsamic reduction for extra flavor.
- Experiment with different varieties of tomatoes or use heirloom tomatoes for a colorful twist.

PAIRING SUGGESTIONS:
- A glass of Prosecco or your favorite white wine
- Serve as an appetizer before a main course

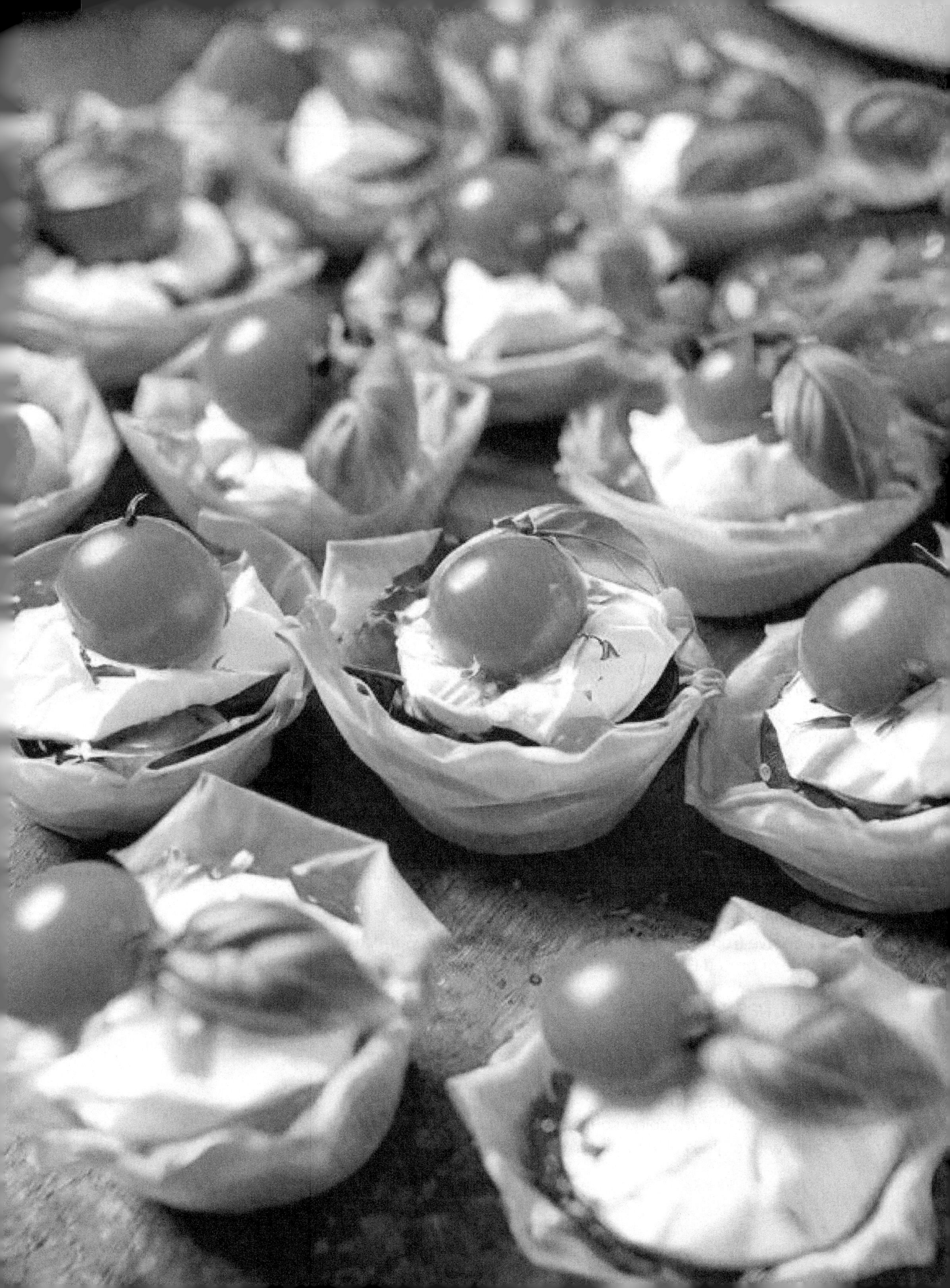

Pizza Roses

Servings: 2 | **Prep Time:** 20 minutes | **Cooking Time:** 25 minutes

INGREDIENTS:
- 1 sheet puff pastry, thawed
- 1/2 cup pizza sauce
- 1 cup shredded mozzarella cheese
- 1/4 cup pepperoni slices
- Fresh basil leaves, for garnish
- Grated Parmesan cheese, for topping
- Olive oil, for brushing

INSTRUCTIONS:
1. *Preheat Oven:*
   - Preheat your oven to 375°F (190°C).
2. *Prepare Puff Pastry:*
   - Roll out the puff pastry sheet on a lightly floured surface.
3. *Cut Strips:*
   - Cut the puff pastry into strips, about 2 inches wide.
4. *Spread Pizza Sauce:*
   - Spread a thin layer of pizza sauce on each strip.
5. *Add Cheese and Pepperoni:*
   - Sprinkle shredded mozzarella cheese over the sauce. Place pepperoni slices along the strip.
6. *Roll into Roses:*
   - Carefully roll each strip into a rose shape, starting from one end and coiling toward the center.
7. *Place in Muffin Tin:*
   - Place the pizza roses in a greased muffin tin, with the open end facing up.
8. *Brush with Olive Oil:*
   - Lightly brush the tops of the pizza roses with olive oil.
9. *Bake:*
   - Bake in the preheated oven for 20-25 minutes or until the puff pastry is golden and cooked through.
10. *Garnish and Serve:*
    - Remove from the oven and let them cool slightly. Garnish with fresh basil leaves and a sprinkle of grated Parmesan cheese.

EXPERT TIPS & VARIATIONS:
- Customize with your favorite pizza toppings like olives, bell peppers, or mushrooms.
- Experiment with different types of cheese for added flavor.

PAIRING SUGGESTIONS:
- Marinara or garlic dipping sauce on the side
- Enjoy with a glass of your preferred wine or sparkling water

Baked Brie in Puff Pastry

Servings: 2 | Prep Time: 15 minutes | Cooking Time: 20 minutes

INGREDIENTS:
- 1 sheet puff pastry, thawed
- 1 round of Brie cheese (about 8 oz)
- 2 tablespoons fruit preserves (apricot, raspberry, or fig work well)
- 1 egg, beaten (for egg wash)
- Crackers or sliced baguette, for serving

INSTRUCTIONS:
1. *Preheat Oven:*
   - Preheat your oven to 375°F (190°C).
2. *Prepare Puff Pastry:*
   - Roll out the puff pastry sheet on a lightly floured surface.
3. *Wrap Brie:*
   - Place the round of Brie in the center of the puff pastry. Spread fruit preserves on top of the Brie.
4. *Encase Brie in Puff Pastry:*
   - Fold the puff pastry over the Brie, sealing it well. Trim any excess pastry.
5. *Brush with Egg Wash:*
   - Brush the entire puff pastry-wrapped Brie with the beaten egg to give it a golden color when baked.
6. *Bake:*
   - Place the wrapped Brie on a baking sheet and bake in the preheated oven for about 20 minutes or until the pastry is golden brown.
7. *Serve:*
   - Allow the Baked Brie to cool for a few minutes before serving. Serve with crackers or sliced baguette.

EXPERT TIPS & VARIATIONS:
- Experiment with different fruit preserves or add a layer of chopped nuts for extra flavor and texture.
- Drizzle honey or balsamic glaze over the Brie before serving for a sweet touch.

PAIRING SUGGESTIONS:
- Fresh fruits like apple or pear slices
- A selection of nuts for added crunch

Cheese Fondue

Servings: 2 | **Prep Time:** 15 minutes | **Cooking Time:** 15 minutes

INGREDIENTS:
- 1 clove garlic, halved
- 1 cup dry white wine
- 8 oz Gruyère cheese, grated
- 8 oz Emmental cheese, grated
- 1 tablespoon cornstarch
- 1 tablespoon lemon juice
- 1/4 teaspoon nutmeg, freshly grated
- A pinch of white pepper
- 1 French baguette, cubed
- Assorted vegetables for dipping (broccoli, cherry tomatoes, mushrooms)

INSTRUCTIONS:
1. *Rub Pot with Garlic:*
   - Rub the inside of a fondue pot with the halved garlic clove.
2. *Prepare Cheese Mixture:*
   - In a bowl, toss the grated Gruyère and Emmental cheeses with cornstarch until well coated.
3. *Heat Wine:*
   - Pour the dry white wine into the fondue pot and heat it over medium heat until it's hot but not boiling.
4. *Melt Cheese:*
   - Gradually add the cheese mixture to the pot, stirring constantly in a figure-eight motion until the cheese is melted and smooth.
5. *Add Lemon Juice and Seasoning:*
   - Stir in lemon juice, nutmeg, and white pepper. Continue stirring until the mixture is well combined and smooth.
6. *Serve:*
   - Place the fondue pot over a low flame to keep the cheese fondue warm. Serve with cubed French baguette and assorted vegetables for dipping.

EXPERT TIPS & VARIATIONS:
- Experiment with different cheese combinations, such as adding Swiss cheese or Fontina for a unique flavor.
- Enhance the fondue with a splash of Kirsch (cherry brandy) for an authentic touch.

PAIRING SUGGESTIONS:
- Sliced apples or pears
- A bottle of your favorite white wine

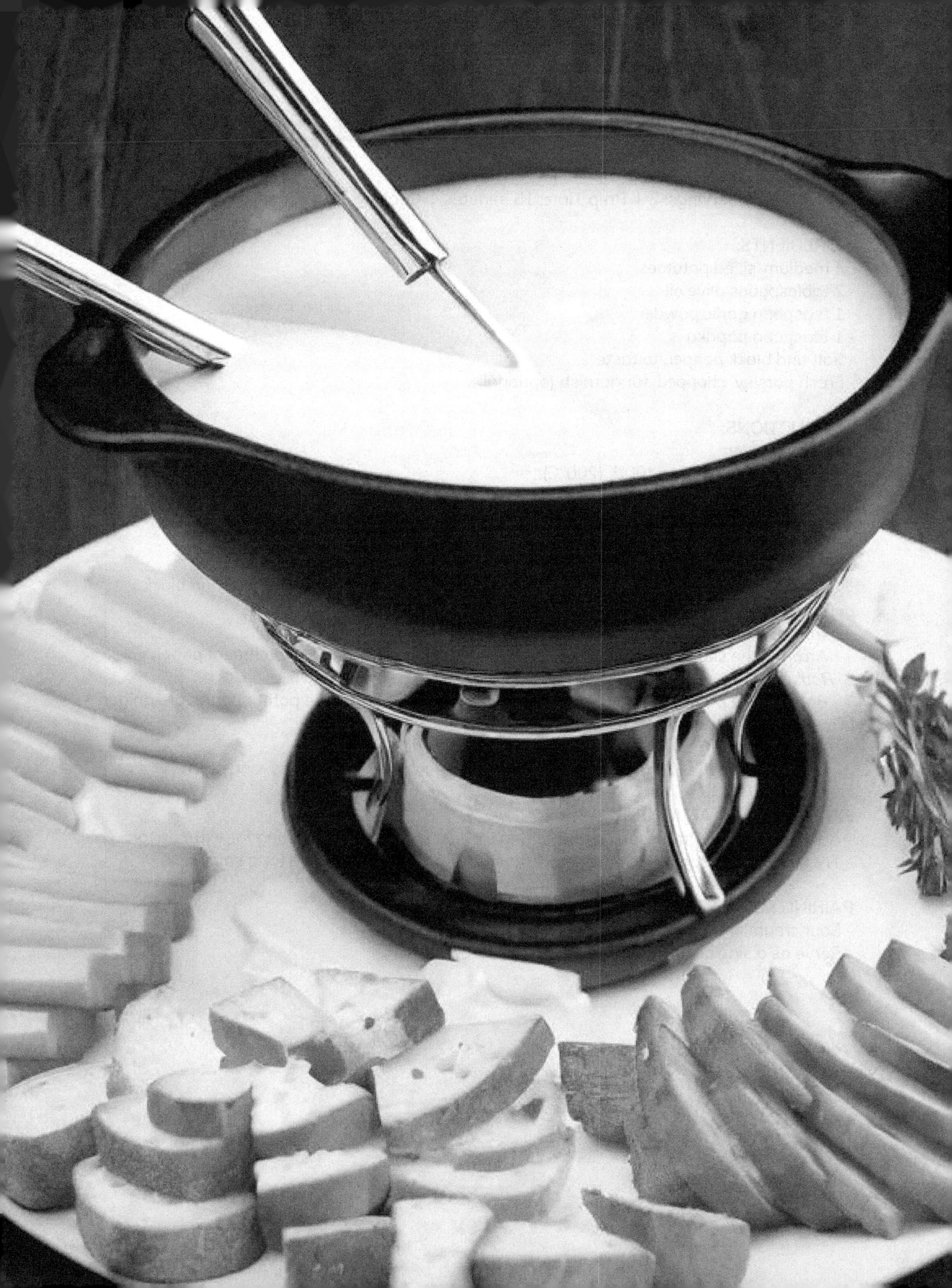

Roasted Potato Hearts

Servings: 2 | **Prep Time:** 15 minutes | **Cooking Time:** 25 minutes

INGREDIENTS:
- 4 medium-sized potatoes
- 2 tablespoons olive oil
- 1 teaspoon garlic powder
- 1 teaspoon paprika
- Salt and black pepper, to taste
- Fresh parsley, chopped, for garnish (optional)

INSTRUCTIONS:
1. *Preheat Oven:*
   - Preheat your oven to 400°F (200°C).
2. *Prepare Potatoes:*
   - Peel and wash the potatoes. Cut them into slices, and then use a heart-shaped cookie cutter to cut heart shapes from the slices.
3. *Toss with Seasonings:*
   - In a bowl, toss the potato hearts with olive oil, garlic powder, paprika, salt, and black pepper until evenly coated.
4. *Arrange on Baking Sheet:*
   - Arrange the seasoned potato hearts on a baking sheet lined with parchment paper.
5. *Roast:*
   - Roast in the preheated oven for about 20-25 minutes or until the potato hearts are golden brown and crispy on the edges.
6. *Garnish and Serve:*
   - Remove from the oven, garnish with chopped fresh parsley if desired, and serve.

EXPERT TIPS & VARIATIONS:
- Add a sprinkle of Parmesan cheese during the last 5 minutes of roasting for extra flavor.
- Try different seasonings like rosemary, thyme, or a pinch of cayenne for a spicy kick.

PAIRING SUGGESTIONS:
- Sour cream or a garlic aioli for dipping
- Serve as a side dish with grilled chicken or steak

Candied Bacon Roses

Servings: 2 | Prep Time: 15 minutes | Cooking Time: 20 minutes

INGREDIENTS:
- 6 slices of bacon
- 2 tablespoons brown sugar
- 1 tablespoon maple syrup
- 1/2 teaspoon black pepper
- Toothpicks

INSTRUCTIONS:
1. *Preheat Oven:*
   - Preheat your oven to 375°F (190°C).
2. *Candy Bacon:*
   - In a bowl, mix brown sugar, maple syrup, and black pepper to create the candied bacon glaze.
3. *Coat Bacon:*
   - Coat each slice of bacon with the candied glaze, ensuring they are evenly coated.
4. *Roll into Roses:*
   - Take each slice of bacon and roll it into a rose shape, starting from one end. Secure with a toothpick.
5. *Bake:*
   - Place the bacon roses on a baking sheet lined with parchment paper and bake in the preheated oven for about 15-20 minutes or until the bacon is crispy and caramelized.
6. *Cool and Serve:*
   - Allow the bacon roses to cool slightly before serving. Remove the toothpicks before enjoying.

EXPERT TIPS & VARIATIONS:
- Experiment with different flavors by adding a pinch of cayenne pepper for a spicy kick.
- Serve with a drizzle of honey or a side of dark chocolate for a sweet-savory combination.

PAIRING SUGGESTIONS:
- Champagne or sparkling wine
- Use as a unique topping for desserts like chocolate mousse or vanilla ice cream

Mini Bacon Ranch Cheese Balls

Servings: 2 | **Prep Time:** 15 minutes | **Chilling Time:** 1 hour

INGREDIENTS:
- 4 oz cream cheese, softened
- 1 cup shredded cheddar cheese
- 2 tablespoons ranch seasoning mix
- 1/4 cup green onions, finely chopped
- 1/2 cup crispy bacon, crumbled
- 1/2 cup chopped pecans or crushed pretzels (for coating)
- Crackers or pretzel sticks, for serving

INSTRUCTIONS:
1. *Mix Cheese Ball Ingredients:*
   - In a bowl, combine softened cream cheese, shredded cheddar cheese, ranch seasoning mix, green onions, and crumbled bacon. Mix until well combined.
2. *Form Mini Cheese Balls:*
   - Scoop out small portions of the mixture and roll them into bite-sized balls.
3. *Coat with Toppings:*
   - Roll each mini cheese ball in chopped pecans or crushed pretzels, ensuring they are evenly coated.
4. *Chill:*
   - Place the mini bacon ranch cheese balls in the refrigerator for at least 1 hour to allow them to firm up.
5. *Serve:*
   - Arrange the mini cheese balls on a serving platter with crackers or pretzel sticks.

EXPERT TIPS & VARIATIONS:
- Customize by adding a dash of hot sauce or a sprinkle of cayenne for a spicy twist.
- Experiment with different coatings like chopped fresh herbs or crispy fried onions.

PAIRING SUGGESTIONS:
- Sliced cucumber or carrot sticks
- Your favorite white wine or craft beer

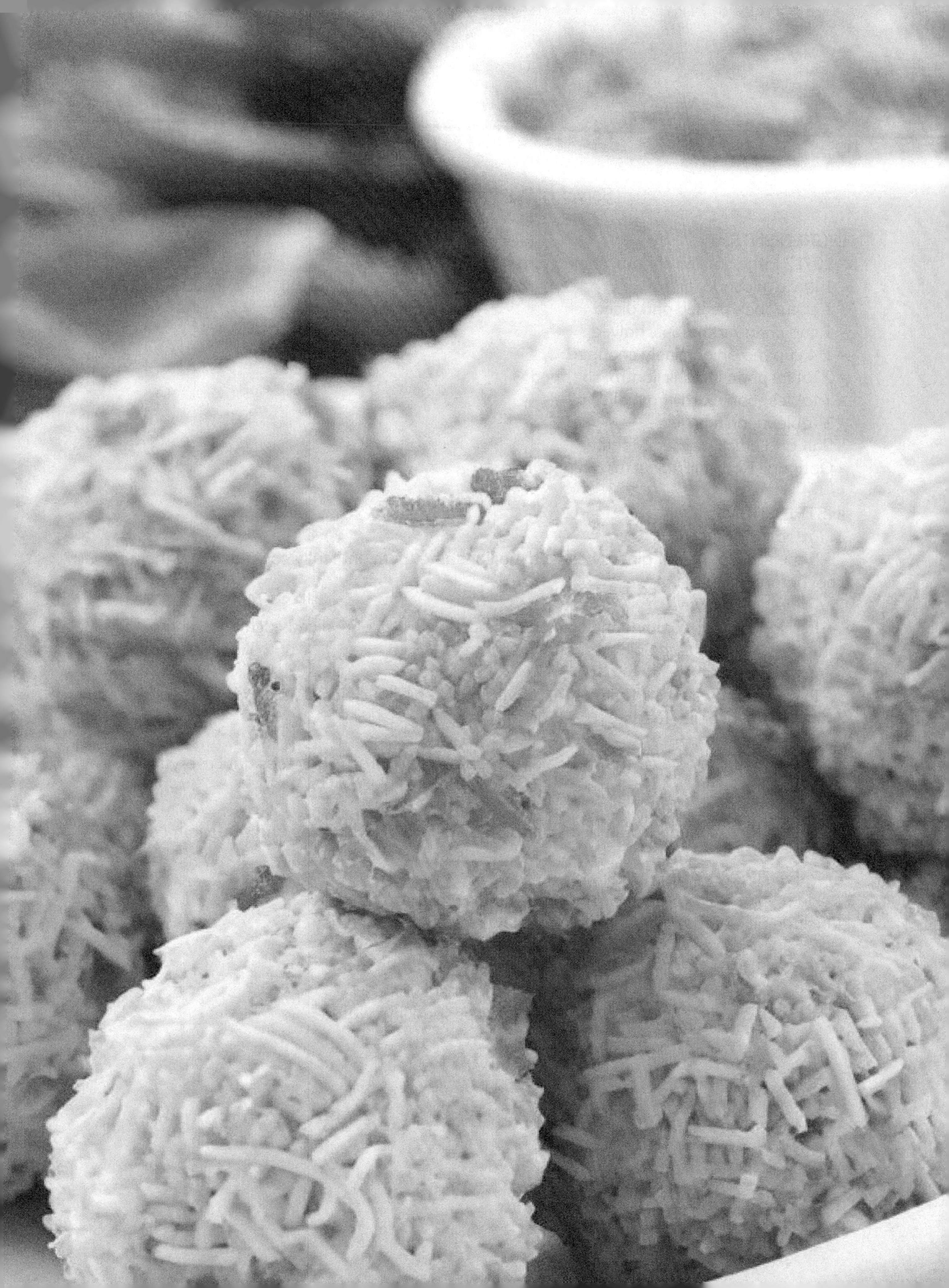

Avocado Cucumber Shrimp Salad

Servings: 2 | **Prep Time:** 15 minutes

INGREDIENTS:
- 10-12 large cooked shrimp, peeled and deveined
- 1 large avocado, diced
- 1 cucumber, peeled and diced
- 1 cup cherry tomatoes, halved
- 1/4 cup red onion, finely chopped
- 2 tablespoons fresh cilantro, chopped
- 1 tablespoon extra virgin olive oil
- 1 tablespoon lime juice
- Salt and black pepper, to taste
- Optional: Red chili flakes for a hint of heat

INSTRUCTIONS:
1. *Prepare Shrimp:*
   - If the shrimp are not already cooked, boil or sauté them until fully cooked. Allow them to cool before using.
2. *Combine Ingredients:*
   - In a large bowl, combine the cooked shrimp, diced avocado, diced cucumber, cherry tomatoes, chopped red onion, and fresh cilantro.
3. *Make Dressing:*
   - In a small bowl, whisk together extra virgin olive oil, lime juice, salt, and black pepper. Adjust the seasoning to taste.
4. *Toss Salad:*
   - Pour the dressing over the shrimp and vegetable mixture. Gently toss until everything is well coated.
5. *Serve:*
   - Divide the Avocado Cucumber Shrimp Salad between two plates and serve immediately.

EXPERT TIPS & VARIATIONS:
- Add a splash of balsamic vinegar or soy sauce for extra flavor.
- Include diced mango or pineapple for a sweet and tropical twist.

PAIRING SUGGESTIONS:
- Serve over a bed of mixed greens for a heartier salad.
- Pair with a chilled glass of Sauvignon Blanc or sparkling water.

Monte Cristo Sliders

Servings: 2 | **Prep Time:** 15 minutes | **Cooking Time:** 15 minutes

INGREDIENTS:
- 4 slider buns
- 4 slices ham
- 4 slices turkey
- 4 slices Swiss cheese
- 2 tablespoons Dijon mustard
- 2 tablespoons raspberry jam
- 2 large eggs
- 1/4 cup milk
- 2 tablespoons butter
- Powdered sugar, for dusting (optional)

INSTRUCTIONS:
1. *Prepare Sliders:*
   - Slice the slider buns in half. On the bottom half of each bun, layer a slice of ham, a slice of turkey, and a slice of Swiss cheese.
2. *Spread Condiments:*
   - Spread Dijon mustard on the top half of each bun and raspberry jam on the bottom half.
3. *Assemble Sliders:*
   - Place the top half of each bun on the layered ingredients to assemble the sliders.
4. *Whisk Egg Mixture:*
   - In a shallow bowl, whisk together eggs and milk to create an egg mixture.
5. *Dip and Coat:*
   - Dip each slider in the egg mixture, ensuring it is well-coated on both sides.
6. *Cook Sliders:*
   - In a skillet over medium heat, melt butter. Cook each slider until golden brown on both sides, approximately 3-4 minutes per side.
7. *Serve:*
   - Remove sliders from the skillet, dust with powdered sugar if desired, and serve warm.

EXPERT TIPS & VARIATIONS:
- Try using different types of cheese for variety, such as Gruyère or cheddar.
- Add a sprinkle of cinnamon to the egg mixture for a hint of warmth.

PAIRING SUGGESTIONS:
- Serve with a side of mixed greens or a light fruit salad.
- Enjoy with a glass of sparkling cider or your favorite brunch beverage.

Pink Moscato Strawberries

Servings: 2 | **Prep Time:** 10 minutes | **Chilling Time:** 1 hour

INGREDIENTS:
- 1 cup fresh strawberries, washed and hulled
- 1/2 cup pink Moscato wine
- 2 tablespoons powdered sugar
- 1 teaspoon lemon zest
- Fresh mint leaves, for garnish (optional)

INSTRUCTIONS:
1. *Prepare Strawberries:*
   - Wash the strawberries and remove the hulls, ensuring they are dry.
2. *Create Wine Soak:*
   - In a bowl, combine pink Moscato wine, powdered sugar, and lemon zest. Stir until the sugar dissolves.
3. *Soak Strawberries:*
   - Place the strawberries in the wine mixture, ensuring they are fully submerged. Allow them to soak for at least 1 hour in the refrigerator.
4. *Serve:*
   - Remove the strawberries from the wine mixture and arrange them on a serving plate. Optionally, drizzle with a bit of the wine mixture.
5. *Garnish:*
   - Garnish with fresh mint leaves for an extra touch of freshness.

EXPERT TIPS & VARIATIONS:
- Experiment with different berries like raspberries or blackberries for a mixed berry treat.
- For a more intense flavor, reduce the wine mixture on the stove before soaking the strawberries.

PAIRING SUGGESTIONS:
- Enjoy as a standalone dessert or serve over vanilla ice cream.
- Pair with a glass of the same pink Moscato wine for a delightful combination.

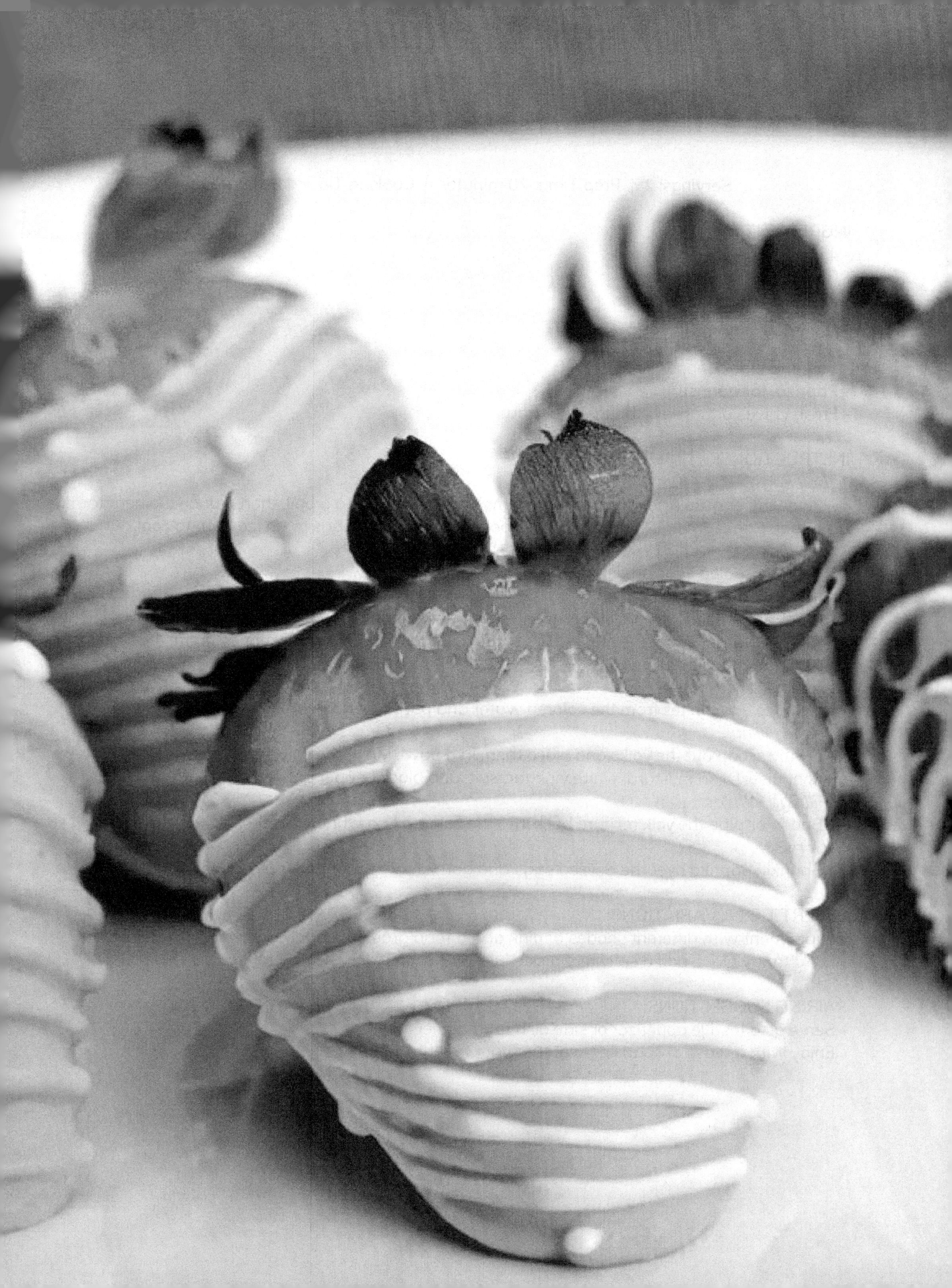

Colored Deviled Eggs

Servings: 2 | Prep Time: 20 minutes | Cooking Time: 12 minutes

INGREDIENTS:
- 4 large eggs
- Red or pink food coloring
- 2 tablespoons mayonnaise
- 1 teaspoon Dijon mustard
- 1 teaspoon white vinegar
- Salt and black pepper, to taste
- Paprika, for garnish
- Fresh chives or parsley, chopped, for garnish

INSTRUCTIONS:
1. *Boil Eggs:*
   - Place the eggs in a saucepan and cover with water. Bring to a boil, then reduce the heat to a simmer. Cook for 10-12 minutes. Once cooked, transfer the eggs to an ice bath to cool.
2. *Peel Eggs:*
   - Peel the cooled eggs and cut them in half lengthwise.
3. *Prepare Coloring Mixture:*
   - In separate bowls, create different shades of pink or red by adding a few drops of food coloring to water. Submerge egg whites in the colored water for a few minutes until the desired hue is achieved.
4. *Remove and Dry:*
   - Remove egg whites from the colored water and pat them dry with a paper towel.
5. *Make Filling:*
   - Gently scoop out the yolks and place them in a bowl. Mash the yolks and mix with mayonnaise, Dijon mustard, white vinegar, salt, and black pepper until smooth.
6. *Fill Egg Whites:*
   - Spoon or pipe the yolk mixture back into the colored egg whites.
7. *Garnish:*
   - Sprinkle paprika over the deviled eggs and garnish with chopped fresh chives or parsley.

EXPERT TIPS & VARIATIONS:
- Experiment with different shades of pink or red for a gradient effect.
- For a tangy twist, add a splash of pickle juice or hot sauce to the yolk mixture.

PAIRING SUGGESTIONS:
- Serve as a festive appetizer or side dish for a dinner.
- Enjoy with a glass of sparkling water or your favorite wine.

Mini Deep Dish Pizzas

Servings: 2 | Prep Time: 15 minutes | Cooking Time: 15 minutes

INGREDIENTS:
- 2 small pizza dough rounds (store-bought or homemade)
- 1/2 cup pizza sauce
- 1 cup shredded mozzarella cheese
- 1/4 cup pepperoni slices
- 1/4 cup sliced black olives
- 1/4 cup diced bell peppers (red and green)
- Fresh basil leaves, for garnish
- Olive oil, for brushing

INSTRUCTIONS:
1. *Preheat Oven:*
   - Preheat your oven to 425°F (220°C).
2. *Prepare Pizza Dough:*
   - Roll out the pizza dough rounds on a floured surface to your desired thickness.
3. *Assemble Mini Pizzas:*
   - Place each rolled-out dough round in a greased mini deep dish pan or a muffin tin, shaping it to form a small pizza crust.
4. *Layer Ingredients:*
   - Spread pizza sauce over each crust. Layer with shredded mozzarella cheese, pepperoni slices, black olives, and diced bell peppers.
5. *Brush with Olive Oil:*
   - Lightly brush the edges of the crust with olive oil for a golden finish.
6. *Bake:*
   - Bake in the preheated oven for approximately 12-15 minutes or until the crust is golden brown and the cheese is melted and bubbly.
7. *Garnish and Serve:*
   - Remove the mini deep dish pizzas from the oven, garnish with fresh basil leaves, and serve hot.

EXPERT TIPS & VARIATIONS:
- Customize with your favorite pizza toppings like mushrooms, onions, or sausage.
- Experiment with different cheeses for added flavor, such as cheddar or provolone.

PAIRING SUGGESTIONS:
- A side of mixed greens with balsamic vinaigrette
- Enjoy with a glass of red wine or your preferred beverage

Air Fryer Mozzarella Sticks

Servings: 2 | **Prep Time:** 15 minutes | **Cooking Time:** 8 minutes

INGREDIENTS:
- 8 mozzarella string cheese sticks
- 1/2 cup all-purpose flour
- 2 large eggs, beaten
- 1 cup Italian-style breadcrumbs
- 1/2 cup grated Parmesan cheese
- 1 teaspoon dried oregano
- 1 teaspoon garlic powder
- Marinara sauce, for dipping

INSTRUCTIONS:
1. *Prepare Cheese Sticks:*
   - Cut each mozzarella stick in half to create 16 shorter sticks.
2. *Set Up Breading Station:*
   - In separate bowls, place the flour, beaten eggs, and a mixture of breadcrumbs, grated Parmesan, dried oregano, and garlic powder.
3. *Coat Cheese Sticks:*
   - Dredge each mozzarella stick in the flour, then dip into the beaten eggs, and finally coat thoroughly with the breadcrumb mixture.
4. *Repeat Breading:*
   - For an extra crispy coating, repeat the egg and breadcrumb steps for each mozzarella stick.
5. *Preheat Air Fryer:*
   - Preheat your air fryer to 375°F (190°C).
6. *Air Fry:*
   - Place the breaded mozzarella sticks in the air fryer basket in a single layer. Cook for 8 minutes, turning halfway through, or until they are golden and crispy.
7. *Serve:*
   - Remove the mozzarella sticks from the air fryer and let them cool for a minute. Serve with marinara sauce for dipping.

EXPERT TIPS & VARIATIONS:
- Freeze the breaded mozzarella sticks for about 30 minutes before air frying for a firmer texture.
- Add a pinch of red pepper flakes to the breadcrumb mixture for a hint of spice.

PAIRING SUGGESTIONS:
- Enjoy as an appetizer or snack on their own.
- Serve alongside a fresh salad for a balanced meal.

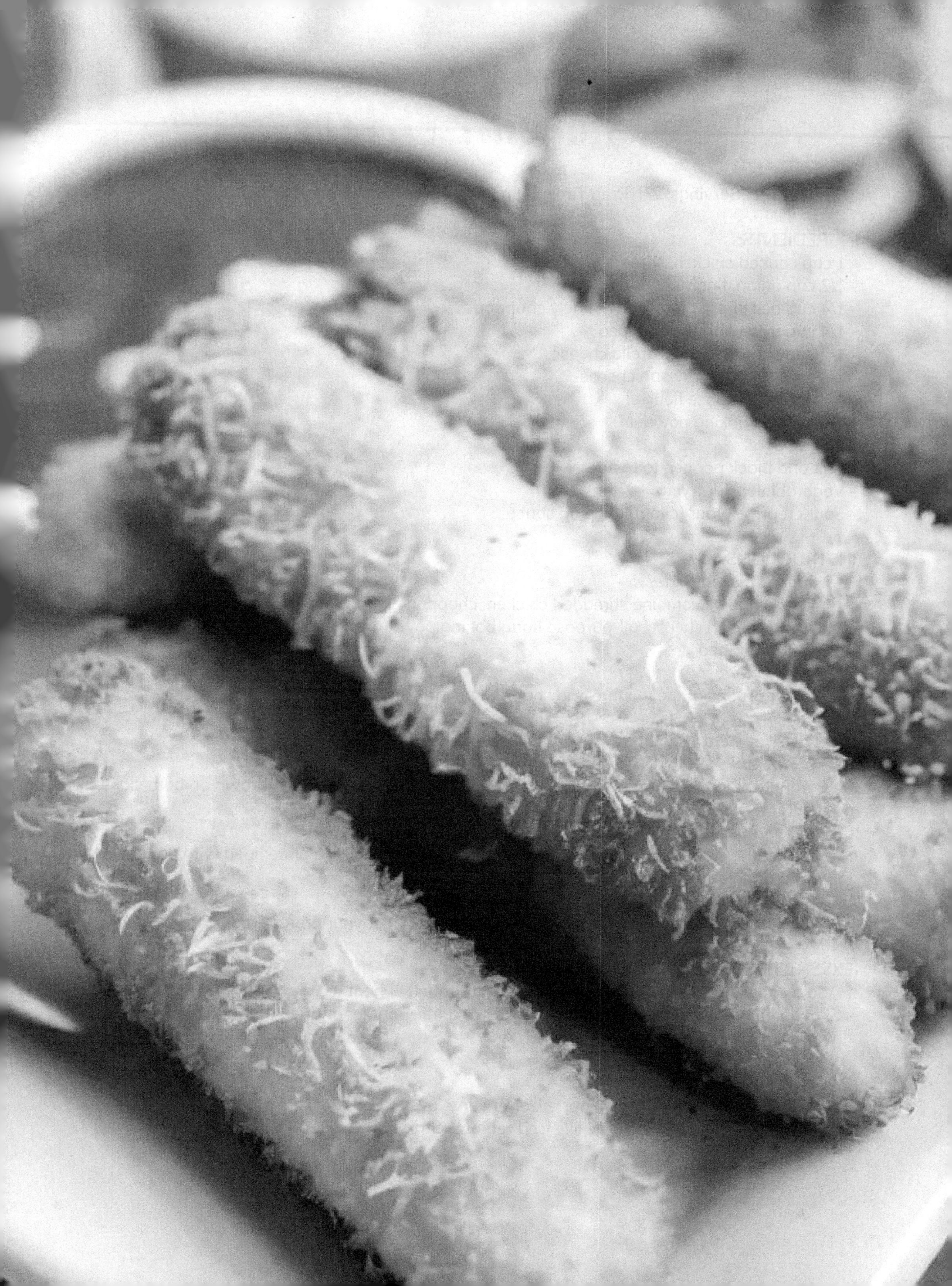

Chicken Fritters

Servings: 2 | **Prep Time:** 20 minutes | **Cooking Time:** 15 minutes

INGREDIENTS:
- 1 cup cooked chicken, shredded
- 1/2 cup onion, finely chopped
- 1/4 cup bell pepper (any color), finely chopped
- 1/4 cup fresh parsley, chopped
- 1/2 cup shredded mozzarella cheese
- 1/4 cup grated Parmesan cheese
- 1/3 cup all-purpose flour
- 1 teaspoon baking powder
- 2 large eggs
- Salt and black pepper, to taste
- Vegetable oil, for frying
- Sour cream or your favorite dipping sauce

INSTRUCTIONS:
1. *Prepare Chicken Mixture:*
   - In a large bowl, combine shredded chicken, chopped onion, bell pepper, parsley, mozzarella cheese, Parmesan cheese, all-purpose flour, baking powder, eggs, salt, and black pepper. Mix until well combined.
2. *Shape Fritters:*
   - Scoop portions of the mixture and shape them into small fritters.
3. *Heat Oil:*
   - In a skillet, heat vegetable oil over medium heat.
4. *Fry Fritters:*
   - Carefully place the shaped fritters in the hot oil and cook until golden brown on both sides, approximately 3-4 minutes per side.
5. *Drain and Serve:*
   - Remove the chicken fritters from the skillet and place them on a plate lined with paper towels to drain excess oil.
6. *Serve with Dipping Sauce:*
   - Serve the chicken fritters hot with a side of sour cream or your preferred dipping sauce.

EXPERT TIPS & VARIATIONS:
- Add a pinch of cayenne pepper or paprika for a touch of heat.
- Experiment with different herbs and spices like garlic powder or dried oregano for added flavor.

PAIRING SUGGESTIONS:
- Enjoy the chicken fritters as an appetizer or serve over a bed of mixed greens for a light meal.
- Pair with a refreshing beverage like iced tea or a citrus-infused sparkling water.

Hot Mini Italian Sliders

Servings: 2 | **Prep Time:** 15 minutes | **Cooking Time:** 20 minutes

INGREDIENTS:
- 4 slider buns
- 8 slices Italian salami
- 4 slices provolone cheese
- 1/2 cup roasted red peppers, sliced
- 1/4 cup banana pepper rings
- 1/4 cup black olives, sliced
- 1/4 cup fresh basil leaves
- 2 tablespoons olive oil
- 1 tablespoon balsamic glaze (optional)
- Salt and black pepper, to taste

INSTRUCTIONS:
1. *Preheat Oven:*
   - Preheat your oven to 375°F (190°C).
2. *Prepare Sliders:*
   - Slice the slider buns in half. On the bottom half of each bun, layer Italian salami, provolone cheese, roasted red peppers, banana pepper rings, black olives, and fresh basil leaves.
3. *Drizzle with Olive Oil:*
   - Drizzle olive oil over the layered ingredients. Season with salt and black pepper to taste.
4. *Assemble Sliders:*
   - Place the top half of each bun on the layered ingredients to assemble the sliders.
5. *Bake:*
   - Bake in the preheated oven for approximately 10-12 minutes or until the cheese is melted, and the sliders are heated through.
6. *Drizzle with Balsamic Glaze:*
   - Optional: Drizzle with balsamic glaze for added flavor.
7. *Serve:*
   - Remove the hot mini Italian sliders from the oven and serve immediately.

EXPERT TIPS & VARIATIONS:
- Customize with your favorite Italian deli meats like ham or prosciutto.
- Add a spread of pesto or sun-dried tomato aioli for extra flavor.

PAIRING SUGGESTIONS:
- Serve with a side of mixed greens or a simple tomato salad.
- Enjoy with a glass of red wine or sparkling water.

Crab Cakes

Servings: 2 | Prep Time: 20 minutes \ Cooking Time: 15 minutes

INGREDIENTS:
- 8 oz lump crabmeat, drained
- 1/4 cup breadcrumbs
- 2 tablespoons mayonnaise
- 1 large egg
- 1 tablespoon Dijon mustard
- 1 tablespoon Worcestershire sauce
- 1 tablespoon fresh parsley, chopped
- 1/2 teaspoon Old Bay seasoning
- 1/4 teaspoon cayenne pepper
- Salt and black pepper, to taste
- 2 tablespoons unsalted butter
- 2 tablespoons olive oil
- Lemon wedges, for serving
- Fresh parsley, chopped, for garnish

INSTRUCTIONS:
1. *Prepare Crab Mixture:*
   - In a bowl, combine lump crabmeat, breadcrumbs, mayonnaise, egg, Dijon mustard, Worcestershire sauce, chopped fresh parsley, Old Bay seasoning, cayenne pepper, salt, and black pepper. Gently fold until well combined.
2. *Shape Crab Cakes:*
   - Form the mixture into 4 crab cakes, ensuring they hold their shape.
3. *Chill:*
   - Place the crab cakes in the refrigerator for at least 15 minutes to firm up.
4. *Heat Butter and Oil:*
   - In a skillet, heat butter and olive oil over medium heat.
5. *Cook Crab Cakes:*
   - Carefully place the crab cakes in the skillet and cook for about 3-4 minutes per side or until golden brown and heated through.
6. *Serve:*
   - Remove the crab cakes from the skillet and place them on a serving plate. Garnish with chopped fresh parsley and serve with lemon wedges.

EXPERT TIPS & VARIATIONS:
- For a crispy exterior, coat the crab cakes with extra breadcrumbs before cooking.
- Add a dash of hot sauce or a squeeze of extra lemon juice for a zesty kick.

PAIRING SUGGESTIONS:
- Serve the crab cakes over a bed of mixed greens for a light and refreshing meal.
- Enjoy with a glass of chilled Sauvignon Blanc or your favorite white wine.

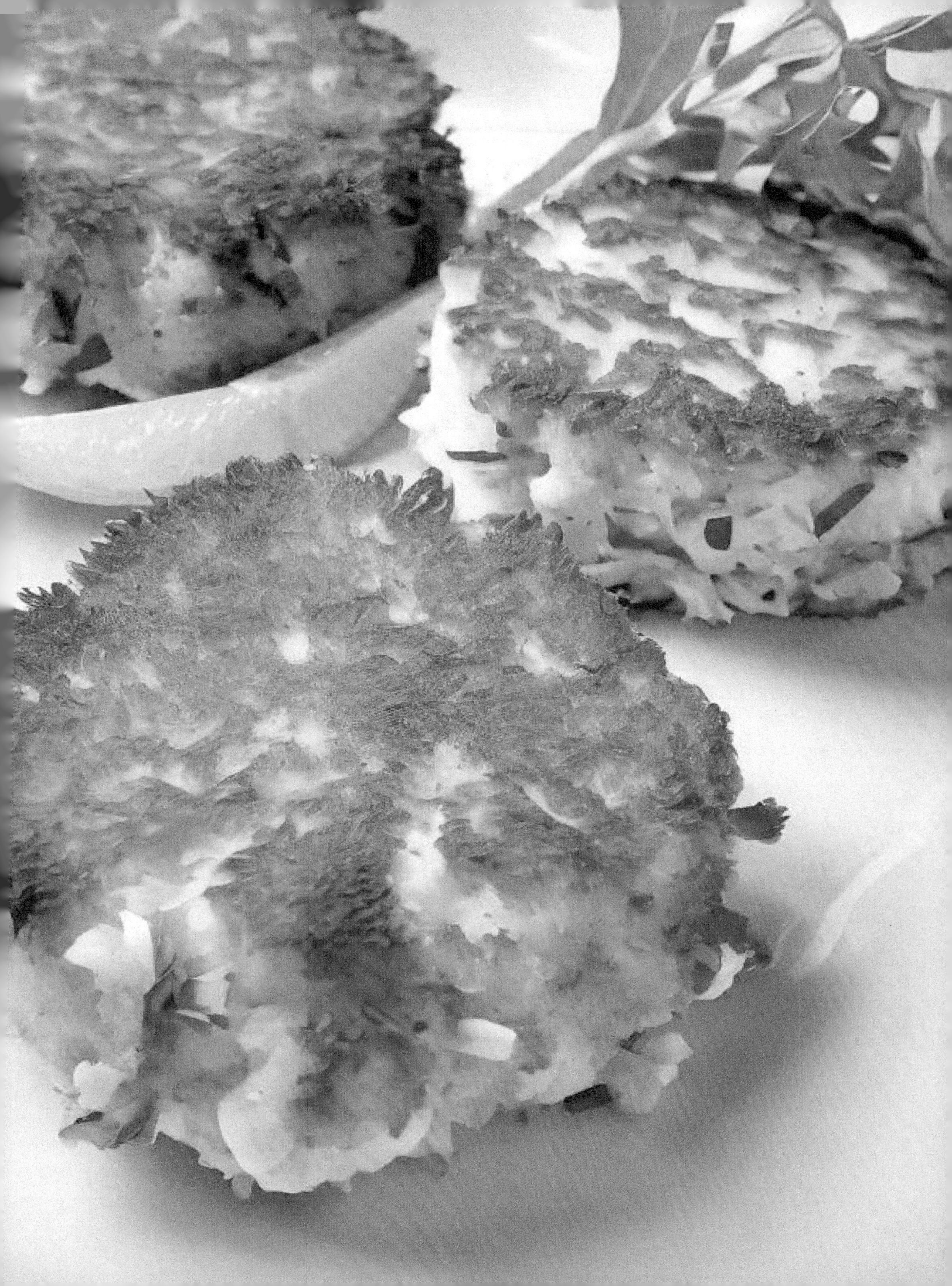

DRINKS

Chocolate Truffle Martini

Servings: 2 | Prep Time: 10 minutes

INGREDIENTS:
- 3 oz chocolate liqueur
- 2 oz vanilla vodka
- 1 oz cream or half-and-half
- 1 oz chocolate syrup
- Ice cubes
- Chocolate shavings or cocoa powder, for garnish

INSTRUCTIONS:
1. *Chill Glassware:*
   - Place martini glasses in the freezer to chill.
2. *Prepare Cocktail Shaker:*
   - Fill a cocktail shaker with ice cubes.
3. *Add Ingredients:*
   - Pour chocolate liqueur, vanilla vodka, cream or half-and-half, and chocolate syrup into the shaker.
4. *Shake Well:*
   - Secure the shaker lid and shake the ingredients vigorously for about 15 seconds to chill the mixture.
5. *Strain into Glasses:*
   - Remove the martini glasses from the freezer and strain the chocolate truffle martini into each glass.
6. *Garnish:*
   - Garnish the martinis with chocolate shavings or a dusting of cocoa powder.
7. *Serve:*
   - Serve the chocolate truffle martinis immediately.

EXPERT TIPS & VARIATIONS:
- For an extra touch, rim the glass with melted chocolate and dip it in crushed nuts or sprinkles.
- Experiment with different flavored liqueurs like hazelnut or mint chocolate.

PAIRING SUGGESTIONS:
- Enjoy the chocolate truffle martini as a dessert cocktail or alongside chocolate-covered strawberries.
- Serve with a plate of assorted chocolates for a decadent experience.

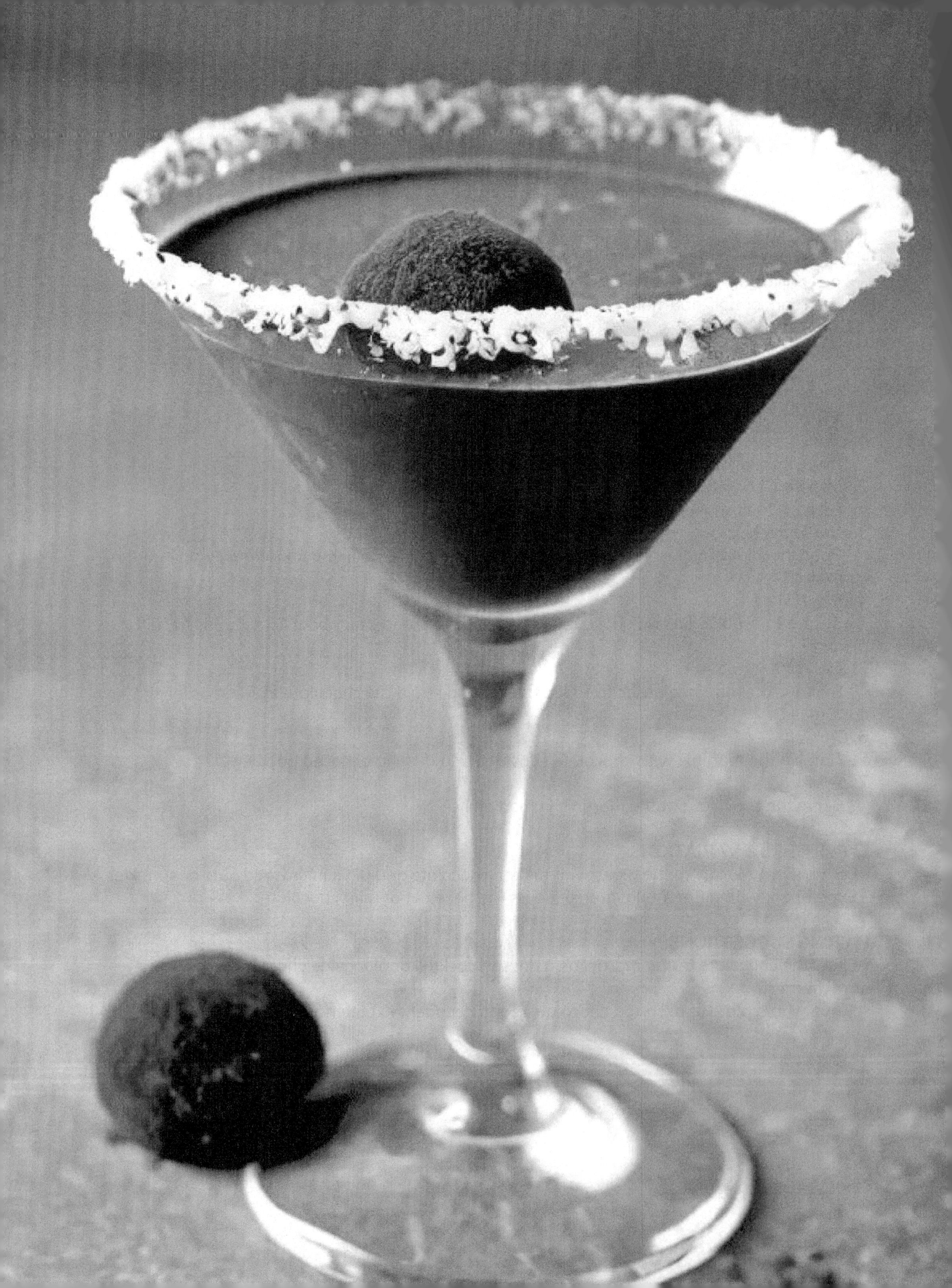

Chocolate Covered Strawberry Shooters

Servings: 2 | **Prep Time:** 15 minutes

INGREDIENTS:
- 6 fresh strawberries, hulled
- 2 oz chocolate liqueur
- 2 oz vanilla vodka
- 1 oz strawberry syrup or puree
- Whipped cream, for garnish
- Chocolate shavings or cocoa powder, for garnish

INSTRUCTIONS:
1. *Prepare Strawberries:*
   - Hull the strawberries, leaving them whole.
2. *Chocolate Dipped Strawberries:*
   - Melt a small amount of chocolate in the microwave or using a double boiler. Dip the hulled end of each strawberry into the melted chocolate and place them on a parchment-lined tray to set.
3. *Chill Glasses:*
   - Chill shot glasses in the freezer for about 10 minutes.
4. *Prepare Cocktail Shaker:*
   - Fill a cocktail shaker with ice cubes.
5. *Add Ingredients:*
   - Pour chocolate liqueur, vanilla vodka, and strawberry syrup or puree into the shake.
6. *Shake Well:*
   - Secure the shaker lid and shake the ingredients vigorously for about 15 seconds to chill the mixture.
7. *Strain into Glasses:*
   - Remove the shot glasses from the freezer and strain the chocolate covered strawberry shooter mixture into each glass.
8. *Garnish:*
   - Top each shooter with a dollop of whipped cream and garnish with chocolate shavings or a dusting of cocoa powder.
9. *Serve:*
   - Serve the chocolate covered strawberry shooters immediately.

EXPERT TIPS & VARIATIONS:
- Experiment with different fruit syrups or purees for a unique twist.
- Rim the shot glasses with chocolate or sugar for an extra decorative touch.

PAIRING SUGGESTIONS:
- Enjoy the chocolate covered strawberry shooters as a delightful dessert drink.
- Serve with additional chocolate-covered strawberries for an extra treat.

Valentine Cupid's Float

Servings: 2 | **Prep Time:** 10 minutes

INGREDIENTS:
- 2 cups strawberry or raspberry sherbet
- 1 cup pink lemonade
- 1 cup strawberry soda
- Vanilla ice cream
- Fresh strawberries, for garnish

INSTRUCTIONS:
1. *Chill Glasses:*
   - Place the glasses in the freezer to chill.
2. *Scoop Sherbet:*
   - Scoop strawberry or raspberry sherbet into each chilled glass.
3. *Pour Pink Lemonade:*
   - Pour pink lemonade over the sherbet in each glass, filling it halfway.
4. *Add Strawberry Soda:*
   - Top off each glass with strawberry soda, allowing the sherbet to create a fizzy reaction.
5. *Top with Ice Cream:*
   - Add a scoop of vanilla ice cream to each glass.
6. *Garnish:*
   - Garnish the floats with fresh strawberries.
7. *Serve with a Straw and Spoon:*
   - Place a straw and a spoon in each glass and serve immediately.

EXPERT TIPS & VARIATIONS:
- For an adult version, add a splash of strawberry liqueur or vodka.
- Experiment with different sherbet flavors for variety.

PAIRING SUGGESTIONS:
- Enjoy Cupid's Float as a sweet and refreshing treat.
- Serve alongside heart-shaped cookies for an extra touch of love.

Strawberries and Champagne Margarita

Servings: 2 | **Prep Time:** 15 minutes

INGREDIENTS:
- 4 oz fresh strawberries, hulled and halved
- 3 oz silver tequila
- 2 oz triple sec
- 1 oz fresh lime juice
- 1 oz simple syrup
- Champagne or sparkling wine, chilled
- Ice cubes
- Lime wedges and whole strawberries, for garnish
- Salt or sugar, for rimming (optional)

INSTRUCTIONS:
1. *Rim Glasses (Optional):*
   - If desired, rim the edges of the glasses with salt or sugar. Dip the rims into a shallow dish with simple syrup, then into the salt or sugar.
2. *Prepare Strawberries:*
   - In a blender, combine fresh strawberries, tequila, triple sec, fresh lime juice, and simple syrup. Blend until smooth.
3. *Strain (Optional):*
   - If you prefer a smoother texture, you can strain the strawberry mixture using a fine-mesh sieve to remove pulp.
4. *Fill Glasses:*
   - Fill each prepared glass with ice cubes.
5. *Pour Strawberry Margarita:*
   - Pour the strawberry margarita mixture over the ice in each glass.
6. *Top with Champagne:*
   - Top off each glass with chilled Champagne or sparkling wine.
7. *Garnish:*
   - Garnish the drinks with lime wedges and whole strawberries.
8. *Serve:*
   - Serve the Strawberries and Champagne Margaritas immediately.

EXPERT TIPS & VARIATIONS:
- Experiment with different berries or a combination of berries for a unique flavor.
- Adjust the sweetness by adding more or less simple syrup to suit your taste.

PAIRING SUGGESTIONS:
- Enjoy the Strawberries and Champagne Margaritas as a festive and romantic drink.
- Serve with a side of chocolate-covered strawberries for an extra sweet treat.

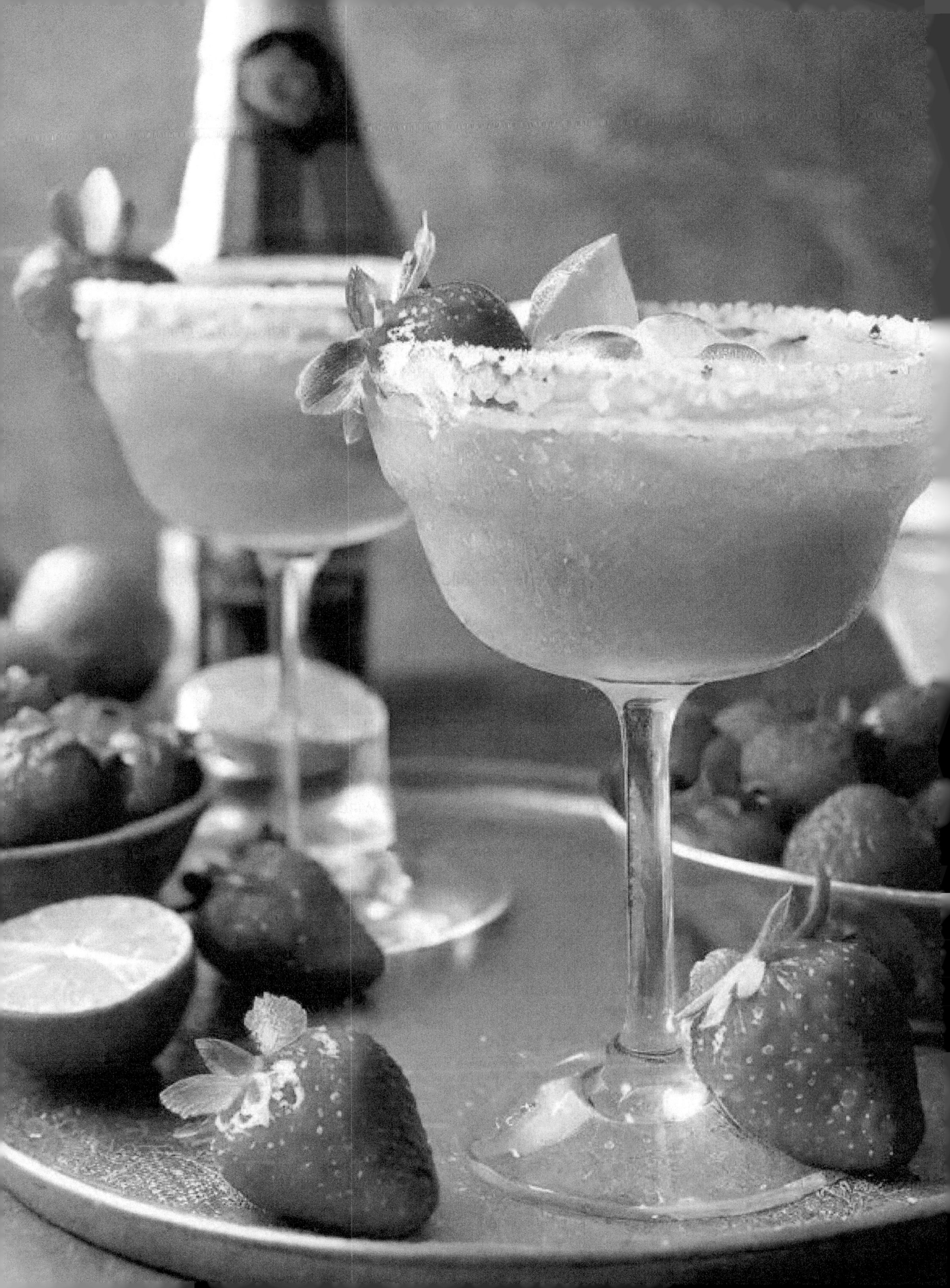

Strawberry Grapefruit Mimosa

Servings: 2 | Prep Time: 10 minutes

INGREDIENTS:
- 1 cup fresh strawberries, hulled and halved
- 1/2 cup pink grapefruit juice
- 2 tablespoons honey or agave syrup
- 1 bottle of chilled sparkling wine or Champagne
- Fresh mint leaves, for garnish
- Strawberry slices, for garnish

INSTRUCTIONS:
1. *Prepare Strawberry Puree:*
   - In a blender, combine fresh strawberries, pink grapefruit juice, and honey or agave syrup. Blend until smooth.
2. *Strain (Optional):*
   - For a smoother consistency, strain the strawberry puree using a fine-mesh sieve to remove pulp.
3. *Chill Glasses:*
   - Place Champagne flutes in the freezer for a few minutes to chill.
4. *Pour Strawberry Mixture:*
   - Divide the strawberry puree equally between the chilled Champagne flutes.
5. *Top with Sparkling Wine:*
   - Slowly pour the chilled sparkling wine or Champagne into each glass, allowing it to mix with the strawberry puree.
6. *Garnish:*
   - Garnish each mimosa with fresh mint leaves and strawberry slices.
7. *Serve:*
   - Serve the Strawberry Grapefruit Mimosas immediately.

EXPERT TIPS & VARIATIONS:
- Adjust the sweetness by adding more or less honey or agave syrup according to your taste.
- Experiment with different citrus juices like blood orange or regular orange for a variation.

PAIRING SUGGESTIONS:
- Enjoy the Strawberry Grapefruit Mimosas as a delightful and refreshing brunch drink.
- Serve with a side of fresh fruit or pastries for a complete breakfast or brunch experience.

Raspberry Rose Bellinis

Servings: 2 | **Prep Time:** 10 minutes

INGREDIENTS:
- 1 cup fresh raspberries
- 1 tablespoon sugar
- 1 teaspoon lemon juice
- 1/2 cup raspberry liqueur
- 1/2 cup rose water
- 1 bottle of chilled prosecco or sparkling wine
- Fresh rose petals, for garnish

INSTRUCTIONS:
1. *Prepare Raspberry Puree:*
   - In a blender, combine fresh raspberries, sugar, and lemon juice. Blend until smooth.
2. *Strain (Optional):*
   - For a smoother texture, strain the raspberry puree using a fine-mesh sieve to remove seeds.
3. *Chill Glasses:*
   - Place Champagne flutes in the freezer for a few minutes to chill.
4. *Pour Raspberry Mixture:*
   - Divide the raspberry puree equally between the chilled Champagne flutes.
5. *Add Raspberry Liqueur and Rose Water:*
   - Pour 1/4 cup of raspberry liqueur and 1/4 cup of rose water into each glass.
6. *Top with Prosecco:*
   - Top off each glass with chilled prosecco or sparkling wine.
7. *Garnish:*
   - Garnish each Raspberry Rose Bellini with fresh rose petals.
8. *Serve:*
   - Serve the bellinis immediately.

EXPERT TIPS & VARIATIONS:
- Adjust sweetness by adding more or less sugar according to your preference.
- Experiment with different edible flowers for a unique garnish.

PAIRING SUGGESTIONS:
- Enjoy Raspberry Rose Bellinis as an elegant and romantic aperitif.
- Serve with a light appetizer like goat cheese and crackers for a delightful pairing.

Cotton Candy Champagne

Servings: 2 | **Prep Time:** 5 minutes

INGREDIENTS:
- 1 bottle of chilled champagne or sparkling wine
- Cotton candy (flavor of your choice)
- Edible flowers, for garnish (optional)

INSTRUCTIONS:
1. *Chill Glasses:*
   - Place Champagne flutes in the freezer for a few minutes to chill.
2. *Pour Champagne:*
   - Pour the chilled champagne or sparkling wine into each of the chilled glasses, filling them about halfway.
3. *Add Cotton Candy:*
   - Place a small bunch of cotton candy on top of each glass, allowing it to float and slowly dissolve into the champagne.
4. *Garnish (Optional):*
   - If desired, garnish the Cotton Candy Champagne with edible flowers for an extra touch of elegance.
5. *Serve:*
   - Serve the Cotton Candy Champagne immediately.

EXPERT TIPS & VARIATIONS:
- Experiment with different flavors of cotton candy for a fun and colorful twist.
- Try using flavored sparkling water for a non-alcoholic version.

PAIRING SUGGESTIONS:
- Enjoy Cotton Candy Champagne as a whimsical and delightful drink.
- Serve with light desserts or fruit for a sweet pairing.

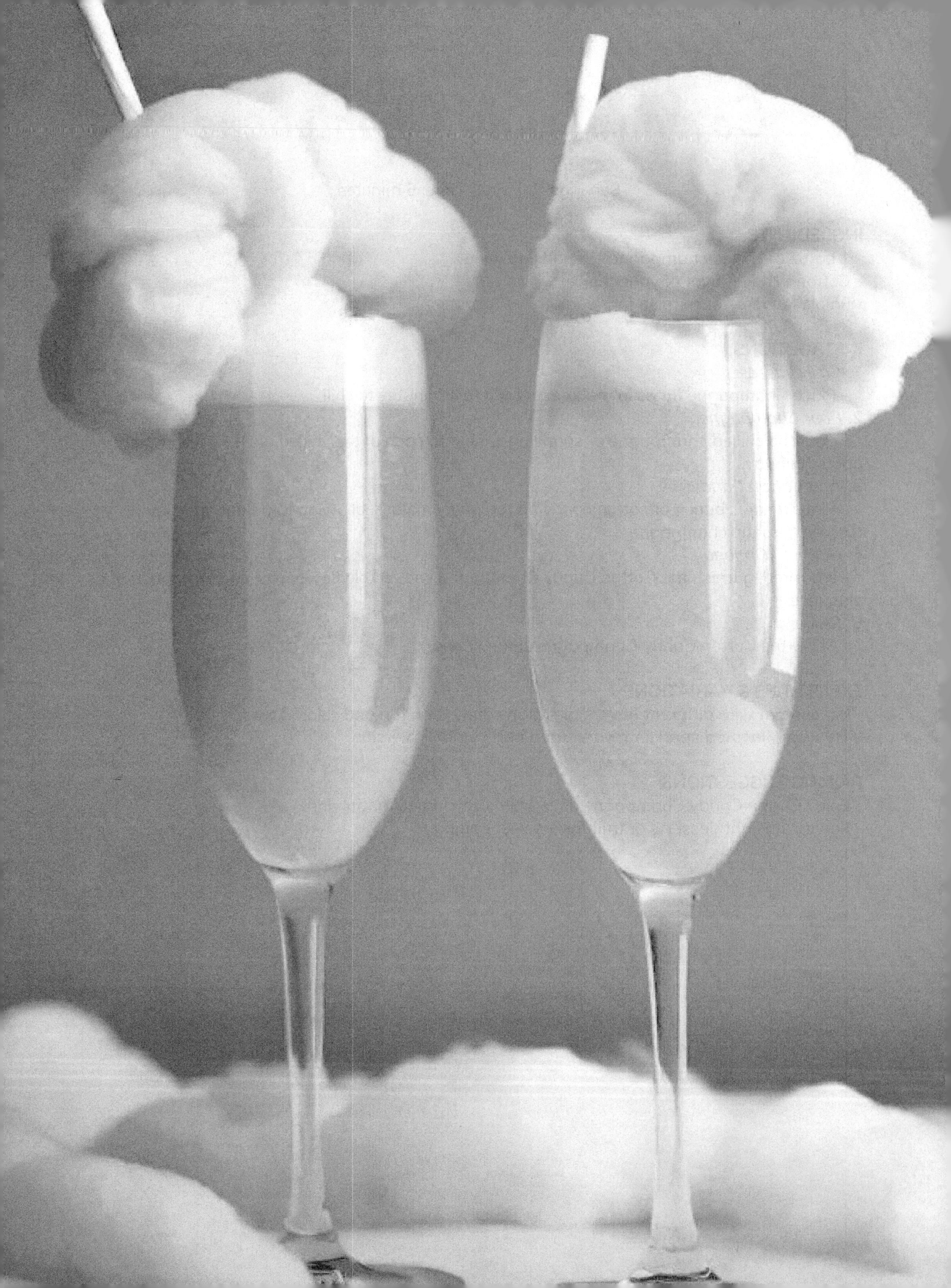

Love Potion Cocktail

Servings: 2 | **Prep Time:** 10 minutes

INGREDIENTS:
- 2 oz raspberry vodka
- 1 oz elderflower liqueur
- 1 oz cranberry juice
- 1 oz freshly squeezed lime juice
- 1/2 oz simple syrup
- Sparkling water or club soda
- Fresh raspberries and mint leaves, for garnish
- Ice cubes

INSTRUCTIONS:
1. *Chill Glasses:*
   - Place cocktail glasses in the freezer for a few minutes to chill.
2. *Prepare Cocktail Shaker:*
   - Fill a cocktail shaker with ice cubes.
3. *Add Ingredients:*
   - Pour raspberry vodka, elderflower liqueur, cranberry juice, freshly squeezed lime juice, and simple syrup into the shaker.
4. *Shake Well:*
   - Secure the shaker lid and shake the ingredients vigorously for about 15 seconds to chill the mixture.
5. *Strain into Glasses:*
   - Remove the chilled glasses from the freezer and strain the Love Potion Cocktail into each glass.
6. *Top with Sparkling Water:*
   - Top off each glass with sparkling water or club soda for a fizzy finish.
7. *Garnish:*
   - Garnish the cocktails with fresh raspberries and mint leaves.
8. *Serve:*
   - Serve the Love Potion Cocktails immediately.

EXPERT TIPS & VARIATIONS:
- Adjust sweetness by adding more or less simple syrup to suit your taste.
- Experiment with different berry-infused vodkas for flavor variations.

PAIRING SUGGESTIONS:
- Enjoy the Love Potion Cocktail as a romantic and flavorful drink.
- Pair with light appetizers or a charcuterie board for an elegant touch.

Love Bug Cocktail

Servings: 2 | **Prep Time:** 10 minutes

INGREDIENTS:
- 3 oz raspberry vodka
- 1 oz peach schnapps
- 1 oz cranberry juice
- 1 oz orange juice
- 1 oz simple syrup
- Ice cubes
- Fresh raspberries or strawberries, for garnish
- Mint leaves, for garnish

INSTRUCTIONS:
1. *Chill Glasses:*
   - Place cocktail glasses in the freezer for a few minutes to chill.
2. *Prepare Cocktail Shaker:*
   - Fill a cocktail shaker with ice cubes.
3. *Add Ingredients:*
   - Pour raspberry vodka, peach schnapps, cranberry juice, orange juice, and simple syrup into the shaker.
4. *Shake Well:*
   - Secure the shaker lid and shake the ingredients vigorously for about 15 seconds to chill the mixture.
5. *Strain into Glasses:*
   - Remove the chilled glasses from the freezer and strain the Love Bug Cocktail into each glass.
6. *Garnish:*
   - Garnish the cocktails with fresh raspberries or strawberries and mint leaves.
7. *Serve:*
   - Serve the Love Bug Cocktails immediately.

EXPERT TIPS & VARIATIONS:
- Adjust sweetness by adding more or less simple syrup according to your taste.
- Experiment with different fruit garnishes for a playful twist.

PAIRING SUGGESTIONS:
- Enjoy the Love Bug Cocktail as a fun and delightful drink.
- Serve with heart-shaped cookies or chocolate-covered fruits for added sweetness.

Raspberry Kiss Cocktail

Servings: 2 | **Prep Time:** 10 minutes

INGREDIENTS:
- 4 oz raspberry-flavored vodka
- 2 oz Chambord (raspberry liqueur)
- 1 oz freshly squeezed lemon juice
- 1 oz simple syrup
- Fresh raspberries, for muddling and garnish
- Ice cubes
- Lemon twists, for garnish

INSTRUCTIONS:
1. *Chill Glasses:*
   - Place cocktail glasses in the freezer for a few minutes to chill.
2. *Prepare Cocktail Shaker:*
   - Fill a cocktail shaker with ice cubes.
3. *Muddle Raspberries:*
   - In the shaker, muddle a few fresh raspberries to release their juices.
4. *Add Ingredients:*
   - Pour raspberry-flavored vodka, Chambord, freshly squeezed lemon juice, and simple syrup into the shaker.
5. *Shake Well:*
   - Secure the shaker lid and shake the ingredients vigorously for about 15 seconds to chill the mixture.
6. *Strain into Glasses:*
   - Remove the chilled glasses from the freezer and strain the Raspberry Kiss Cocktail into each glass.
7. *Garnish:*
   - Garnish the cocktails with fresh raspberries and lemon twists.
8. *Serve:*
   - Serve the Raspberry Kiss Cocktails immediately.

EXPERT TIPS & VARIATIONS:
- Adjust sweetness by adding more or less simple syrup based on your preference.
- Experiment with different berry-flavored vodkas for a unique twist.

PAIRING SUGGESTIONS:
- Enjoy the Raspberry Kiss Cocktail as a flavorful and romantic drink.
- Serve with light appetizers or a cheese board for an elegant pairing.

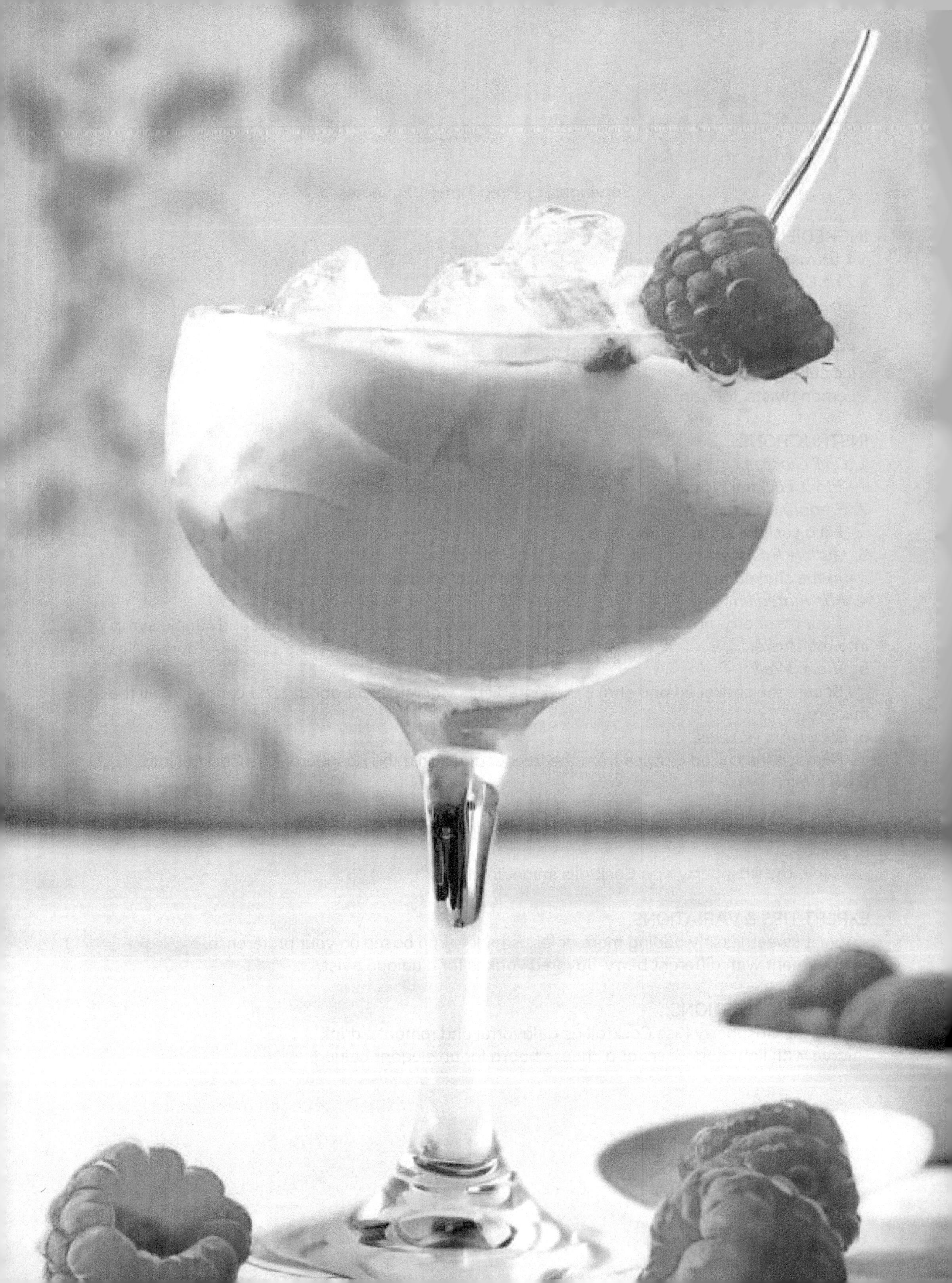

Valentine Moscow Mule Cocktail

Servings: 2 | Prep Time: 10 minutes

INGREDIENTS:
- 4 oz vodka
- 2 oz fresh lime juice
- 1 oz raspberry syrup or puree
- Ginger beer
- Fresh raspberries and lime slices, for garnish
- Ice cubes

INSTRUCTIONS:
1. *Chill Copper Mugs:*
   - Place copper mugs in the freezer for a few minutes to chill.
2. *Prepare Moscow Mule:*
   - In each chilled mug, combine vodka, fresh lime juice, and raspberry syrup or puree.
3. *Stir Well:*
   - Stir the ingredients in each mug to combine.
4. *Add Ice:*
   - Fill each mug with ice cubes.
5. *Top with Ginger Beer:*
   - Top off each mug with ginger beer, leaving some space at the top.
6. *Garnish:*
   - Garnish the Moscow Mule with fresh raspberries and lime slices.
7. *Stir Again (Optional):*
   - Give it a gentle stir if you like your Moscow Mule well mixed.
8. *Serve:*
   - Serve the Valentine Moscow Mule immediately.

EXPERT TIPS & VARIATIONS:
- Adjust sweetness by adding more or less raspberry syrup based on your taste.
- Experiment with flavored ginger beer for added depth of flavor.

PAIRING SUGGESTIONS:
- Enjoy the Valentine Moscow Mule as a refreshing and crisp drink.
- Pair with spicy snacks or appetizers for a delightful contrast.

Pink Squirrel

Servings: 2 | **Prep Time:** 10 minutes

INGREDIENTS:
- 2 oz crème de noyaux (almond-flavored liqueur)
- 2 oz white crème de cacao
- 2 oz heavy cream
- Maraschino cherries, for garnish
- Ice cubes

INSTRUCTIONS:
1. *Chill Glasses:*
   - Place cocktail glasses in the freezer for a few minutes to chill.
2. *Prepare Pink Squirrel:*
   - In a cocktail shaker, combine crème de noyaux, white crème de cacao, and heavy cream.
3. *Add Ice:*
   - Add ice cubes to the shaker.
4. *Shake Well:*
   - Secure the shaker lid and shake the ingredients vigorously for about 15 seconds to chill the mixture.
5. *Strain into Glasses:*
   - Remove the chilled glasses from the freezer and strain the Pink Squirrel into each glass.
6. *Garnish:*
   - Garnish each cocktail with a maraschino cherry.
7. *Serve:*
   - Serve the Pink Squirrel cocktails immediately.

EXPERT TIPS & VARIATIONS:
- Adjust the sweetness by adding more or less crème de noyaux based on your preference.
- You can use pink crème de cacao for a more vibrant color.

PAIRING SUGGESTIONS:
- Enjoy the Pink Squirrel as a delightful and nostalgic treat.
- Serve with chocolate-covered strawberries for an indulgent pairing.

Love Martini

Servings: 2 | **Prep Time:** 10 minutes

INGREDIENTS:
- 3 oz vanilla vodka
- 1 oz raspberry liqueur
- 1 oz cranberry juice
- 1/2 oz simple syrup
- Fresh raspberries, for garnish
- Ice cubes

INSTRUCTIONS:
1. *Chill Glasses:*
   - Place martini glasses in the freezer for a few minutes to chill.
2. *Prepare Love Martini:*
   - In a cocktail shaker, combine vanilla vodka, raspberry liqueur, cranberry juice, and simple syrup.
3. *Add Ice:*
   - Add ice cubes to the shaker.
4. *Shake Well:*
   - Secure the shaker lid and shake the ingredients vigorously for about 15 seconds to chill the mixture.
5. *Strain into Glasses:*
   - Remove the chilled glasses from the freezer and strain the Love Martini into each glass.
6. *Garnish:*
   - Garnish each martini with fresh raspberries.
7. *Serve:*
   - Serve the Love Martinis immediately.

EXPERT TIPS & VARIATIONS:
- Adjust sweetness by adding more or less simple syrup according to your taste.
- You can rim the glasses with sugar for an extra decorative touch.

PAIRING SUGGESTIONS:
- Enjoy the Love Martini as a romantic and flavorful drink.
- Pair with light appetizers or a cheese platter for a sophisticated touch.

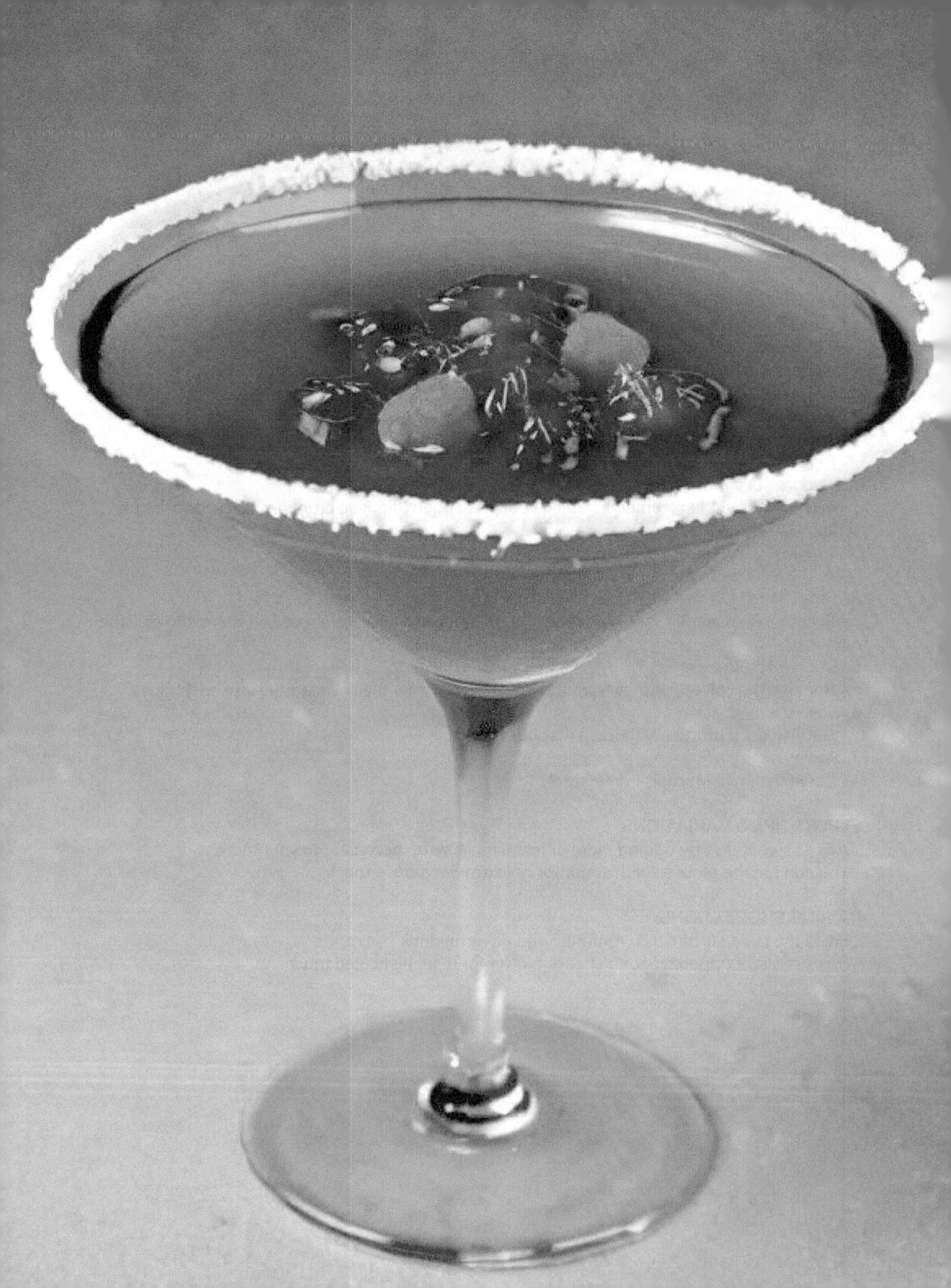

DESSERTS

Chocolate Strawberries

Servings: Varies | **Prep Time:** 30 minutes

INGREDIENTS:
- Fresh strawberries, washed and dried
- Dark, milk, or white chocolate (8-10 ounces)
- Optional: White chocolate drizzle, chopped nuts, coconut flakes for decoration

INSTRUCTIONS:
1. *Prepare Strawberries:*
   - Ensure strawberries are completely dry to help the chocolate adhere. Leave the stems for a decorative touch.
2. *Melt Chocolate:*
   - In a heatproof bowl, melt the chocolate using a microwave or a double boiler. Stir occasionally until smooth.
3. *Dip Strawberries:*
   - Holding each strawberry by the stem, dip it into the melted chocolate, covering about two-thirds of the strawberry.
4. *Allow Excess to Drip:*
   - Allow excess chocolate to drip back into the bowl.
5. *Optional Decoration:*
   - If desired, roll the chocolate-covered part of the strawberry in chopped nuts or coconut flakes while the chocolate is still wet.
6. *Set on Parchment Paper:*
   - Place the dipped strawberries on a parchment paper-lined tray.
7. *Cool and Harden:*
   - Allow the chocolate to cool and harden. You can speed up the process by placing the tray in the refrigerator for about 15-20 minutes.
8. *Optional Drizzle:*
   - If using white chocolate for drizzling, melt it similarly to the first chocolate and use a fork to drizzle over the hardened chocolate-covered strawberries.
9. *Final Set:*
   - Allow the chocolate to fully set before serving.
10. *Serve:*
    - Arrange the chocolate-covered strawberries on a plate and serve.

EXPERT TIPS:
- Use good quality chocolate for a richer flavor.
- Experiment with different toppings like crushed cookies, sprinkles, or edible gold dust for a creative touch.

PAIRING SUGGESTIONS:
- Enjoy the chocolate-covered strawberries on their own or pair them with a glass of champagne for a classic and romantic treat.

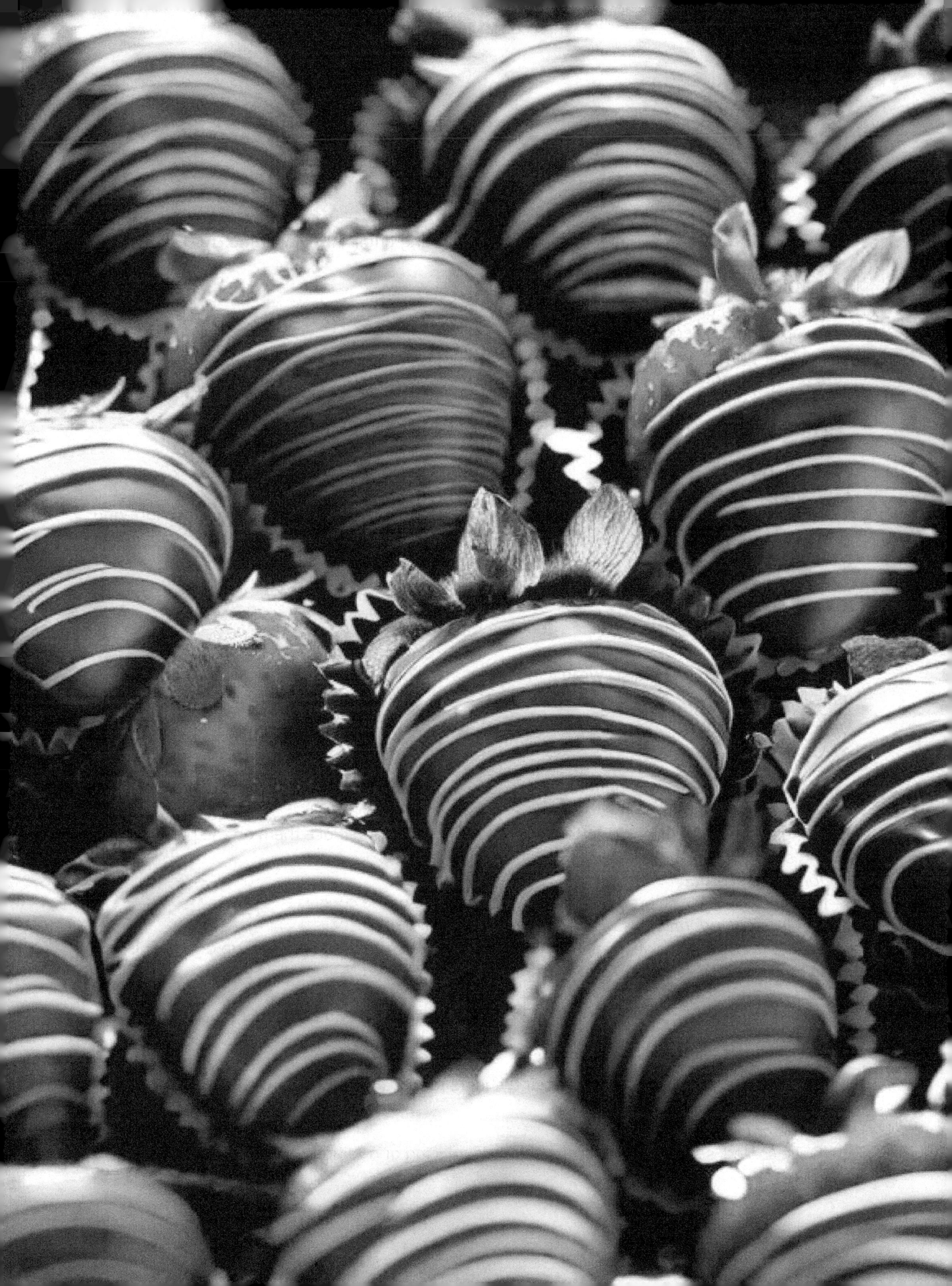

Shortbread Heart-Shaped Cookies

Servings: Varies | **Prep Time:** 20 minutes (plus chilling time) | **Baking Time:** 10-12 minutes

INGREDIENTS:
- 1 cup (2 sticks) unsalted butter, softened
- 1/2 cup confectioners' sugar
- 2 cups all-purpose flour
- 1/4 teaspoon salt
- 1 teaspoon vanilla extract
- Optional: Colored sugar or sprinkles for decorating

INSTRUCTIONS:
1. *Prepare Dough:*
   - In a large bowl, cream together the softened butter and confectioners' sugar until light and fluffy.
2. *Add Dry Ingredients:*
   - Sift in the flour and add the salt. Mix until just combined.
3. *Add Vanilla Extract:*
   - Stir in the vanilla extract until the dough comes together.
4. *Chill Dough:*
   - Form the dough into a disc, wrap it in plastic wrap, and refrigerate for at least 1-2 hours or until firm.
5. *Preheat Oven:*
   - Preheat your oven to 350°F (180°C). Line baking sheets with parchment paper.
6. *Roll Out Dough:*
   - On a floured surface, roll out the chilled dough to about 1/4-inch thickness.
7. *Cut Heart Shapes:*
   - Using heart-shaped cookie cutters, cut out the cookies and place them on the prepared baking sheets.
8. *Optional Decoration:*
   - If desired, sprinkle colored sugar or sprinkles on top of the cookies.
9. *Chill Again (Optional):*
   - Place the cut-out cookies in the refrigerator for about 15 minutes to firm up again. This helps them keep their shape while baking.
10. *Bake:*
    - Bake in the preheated oven for 10-12 minutes or until the edges are just starting to turn golden.
11. *Cool:*
    - Allow the cookies to cool on the baking sheets for a few minutes before transferring them to a wire rack to cool completely.
12. *Serve or Decorate (Optional):*
    - Once cooled, serve as is or decorate with royal icing or additional sprinkles.

EXPERT TIPS:
- Be sure not to overmix the dough to maintain a tender texture.
- If you don't have heart-shaped cookie cutters, you can use a knife to carefully cut heart shapes.

PAIRING SUGGESTIONS:
- Enjoy these heart-shaped shortbread cookies with a cup of hot tea or coffee for a delightful treat.

Chocolate-Covered Strawberry Brownies

Servings: 12 brownies | **Prep Time:** 20 minutes | **Baking Time:** 25-30 minutes

INGREDIENTS:

For Brownies:
- 1/2 cup (1 stick) unsalted butter
- 1 cup granulated sugar
- 2 large eggs
- 1 teaspoon vanilla extract
- 1/3 cup unsweetened cocoa powder
- 1/2 cup all-purpose flour
- 1/4 teaspoon salt

For Topping:
- 1 cup fresh strawberries, hulled and sliced
- 4 oz dark chocolate, chopped
- 1 tablespoon unsalted butter
- Optional: Powdered sugar for dusting

INSTRUCTIONS:

1. *Preheat Oven:*
   - Preheat your oven to 350°F (180°C). Grease and line a square baking pan with parchment paper, leaving an overhang for easy removal.
2. *Prepare Brownie Batter:*
   - In a saucepan, melt the butter over medium heat. Remove from heat and whisk in sugar, eggs, and vanilla extract until well combined.
3. *Add Dry Ingredients:*
   - Sift in cocoa powder, all-purpose flour, and salt. Stir until just combined; do not overmix.
4. *Bake:*
   - Pour the brownie batter into the prepared pan and spread it evenly. Bake in the preheated oven for 25-30 minutes or until a toothpick inserted into the center comes out with a few moist crumbs.
5. *Cool:*
   - Allow the brownies to cool completely in the pan.
6. *Prepare Topping:*
   - In a heatproof bowl, melt the dark chocolate and butter together. Stir until smooth.
7. *Cover Brownies:*
   - Spread the melted chocolate over the cooled brownies, creating a smooth layer.
8. *Arrange Strawberries:*
   - Arrange sliced strawberries on top of the chocolate layer, pressing them slightly into the chocolate.

9. *Optional Decoration:*
   - If desired, dust the top with powdered sugar for an extra touch.
10. *Chill (Optional):*
    - Place the brownies in the refrigerator for about 30 minutes to allow the chocolate to set.
11. *Slice and Serve:*
    - Use the parchment paper overhang to lift the brownies from the pan. Slice into squares and serve.

EXPERT TIPS:
- Ensure the brownies are completely cooled before adding the chocolate topping to prevent it from melting.
- Experiment with different types of chocolate or add a touch of strawberry jam to the melted chocolate for extra flavor.

PAIRING SUGGESTIONS:
- Enjoy these Chocolate-Covered Strawberry Brownies with a scoop of vanilla ice cream for a decadent dessert.

Red Velvet Cheesecake Bites

Servings: 24 cheesecake bites | **Prep Time:** 30 minutes (plus chilling time) | **Baking Time:** 20-25 minutes

INGREDIENTS:

For Red Velvet Crust:
- 1 1/2 cups red velvet cake crumbs (prepared cake, crumbled)
- 4 tablespoons unsalted butter, melted

For Cheesecake Filling:
- 16 oz cream cheese, softened
- 1/2 cup granulated sugar
- 2 large eggs
- 1 teaspoon vanilla extract
- 1/4 cup sour cream

For Chocolate Ganache:
- 4 oz semi-sweet chocolate, chopped
- 1/2 cup heavy cream

INSTRUCTIONS:

1. *Preheat Oven:*
   - Preheat your oven to 325°F (163°C). Line a square baking pan with parchment paper, leaving an overhang for easy removal.
2. *Prepare Red Velvet Crust:*
   - In a bowl, combine red velvet cake crumbs and melted butter. Press the mixture evenly into the bottom of the prepared pan to create the crust.
3. *Bake Crust:*
   - Bake the crust in the preheated oven for 8-10 minutes. Remove from the oven and allow it to cool while preparing the cheesecake filling.
4. *Prepare Cheesecake Filling:*
   - In a large mixing bowl, beat the cream cheese and sugar until smooth. Add eggs one at a time, beating well after each addition. Stir in vanilla extract and sour cream until combined.
5. *Pour Filling Over Crust:*
   - Pour the cheesecake filling over the cooled red velvet crust, spreading it evenly.
6. *Bake Cheesecake:*
   - Bake in the preheated oven for 20-25 minutes or until the edges are set and the center is slightly jiggly.
7. *Cool and Chill:*
   - Allow the cheesecake to cool in the pan, then refrigerate for at least 2 hours or until completely chilled.
8. *Prepare Chocolate Ganache:*
   - In a heatproof bowl, melt the semi-sweet chocolate with the heavy cream. Stir until smooth.
9. *Pour Ganache Over Cheesecake:*

- Pour the chocolate ganache over the chilled cheesecake, spreading it evenly.
10. *Chill Again (Optional):*
   - Place the pan back in the refrigerator for about 30 minutes to let the ganache set.
11. *Slice Into Bites:*
   - Use the parchment paper overhang to lift the cheesecake from the pan. Slice into bite-sized squares.
12. *Serve:*
   - Serve the Red Velvet Cheesecake Bites and enjoy!

EXPERT TIPS:
- For a more intense red color in the crust, you can add a few drops of red food coloring to the prepared cake crumbs.
- Experiment with different chocolate types for the ganache to suit your taste.

PAIRING SUGGESTIONS:
- Enjoy these Red Velvet Cheesecake Bites with a cup of coffee or a glass of milk for a delightful treat.

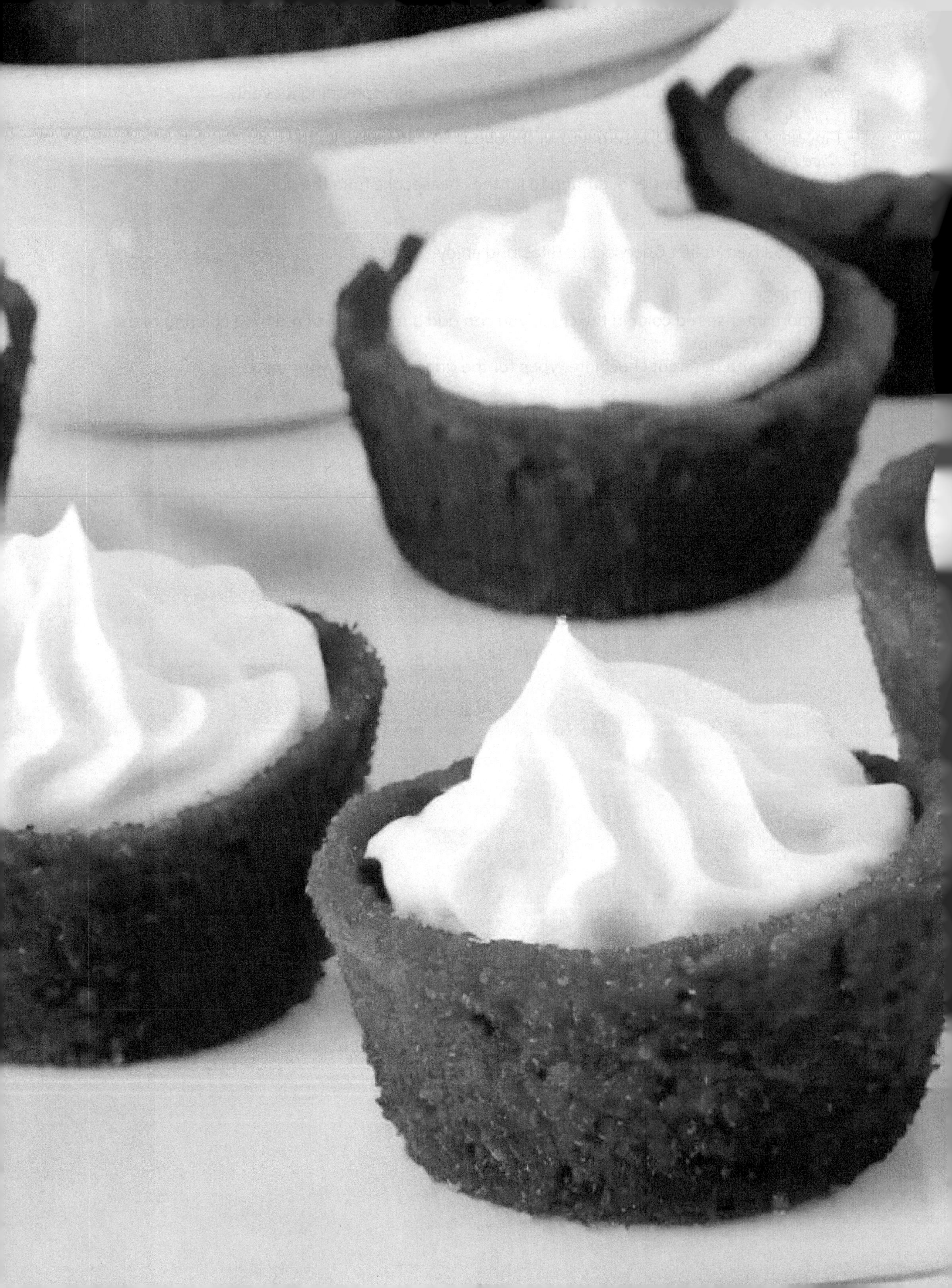

Sparkle Heart Cookies

Servings: 24 cookies | **Prep Time:** 30 minutes (plus chilling time) | **Baking Time:** 8-10 minutes

INGREDIENTS:
For Cookies:
- 2 1/2 cups all-purpose flour
- 1/2 teaspoon baking powder
- 1/4 teaspoon salt
- 1 cup unsalted butter, softened
- 1 cup granulated sugar
- 1 large egg
- 2 teaspoons vanilla extract

For Decoration:
- Colored sanding sugar or edible glitter
- Royal icing (optional)

INSTRUCTIONS:
1. *Prepare Cookie Dough:*
   - In a bowl, whisk together flour, baking powder, and salt. Set aside.
   - In another bowl, cream together softened butter and sugar until light and fluffy. Add the egg and vanilla extract, mixing until well combined.
   - Gradually add the dry ingredients to the wet ingredients, mixing until a soft dough forms.
2. *Chill Dough:*
   - Divide the dough in half, shape each half into a disk, wrap in plastic wrap, and refrigerate for at least 2 hours or until firm.
3. *Preheat Oven:*
   - Preheat your oven to 350°F (180°C). Line baking sheets with parchment paper.
4. *Roll Out Dough:*
   - On a floured surface, roll out one disk of chilled dough to about 1/4-inch thickness.
5. *Cut Heart Shapes:*
   - Use heart-shaped cookie cutters to cut out cookies and place them on the prepared baking sheets.
6. *Decorate with Sparkle:*
   - Sprinkle colored sanding sugar or edible glitter over the heart-shaped cookies before baking for a sparkling effect.
7. *Bake:*
   - Bake in the preheated oven for 8-10 minutes or until the edges are lightly golden.
8. *Cool:*
   - Allow the cookies to cool on the baking sheets for a few minutes before transferring them to a wire rack to cool completely.
9. *Optional: Decorate with Royal Icing:*
   - If desired, you can decorate the cooled cookies with royal icing in various colors.
10. *Serve:*

- Serve the Sparkle Heart Cookies and enjoy!

EXPERT TIPS:
- For a more defined sparkle effect, you can brush the cookies lightly with edible glue before sprinkling the sanding sugar.
- Make sure the cookie dough is thoroughly chilled for easier handling and better shapes.

PAIRING SUGGESTIONS:
- Enjoy these Sparkle Heart Cookies with a cup of hot cocoa or your favorite tea for a delightful treat.

Double Chocolate Mascarpone Raspberry Pie

Servings: 8 slices | **Prep Time:** 30 minutes (plus chilling time) | **Baking Time:** 15-20 minutes

INGREDIENTS:
For Chocolate Crust:
- 1 1/2 cups chocolate cookie crumbs
- 1/3 cup unsalted butter, melted

For Mascarpone Filling:
- 8 oz mascarpone cheese, softened
- 1/2 cup powdered sugar
- 1 teaspoon vanilla extract

For Chocolate Ganache:
- 6 oz dark chocolate, chopped
- 1/2 cup heavy cream

For Raspberry Topping:
- 1 cup fresh raspberries
- 2 tablespoons raspberry jam (seedless)

INSTRUCTIONS:
1. *Preheat Oven:*
   - Preheat your oven to 350°F (180°C).
2. *Prepare Chocolate Crust:*
   - In a bowl, combine chocolate cookie crumbs and melted butter. Press the mixture into the bottom of a pie pan to create the crust.
3. *Bake Crust:*
   - Bake the crust in the preheated oven for 8-10 minutes. Allow it to cool while preparing the filling.
4. *Prepare Mascarpone Filling:*
   - In a mixing bowl, beat together softened mascarpone cheese, powdered sugar, and vanilla extract until smooth and creamy.
5. *Spread Filling Over Crust:*
   - Spread the mascarpone filling evenly over the cooled chocolate crust.
6. *Prepare Chocolate Ganache:*
   - In a heatproof bowl, melt the dark chocolate with the heavy cream. Stir until smooth.
7. *Pour Ganache Over Filling:*
   - Pour the chocolate ganache over the mascarpone filling, spreading it evenly.
8. *Chill Pie:*
   - Place the pie in the refrigerator and allow it to chill for at least 2 hours or until set.

9. *Prepare Raspberry Topping:*
   - In a small saucepan, heat raspberry jam until it becomes a smooth liquid. Remove from heat.
10. *Add Fresh Raspberries:*
    - Gently fold fresh raspberries into the raspberry jam mixture.
11. *Top the Pie:*
    - Spread the raspberry topping over the chilled chocolate ganache layer.
12. *Chill Again (Optional):*
    - Place the pie back in the refrigerator for about 30 minutes to let the raspberry topping set.
13. *Slice and Serve:*
    - Slice the Double Chocolate Mascarpone Raspberry Pie into wedges and serve.

EXPERT TIPS:
- Ensure the mascarpone cheese is softened for a smooth and creamy filling.
- Feel free to experiment with different chocolate types for the ganache.

PAIRING SUGGESTIONS:
- Enjoy a slice of this indulgent pie with a dollop of whipped cream or a scoop of vanilla ice cream for a decadent dessert.

French Silk Pie

Servings: 8 slices | **Prep Time:** 20 minutes (plus chilling time)

INGREDIENTS:

For Chocolate Cookie Crust:
- 1 1/2 cups chocolate cookie crumbs
- 1/3 cup unsalted butter, melted

For French Silk Filling:
- 1 cup unsalted butter, softened
- 1 1/2 cups granulated sugar
- 4 oz unsweetened chocolate, melted and cooled
- 1 teaspoon vanilla extract
- 4 large eggs

For Whipped Cream Topping:
- 1 cup heavy cream
- 2 tablespoons powdered sugar
- Chocolate shavings or cocoa powder for garnish (optional)

INSTRUCTIONS:

1. *Prepare Chocolate Cookie Crust:*
   - In a bowl, combine chocolate cookie crumbs and melted butter. Press the mixture into the bottom of a pie pan to create the crust.
2. *Prepare French Silk Filling:*
   - In a large mixing bowl, beat softened butter and sugar until creamy. Add melted and cooled unsweetened chocolate and vanilla extract, continuing to beat until well combined.
3. *Add Eggs:*
   - Add the eggs one at a time, beating well after each addition. Continue beating the mixture until it becomes light and fluffy.
4. *Fill Crust:*
   - Spoon the French Silk filling into the chocolate cookie crust, spreading it evenly.
5. *Chill Pie:*
   - Place the pie in the refrigerator and allow it to chill for at least 4 hours or overnight to set.
6. *Prepare Whipped Cream Topping:*
   - In a separate bowl, whip the heavy cream and powdered sugar until stiff peaks form.
7. *Top the Pie:*
   - Spread the whipped cream over the chilled French Silk filling.
8. *Optional Garnish:*
   - Garnish with chocolate shavings or a dusting of cocoa powder for an elegant touch.
   - Slice the French Silk Pie into wedges and serve.

EXPERT TIPS:

- Ensure the melted chocolate is completely cooled before adding it to the butter-sugar mixture.
- For a silkier texture, beat the filling for an extra minute or two until it reaches a smooth consistency.

PAIRING SUGGESTIONS:
- Enjoy a slice of this French Silk Pie with a cup of coffee or a glass of red wine for a luxurious dessert.

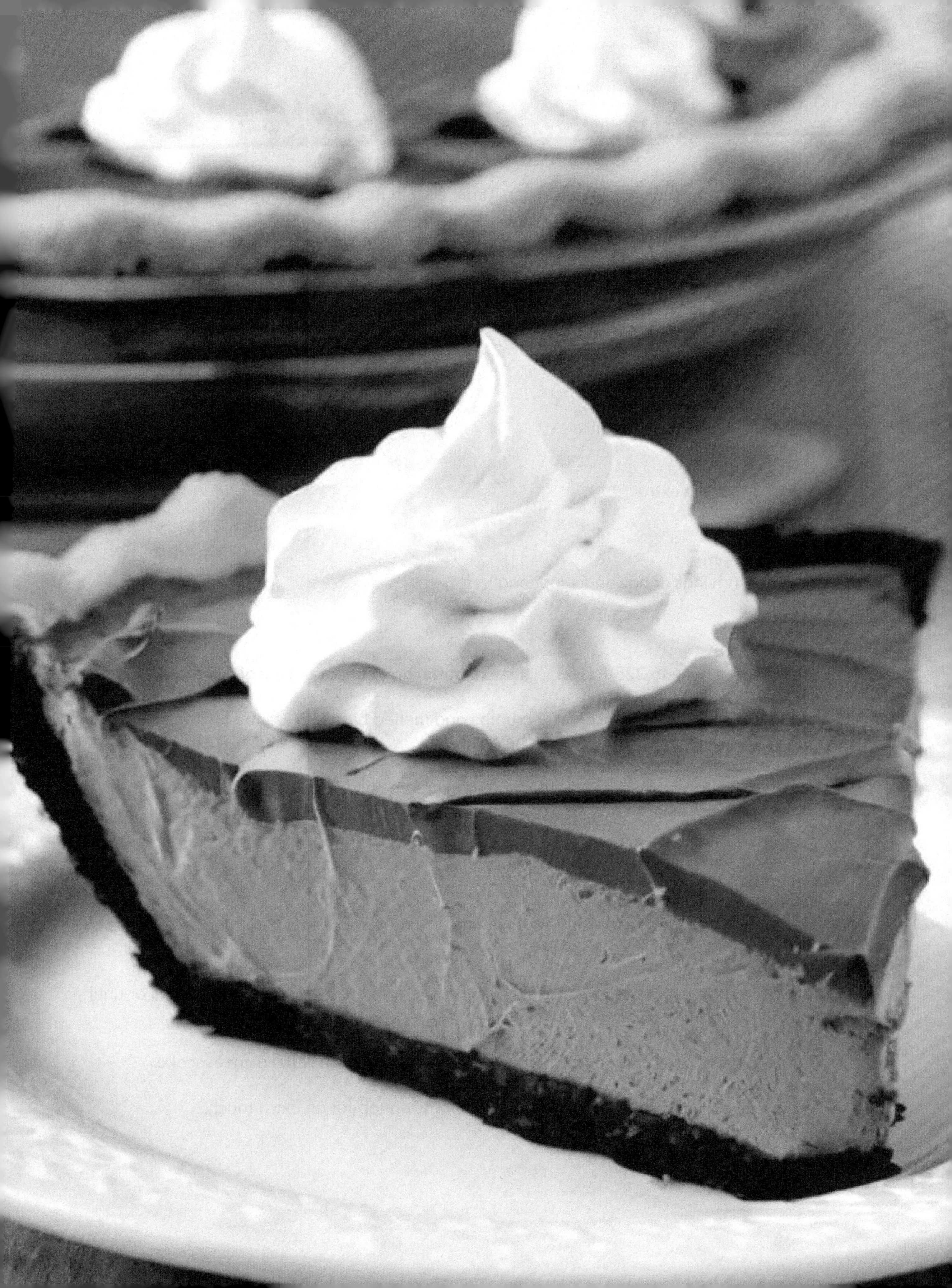

Nutella Cheesecakes

Servings: 6 individual cheesecakes | **Prep Time:** 20 minutes (plus chilling time) | **Baking Time:** 20-25 minutes

INGREDIENTS:
For Crust:
- 1 cup graham cracker crumbs
- 3 tablespoons unsalted butter, melted

For Nutella Cheesecake Filling:
- 16 oz cream cheese, softened
- 2/3 cup granulated sugar
- 2/3 cup Nutella
- 2 large eggs
- 1 teaspoon vanilla extract

For Topping:
- Whipped cream
- Chocolate shavings or hazelnuts (optional)

INSTRUCTIONS:
1. *Preheat Oven:*
   - Preheat your oven to 325°F (163°C). Line a muffin tin with paper cupcake liners.
2. *Prepare Crust:*
   - In a bowl, combine graham cracker crumbs and melted butter. Press the mixture into the bottom of each cupcake liner to create the crust.
3. *Prepare Nutella Cheesecake Filling:*
   - In a large mixing bowl, beat together softened cream cheese, sugar, Nutella, eggs, and vanilla extract until smooth and well combined.
4. *Fill Cupcake Liners:*
   - Spoon the Nutella cheesecake filling over the crust in each cupcake liner, filling them almost to the top.
5. *Bake:*
   - Bake in the preheated oven for 20-25 minutes or until the edges are set and the centers are slightly jiggly.
6. *Cool and Chill:*
   - Allow the cheesecakes to cool in the muffin tin, then refrigerate for at least 2 hours or until completely chilled.
7. *Top with Whipped Cream:*
   - Before serving, add a dollop of whipped cream on top of each Nutella cheesecake.
8. *Optional Toppings:*
   - Sprinkle chocolate shavings or chopped hazelnuts on top for an extra touch.

EXPERT TIPS:
- Use room temperature cream cheese for a smoother filling.
- Adjust the sweetness by adding more or less sugar based on your preference.

PAIRING SUGGESTIONS:
- Enjoy these Nutella Cheesecakes on their own or with a drizzle of warm Nutella for an irresistible treat.

Red Velvet Cake Mix Bars

Servings: 12 bars | Prep Time: 15 minutes | Baking Time: 20-25 minutes

INGREDIENTS:
For Bars:
- 1 box red velvet cake mix (15.25 oz)
- 1/2 cup unsalted butter, melted
- 1 large egg
- 1 cup white chocolate chips

For Cream Cheese Swirl:
- 8 oz cream cheese, softened
- 1/4 cup granulated sugar
- 1 large egg
- 1 teaspoon vanilla extract

INSTRUCTIONS:
1. *Preheat Oven:*
   - Preheat your oven to 350°F (180°C). Grease or line a baking pan with parchment paper.
2. *Prepare Cake Mix Base:*
   - In a large bowl, combine the red velvet cake mix, melted butter, and 1 egg. Mix until well combined.
3. *Add White Chocolate Chips:*
   - Stir in the white chocolate chips into the cake mix batter.
4. *Press Into Pan:*
   - Press the cake mix batter evenly into the bottom of the prepared baking pan.
5. *Prepare Cream Cheese Swirl:*
   - In a separate bowl, beat together the softened cream cheese, granulated sugar, 1 egg, and vanilla extract until smooth.
6. *Swirl Cream Cheese Mixture:*
   - Drop spoonfuls of the cream cheese mixture over the red velvet batter. Use a knife or skewer to create swirl patterns.
7. *Bake:*
   - Bake in the preheated oven for 20-25 minutes or until a toothpick inserted into the center comes out with a few moist crumbs.
8. *Cool:*
   - Allow the bars to cool in the pan before transferring to a wire rack to cool completely.
9. *Chill (Optional):*
   - For a firmer texture, you can refrigerate the bars for a few hours before slicing.
10. *Slice and Serve:*
    - Slice the Red Velvet Cake Mix Bars into squares and serve.

EXPERT TIPS:
- Experiment with different types of chocolate chips or add chopped nuts for extra texture.

- Ensure the cream cheese is softened for a smooth swirl.

PAIRING SUGGESTIONS:
- Enjoy these Red Velvet Cake Mix Bars with a cup of hot cocoa or a scoop of vanilla ice cream for a delightful treat.

Dark Chocolate Cherry Brownies

Servings: 16 brownies | **Prep Time:** 15 minutes | **Baking Time:** 25-30 minutes

INGREDIENTS:
- 1 cup unsalted butter
- 2 cups granulated sugar
- 4 large eggs
- 1 teaspoon vanilla extract
- 1 cup all-purpose flour
- 1/2 cup dark cocoa powder
- 1/4 teaspoon salt
- 1 cup dark chocolate chips or chunks
- 1 cup chopped fresh or dried cherries (pitted and halved
)

INSTRUCTIONS:
1. *Preheat Oven:*
   - Preheat your oven to 350°F (180°C). Grease or line a square baking pan with parchment paper.
2. *Melt Butter:*
   - In a saucepan, melt the butter over low heat. Remove from heat and let it cool slightly.
3. *Combine Wet Ingredients:*
   - In a large mixing bowl, whisk together the melted butter, granulated sugar, eggs, and vanilla extract until well combined.
4. *Add Dry Ingredients:*
   - Sift in the flour, dark cocoa powder, and salt. Stir until just combined; do not overmix.
5. *Fold in Chocolate and Cherries:*
   - Gently fold in the dark chocolate chips or chunks and the chopped cherries into the brownie batter.
6. *Transfer to Pan:*
   - Pour the batter into the prepared baking pan, spreading it evenly.
7. *Bake:*
   - Bake in the preheated oven for 25-30 minutes or until a toothpick inserted into the center comes out with a few moist crumbs.
8. *Cool:*
   - Allow the brownies to cool in the pan before transferring them to a wire rack to cool completely.
   - Slice the Dark Chocolate Cherry Brownies into squares and serve.

EXPERT TIPS:
- If using dried cherries, you can soak them in warm water for about 15 minutes to plump them up before chopping.
- For an extra indulgence, drizzle melted dark chocolate over the cooled brownies.

PAIRING SUGGESTIONS:
- Enjoy these Dark Chocolate Cherry Brownies with a cup of hot coffee or a glass of red wine for a decadent treat.

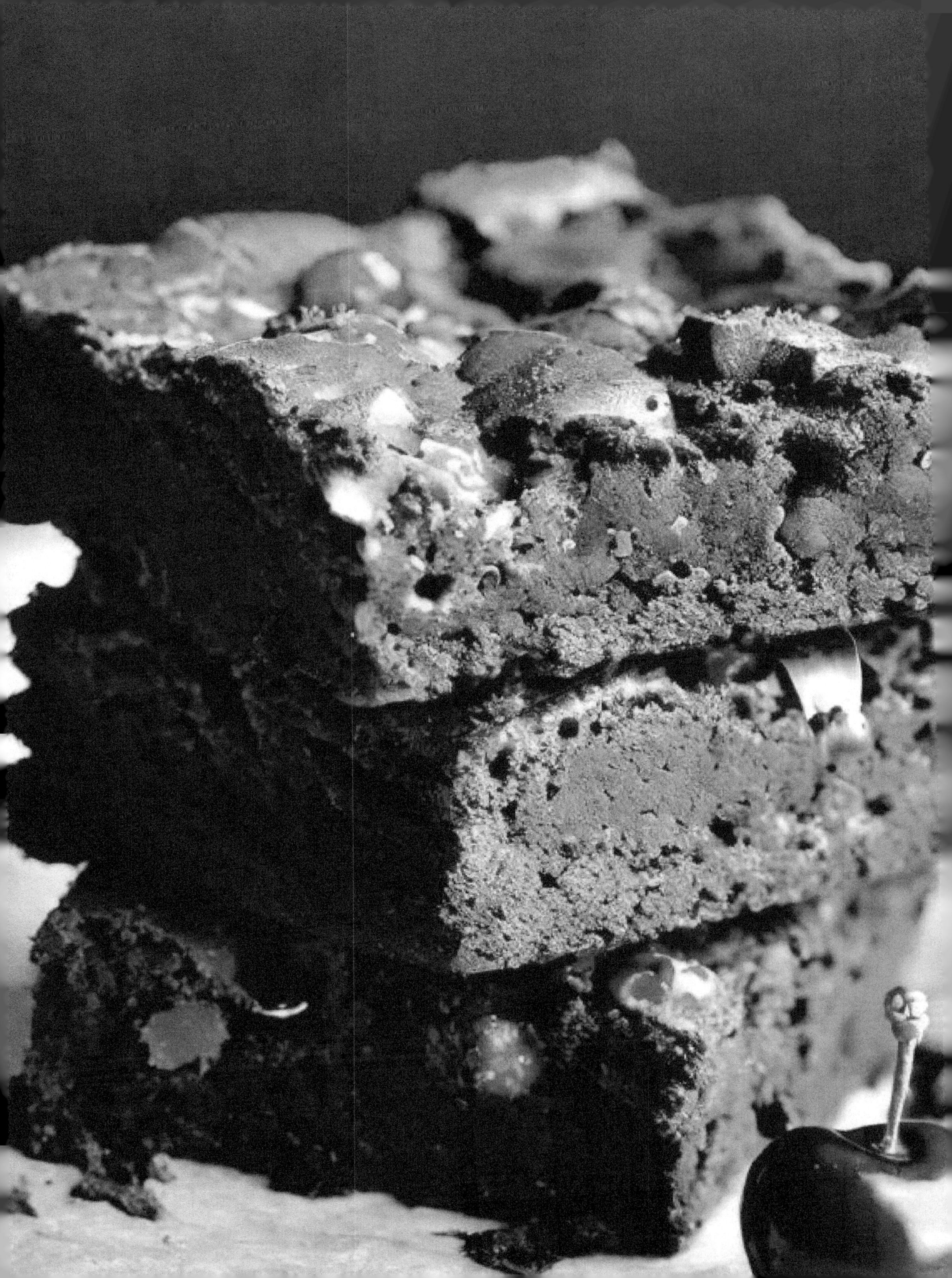

Frosted Sugar Cookie Bars

Servings: 16 bars | **Prep Time:** 20 minutes | **Baking Time:** 15-20 minutes

INGREDIENTS:
For Sugar Cookie Bars:
- 1 cup unsalted butter, softened
- 1 1/2 cups granulated sugar
- 2 large eggs
- 2 teaspoons vanilla extract
- 3 cups all-purpose flour
- 1/2 teaspoon baking powder
- 1/2 teaspoon salt

For Frosting:
- 1/2 cup unsalted butter, softened
- 2 cups powdered sugar
- 1 teaspoon vanilla extract
- 2-3 tablespoons milk
- Food coloring (optional)
- Sprinkles for decoration (optional)

INSTRUCTIONS:
1. *Preheat Oven:*
   - Preheat your oven to 350°F (180°C). Grease or line a square baking pan with parchment paper.
2. *Prepare Sugar Cookie Bars:*
   - In a large bowl, cream together the softened butter and granulated sugar until light and fluffy. Add the eggs and vanilla extract, beating well.
3. *Combine Dry Ingredients:*
   - In a separate bowl, whisk together the flour, baking powder, and salt.
4. *Mix Wet and Dry Ingredients:*
   - Gradually add the dry ingredients to the wet ingredients, mixing until a soft dough forms.
5. *Press into Pan:*
   - Press the cookie dough evenly into the bottom of the prepared baking pan.
6. *Bake:*
   - Bake in the preheated oven for 15-20 minutes or until the edges are lightly golden. The center should be set.
7. *Cool:*
   - Allow the sugar cookie bars to cool completely in the pan.
8. *Prepare Frosting:*
   - In a mixing bowl, beat together the softened butter, powdered sugar, vanilla extract, and milk until smooth and creamy. Add food coloring if desired.
9. *Frost Bars:*
   - Once the bars are completely cooled, spread the frosting evenly over the top.

10. *Decorate (Optional):*
    - Add sprinkles or other decorations over the frosting for a festive touch.
11. *Chill (Optional):*
    - For a firmer frosting, you can refrigerate the bars for about 30 minutes before slicing.
12. *Slice and Serve:*
    - Slice the Frosted Sugar Cookie Bars into squares and serve.

EXPERT TIPS:
- Ensure the butter is softened for both the cookie bars and frosting for smoother textures.
- Experiment with different food coloring and sprinkle combinations for a personalized touch.

PAIRING SUGGESTIONS:
- Enjoy these Frosted Sugar Cookie Bars with a cup of hot tea or a glass of milk for a delightful treat.

Chocolate Pillows

Servings: 24 chocolate pillows | **Prep Time:** 20 minutes | **Chilling Time:** 2 hours

INGREDIENTS:
For Chocolate Filling:
- 1 cup semisweet chocolate chips
- 1/2 cup heavy cream
- 2 tablespoons unsalted butter

For Pillow Dough:
- 2 1/2 cups all-purpose flour
- 1/2 cup granulated sugar
- 1 teaspoon baking powder
- 1/4 teaspoon salt
- 1 cup unsalted butter, chilled and cubed
- 2 large egg yolks
- 1/2 cup cold water

For Chocolate Coating:
- 1 cup dark chocolate, melted
- Sprinkles or powdered sugar for decoration (optional)

INSTRUCTIONS:
1. *Prepare Chocolate Filling:*
   - In a heatproof bowl, combine chocolate chips, heavy cream, and butter. Microwave in 20-second intervals, stirring between each, until smooth. Set aside to cool.
2. *Prepare Pillow Dough:*
   - In a large bowl, whisk together flour, sugar, baking powder, and salt. Add chilled and cubed butter, using a pastry cutter or your fingers to incorporate until the mixture resembles coarse crumbs.
3. *Add Egg Yolks and Water:*
   - Add egg yolks and cold water to the flour mixture. Stir until the dough comes together. Divide the dough into two portions, wrap in plastic wrap, and refrigerate for 1 hour.
4. *Roll Out Dough:*
   - On a lightly floured surface, roll out one portion of the chilled dough into a rectangle. Repeat with the second portion.
5. *Fill Dough with Chocolate:*
   - Spread the cooled chocolate filling over one of the rolled-out dough rectangles. Place the second rectangle on top, pressing the edges to seal.
6. *Chill Again:*
   - Place the assembled dough in the refrigerator and chill for at least 1 hour.
7. *Preheat Oven:*
   - Preheat your oven to 350°F (180°C). Line a baking sheet with parchment paper.
8. *Slice into Pillows:*

- Remove the chilled dough from the refrigerator and slice it into small squares to form chocolate pillows

9. *Bake:*
    - Place the chocolate pillows on the prepared baking sheet and bake in the preheated oven for 12-15 minutes or until the edges are lightly golden.

10. *Cool:*
    - Allow the chocolate pillows to cool on the baking sheet for a few minutes before transferring them to a wire rack to cool completely.

11. *Coat with Chocolate:*
    - Dip each chocolate pillow into melted dark chocolate, ensuring they are fully coated. Place them back on the parchment paper.

12. *Decorate (Optional):*
    - Add sprinkles or dust with powdered sugar for a decorative touch while the chocolate coating is still soft.

13. *Chill Again:*
    - Place the chocolate pillows in the refrigerator for about 30 minutes to set the chocolate coating.

14. *Serve:*
    - Serve the Chocolate Pillows and enjoy!

EXPERT TIPS:
- Ensure the chocolate filling is completely cooled before spreading it on the dough.
- Experiment with different chocolate coatings or add a touch of sea salt for extra flavor.

PAIRING SUGGESTIONS:
- Enjoy these Chocolate Pillows with a cup of hot cocoa or a glass of red wine for a delightful treat.

Mini Red Velvet Donuts

Servings: 24 mini donuts | **Prep Time:** 15 minutes | **Baking Time:** 8-10 minutes

INGREDIENTS:
For Donuts:
- 1 cup all-purpose flour
- 1/4 cup cocoa powder
- 1/2 teaspoon baking powder
- 1/4 teaspoon baking soda
- 1/4 teaspoon salt
- 1/2 cup granulated sugar
- 1/2 cup buttermilk
- 1 large egg
- 2 tablespoons unsalted butter, melted
- 1 teaspoon vanilla extract
- 1 tablespoon red food coloring

For Cream Cheese Glaze:
- 4 oz cream cheese, softened
- 1 cup powdered sugar
- 1/2 teaspoon vanilla extract
- 2-3 tablespoons milk

INSTRUCTIONS:
1. *Preheat Oven:*
   - Preheat your oven to 375°F (190°C). Grease a mini donut pan.
2. *Prepare Dry Ingredients:*
   - In a bowl, whisk together the flour, cocoa powder, baking powder, baking soda, and salt.
3. *Mix Wet Ingredients:*
   - In another bowl, whisk together the sugar, buttermilk, egg, melted butter, vanilla extract, and red food coloring.
4. *Combine Wet and Dry Ingredients:*
   - Add the wet ingredients to the dry ingredients, stirring until just combined.
5. *Fill Donut Pan:*
   - Spoon the batter into a piping bag or a ziplock bag with the corner snipped off. Pipe the batter into the mini donut pan, filling each cavity about halfway.
6. *Bake:*
   - Bake in the preheated oven for 8-10 minutes or until a toothpick inserted into a donut comes out clean.
7. *Cool:*
   - Allow the mini red velvet donuts to cool in the pan for a few minutes before transferring them to a wire rack to cool completely.
8. *Prepare Cream Cheese Glaze:*

- In a bowl, beat together the softened cream cheese, powdered sugar, vanilla extract, and enough milk to achieve a smooth glaze consistency.

9. *Glaze Donuts:*
   - Dip the cooled mini donuts into the cream cheese glaze, ensuring they are coated on one side.

10. *Decorate (Optional):*
    - Add sprinkles, chopped nuts, or edible pearls on top for a festive touch.

11. *Serve:*
    - Serve the Mini Red Velvet Donuts and enjoy!

EXPERT TIPS:
- Be cautious not to overmix the batter to maintain a soft texture.
- If you don't have a mini donut pan, you can use a mini muffin pan and adjust the baking time accordingly.

PAIRING SUGGESTIONS:
- Enjoy these Mini Red Velvet Donuts with a cup of coffee or a glass of cold milk for a delightful treat.

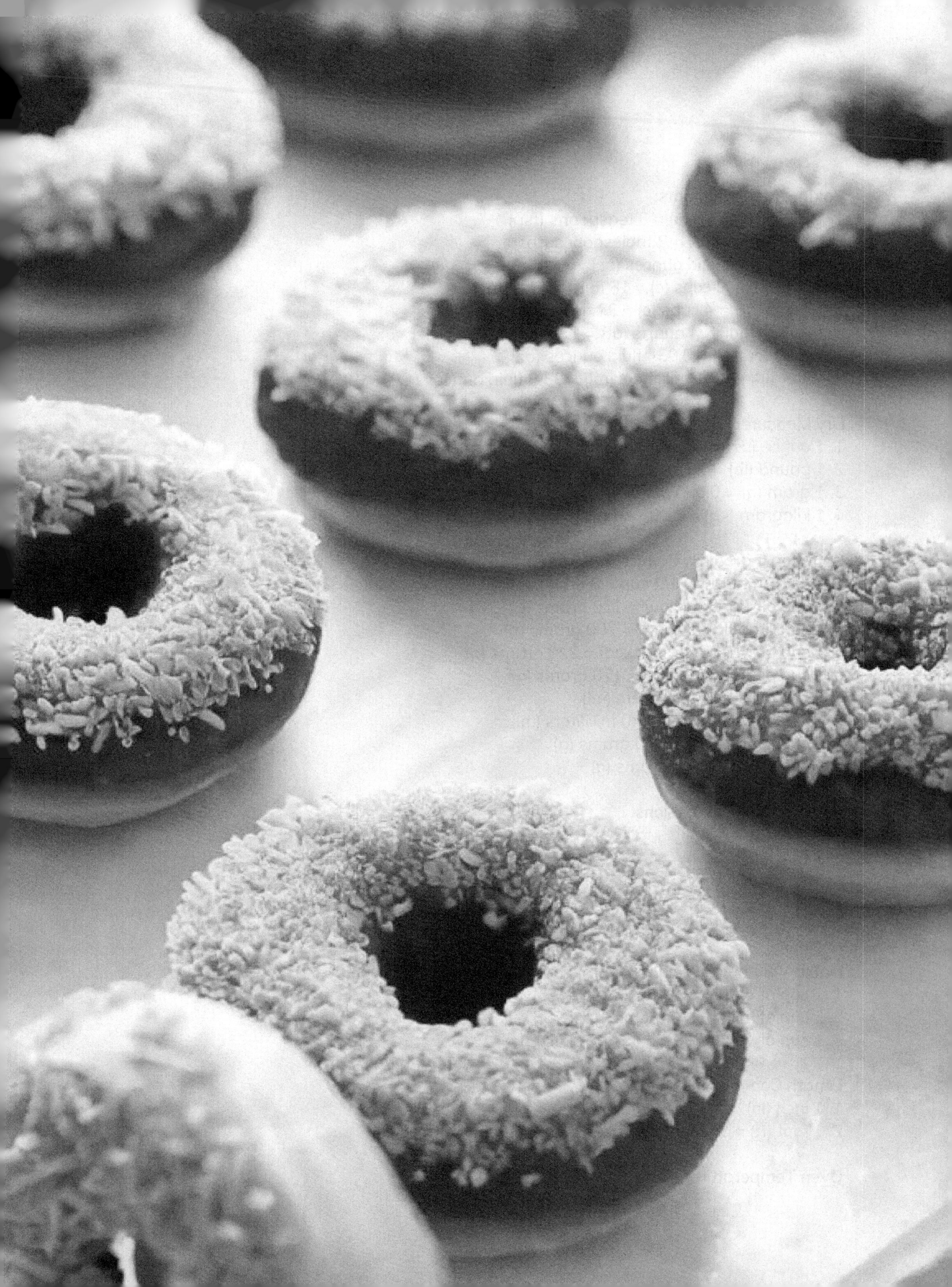

KITCHEN CONVERSION CHART

Volume Measurements:
1. 1 tablespoon (tbsp) = 3 teaspoons (tsp)
2. 1 fluid ounce (oz) = 2 tablespoons (tbsp)
3. 1 cup (c) = 8 fluid ounces (oz)
4. 1 pint (pt) = 2 cups (c) = 16 fluid ounces (oz)
5. 1 quart (qt) = 4 cups (c) = 32 fluid ounces (oz)
6. 1 gallon (gal) = 4 quarts (qt) = 128 fluid ounces (oz)
7. 1 milliliter (ml) = 0.034 fluid ounces (oz)
8. 1 liter (l) = 1,000 milliliters (ml) = 33.8 fluid ounces (oz)

Dry Measurements:
1. 1 ounce (oz) = 28.35 grams (g)
2. 1 pound (lb) = 16 ounces (oz) = 453.59 grams (g)
3. 1 gram (g) = 0.035 ounces (oz)
4. 1 kilogram (kg) = 1,000 grams (g) = 2.2 pounds (lb)

Common Ingredient Conversions:
1. 1 stick of butter = 1/2 cup = 8 tablespoons (tbsp) = 4 ounces (oz)
2. 1 cup all-purpose flour = 120 grams (g)
3. 1 cup granulated sugar = 200 grams (g)
4. 1 cup brown sugar (packed) = 220 grams (g)
5. 1 cup powdered sugar = 120 grams (g)
6. 1 cup milk = 240 milliliters (ml)
7. 1 cup heavy cream = 240 milliliters (ml)
8. 1 cup sour cream = 240 grams (g)
9. 1 cup yogurt = 240 grams (g)

Temperature Conversions:
1. 350°F = 180°C
2. 375°F = 190°C
3. 400°F = 200°C
4. 425°F = 220°C
5. 450°F = 230°C

Liquid Volume to Weight (Approximate):
1. 1 cup of water = 240 grams (g)
2. 1 cup of milk = 240 grams (g)
3. 1 cup of vegetable oil = 218 grams (g)

Length Conversions:
1. 1 inch (in) = 2.54 centimeters (cm)
2. 1 foot (ft) = 12 inches (in) = 30.48 centimeters (cm)

Oven Temperatures:

1. Very slow oven = 250°F (120°C)
2. Slow oven = 300°F (150°C)
3. Moderate oven = 350°F (180°C)
4. Moderately hot oven = 375°F (190°C)
5. Hot oven = 400°F (200°C)
6. Very hot oven = 450°F (230°C)

Miscellaneous:
1. 1 pinch = 1/16 teaspoon (tsp)
2. 1 dash = 1/8 teaspoon (tsp)
3. 1 smidgen = 1/32 teaspoon (tsp)

Keep this kitchen conversion chart handy for all your cooking and baking adventures. It will help you easily convert measurements and ensure your recipes turn out just right.

KITCHEN CHEAT SHEET FOR COOKING

Essential Ingredients:
 - **Olive Oil**: Use extra virgin olive oil for most cooking and as a finishing drizzle.
 - **Herbs and Spices:** Common choices include oregano, basil, thyme, rosemary, parsley, mint, and garlic.
 - **Fresh Produce:** Embrace a variety of fruits and vegetables like tomatoes, eggplants, zucchini, bell peppers, onions, and citrus fruits.
 - **Legumes:** Include chickpeas, lentils, and beans for protein and fiber.
 - **Grains:** Opt for whole grains like bulgur, couscous, and quinoa.
 - **Nuts:** Almonds, walnuts, and pine nuts add texture and flavor.
 - **Fish:** Incorporate seafood, especially oily fish like salmon and mackerel.
 - **Dairy:** Use yogurt and cheese, especially feta and goat cheese, in moderation.
 - **Poultry:** Lean cuts of chicken and turkey are used occasionally.
 - **Wine:** Consider using wine for cooking and pair it with your meal.

Cooking Techniques:
 - **Grilling:** Grill meats, seafood, and vegetables for that signature Mediterranean smokiness.
 - **Roasting:** Roast vegetables with olive oil and herbs for added depth of flavor.
 - **Sauteing:** Use olive oil to sauté onions, garlic, and other aromatics.
 - **Baking:** Make dishes like moussaka, pastitsio, and baklava with this method.
 - **Braising:** Slow-cook meats and stews in flavorful tomato-based sauces.
 - **Steaming:** Steam vegetables and fish to preserve nutrients.
 - **Marinating:** Marinate proteins in olive oil, herbs, and citrus before cooking.
 - **Mezze:** Create a variety of small dishes and appetizers for sharing.

Tips for Authentic Flavor:
 - Use fresh, high-quality ingredients.
 - Experiment with Mediterranean herbs and spices for flavor.

- Balance flavors with lemon juice and vinegar
- Let dishes marinate for enhanced taste.
- Incorporate olives, capers, and preserved lemons for depth.
- Practice moderation with dairy and meat.
- Toast nuts for added crunch and aroma.
- Explore regional variations and traditions.

CONCLUSION

Thank you for getting this date night cookbook for couples! We hope you've enjoyed the diverse range of dishes across different categories.

But remember, this is just the start. Explore more homemade recipes and savor the flavors while spending quality time together. Let's keep cooking and nourishing ourselves, one meal at a time!
Bon appétit and here's to your continued culinary journey!

Share Your Thoughts:
We value your feedback! If you found joy in the recipes or have suggestions, kindly leave a review to guide us and inspire others.

Pass It On:
If this cookbook has enlightened your culinary journey, consider sharing it with friends and family. Your recommendation could brighten someone else's health journey.

Stay Connected:
For more recipes, tips, and updates, follow our author's page

Remember, your health is a lifelong journey, and each sauce and dips choice is a step forward. Thank you for choosing this cookbook as a companion in your pursuit of health.

Happy cooking, my friends!

Jane Garraway

Made in the USA
Columbia, SC
19 January 2025